Briefcase on

CONSTITUTIONAL

&

ADMINISTRATIVE LAW

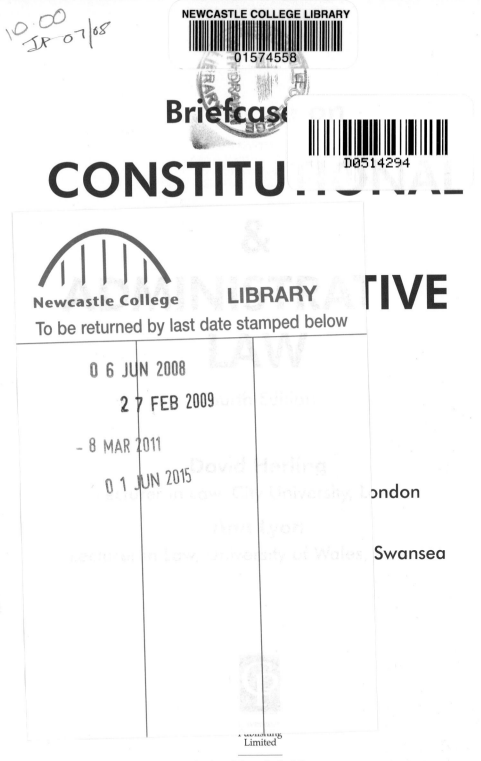
Third Edition

David Herling
Barrister in Law, City University, London

Huw Yorke
Lecturer in Law, University of Wales, Swansea

Cavendish
Publishing
Limited

London • Sydney • Portland, Oregon

Fourth edition first published in Great Britain 2004 by
Cavendish Publishing Limited, The Glass House,
Wharton Street, London WC1X 9PX, United Kingdom
Telephone: + 44 (0)20 7278 8000   Facsimile: + 44 (0)20 7278 8080
Email: info@cavendishpublishing.com
Website: www.cavendishpublishing.com

Published in the United States by Cavendish Publishing
c/o International Specialized Book Services,
5824 NE Hassalo Street, Portland,
Oregon 97213-3644, USA

Published in Australia by Cavendish Publishing (Australia) Pty Ltd
45 Beach Street, Coogee, NSW 2034, Australia
Telephone: + 61 (2)9664 0909   Facsimile: + 61 (2)9664 5420
Email: info@cavendishpublishing.com.au
Website: www.cavendishpublishing.com.au

British Library Cataloguing in Publication Data
Herling, David
Briefcase on constitutional & administrative law – 4th ed
1 Administrative law – England 2 Administrative law – Wales
3 England – constitutional law 4 Wales – constitutional law
I Title II Lyon, Ann III Constitutional & administrative law
342.4'2

Library of Congress Cataloguing in Publication Data
Data available

ISBN 1-85941-760-4

1 3 5 7 9 10 8 6 4 2

Printed and bound in Great Britain

CONTENTS

TABLE OF CASES

TABLE OF STATUTES

CHAPTER 1

CONSTITUTIONAL CONVENTIONS

1.1 The nature of conventions

Sir Ivor Jennings: *The Law and the Constitution* (3rd edn, 1943), pp 80–81:

… [Constitutional conventions] provide the flesh which clothes the dry bones of the law; they make the legal constitution work; they keep it in touch with the growth of ideas.

Constitutional conventions are rules of practice considered binding on those to whom they apply, but they are not legally enforceable. They are of immense importance in regulating the ways in which the legal framework of the British Constitution is operated in reality. Good examples of constitutional practice governed by convention are the office of Prime Minister (not recognised by statute until 1905), the system of Cabinet government, and the principle that the Sovereign does not refuse royal assent to Bills passed by Parliament. All these emerged in the 18th century.

Most of the conventions identifiable within the British Constitution have emerged by evolution, but some have been formally agreed. The best example is that contained in the Preamble to the Statute of Westminster 1931, that the UK Parliament would not, in the future, legislate for the Dominions (then Canada, Newfoundland, Australia, New Zealand, South Africa and the Irish Free State (now the Irish Republic)) except at the request of the Dominion concerned.

AV Dicey: *An Introduction to the Study of the Law of the Constitution* (10th edn, 1965), pp 23–24:

The rules which make up constitutional law, as the term is used in England, include two sets of principles or maxims of a totally different character.

The one set of rules are in the strictest sense 'laws', since they are rules which (either written or unwritten, whether enacted by statute or derived from the mass of custom, tradition, or judge made maxims known as the common law) are enforced by the courts; these rules constitute 'constitutional law' in the proper sense of that term …

The other set of rules consist of conventions, understandings, habits, or practices which, though they may regulate the conduct of the several members of the sovereign power, of the ministry, or of other officials, are not in reality laws at all, since they are not enforced by the courts. This portion of constitutional law may, for the sake of distinction, be termed the 'conventions of the constitution', or 'constitutional morality'.

In *The Law and the Constitution* (3rd edn, p 131), Jennings considers a test of when a convention existed:

We have to ask ourselves three questions: first, what are the precedents; secondly, did the actors in the precedents believe that they were bound by a rule; and, thirdly, is there a reason for the rule? A whole string of precedents without such a reason will be of no avail, unless it is perfectly certain that the persons concerned regarded themselves as bound by it.

1.2   The distinction between laws and conventions

Madzimbamuto v Lardner-Burke **(1969) PC:** Convention not legally enforceable

Facts
When the British colony of Southern Rhodesia (now Zimbabwe) was given autonomy in domestic affairs, a convention was agreed that the UK Parliament would not legislate for Rhodesia in internal matters without the agreement of the Rhodesian Government. The appellant's husband was detained under regulations made by a new regime in Rhodesia, which had assumed power upon the Rhodesian Prime Minister's Unilateral Declaration of Independence of 1965. Six days after the Declaration, the UK Parliament passed the Southern Rhodesia Act 1965, which declared that Rhodesia was still part of Her Majesty's Dominions and that the UK Government and Parliament still had responsibility for and jurisdiction over it. The Southern Rhodesia (Constitution) Order 1965, made under the Act, declared that no laws might be made by the Legislature of Southern Rhodesia. The Rhodesian courts held that, although the new regime was unlawful, it was necessary to give effect to its laws, as it was the only effective government in Rhodesia. Mrs Madzimbamuto appealed to the Privy Council.

Decision
Allowing the appeal by a majority, the Privy Council held that it was for Parliament alone to determine whether the maintenance of law and order would justify giving effect to laws made by the usurping government. In the absence of any such determination, the UK Parliament's laws should continue to be regarded as binding by the courts, whatever the political reality of the situation.

Per Lord Reid:
It is often said that it would be unconstitutional for the UK Parliament to do certain things, meaning that the moral, political and other reasons against doing them are so strong that most people would regard it as highly improper if Parliament did these things. But that does not mean that it is beyond the power of Parliament to do such things. If Parliament chose to do any of them, the courts could not hold the Act of Parliament invalid. It may be that it would be unconstitutional to disregard this convention ... Their Lordships in declaring the law are not concerned with these matters. They are only concerned with the legal powers of Parliament.

1.3   The courts will admit evidence of conventions to establish a cause of action

Attorney General v Jonathan Cape Ltd **(1976):** Convention may have indirect effect

Facts
The Secretary to the Cabinet had refused to approve publication of extracts from the Cabinet diaries of Richard Crossman, a Labour minister during the 1960s, on the ground that it would be contrary to the public interest. He argued that revelation of discussions in Cabinet would breach the convention of collective ministerial

responsibility. The Attorney General sought injunctions to prevent the publication of the diaries in *The Sunday Times*. He submitted that the information contained in the diaries was confidential in character and publication would tend to undermine the future operation of the convention. The defendants contended that the evidence did not prove the existence of a convention of collective Cabinet responsibility, and that if it did, the convention was binding in conscience only.

Decision

The court held, refusing the injunctions, that the general effect of the evidence was that the convention was an established feature of the English form of government. However, although the maintenance of the convention of collective responsibility in Cabinet was in the public interest, and the court would therefore intervene in a clear case to uphold it by injunction where the public interest demanded, the information in the present case was nearly 10 years old and its publication would not inhibit the continued freedom of discussion in Cabinet.

1.4   Conventions cannot crystallise into law

Reference Re Amendment of the Constitution of Canada (1982)
Supreme Court of Canada: Convention cannot itself become law

Facts

Under the British North America Act 1867, which made Canada an independent Dominion within the British Empire, amendments to the Canadian Constitution could only be given effect by an amendment to the 1867 Act made by the UK Parliament. In the early 1980s, Canada sought to 'patriate' its constitution by creating a mechanism for amendment without reference to the UK (enacted as the Constitution Act 1982). This, however, required a final amendment to the 1867 Act (passed as the Canada Act 1982). A convention had developed within the Canadian Constitution that amendments to the 1867 Act which affected the relationship of the federal government and the provinces (as this amendment did) had to be supported by a 'substantial body' of the provincial governments before it could be referred to the UK Parliament. Among a number of questions put to the Supreme Court of Canada was the following:

Does the Canadian Constitution empower, whether by statute, convention or otherwise, the Senate and the House of Commons of Canada to cause the Canadian Constitution to be amended without the consent of the provinces and in spite of the objection of several of them …?

The Attorney General of Manitoba submitted that the amendment before the court was contrary to convention, that a convention may crystallise into law and that, in consequence, the federal government could not legally request the amendment.

Decision

The majority of the House of Lords accepted that a convention existed, on the basis of the Jennings test (see 1.1 above). There were ample precedents to demonstrate that no amendment which affected the position of the provinces had previously been sought without a substantial measure of provincial approval, that the ministers responsible for the amendments had considered themselves bound by a requirement for provincial approval, and that there was a clear reason for the rule – to preserve the federal character of the Canadian Constitution. However, that convention was not legally enforceable and could not be regarded as having crystallised into law.

CHAPTER 2

THE RULE OF LAW

2.1   Government according to the law

The rule of law is an important concept of constitutional law, enunciated by the 19th century writer AV Dicey.

AV Dicey: *An Introduction to the Study of the Law of the Constitution* (10th edn, 1965), pp 188, 202:

We mean, in the first place, that no man is punishable or can be lawfully made to suffer in body or goods except for a distinct breach of law established in the ordinary legal manner before the ordinary courts of the land. In this sense, the rule of law is contrasted with every system of government based on the exercise by persons in authority of wide, arbitrary, or discretionary powers of constraint ... It means ... the absolute supremacy or predominance of regular law as opposed to the influence of arbitrary power, and excludes the existence of arbitrariness, of prerogative, or even of wide discretionary authority on the part of the government. Englishmen are ruled by the law, and by the law alone; a man may with us be punished for a breach of the law, but he can be punished for nothing else.

R v Coventry City Council ex p Phoenix Aviation (and Other Applications) (1995): All lawful activities are entitled to protection of law

Facts
During 1994 and 1995, protesters sought to disrupt and prevent the export of live animals through British ports and airports. This trade was lawful; those demonstrating against it had regularly exceeded their lawful right of protest. The Divisional Court heard three separate applications for judicial review together, each arising in connection with the response of transport authorities to the disruption caused by these demonstrations. The first and second applications were brought by businesses involved in the livestock export trade against decisions to close Coventry City Airport and Dover Harbour respectively to that trade. In the third application, a local authority challenged the failure of a statutory port authority to ban the export of live animals through Millbay Docks at Plymouth. Each application called for consideration of the relevant transport authority's statutory duties, the extent of its statutory discretions (if any) in the discharge of such duties and the factors which might properly influence the exercise of discretion.

Decision
The Divisional Court held that the first two applications would be granted and the third would be refused. In each case, the transport authority enjoyed no general discretion to distinguish between lawful trades. Even were this incorrect, discretion could not properly be exercised to ban the livestock trade on the ground that it would cause unlawful disruption.

Per Simon Brown LJ:
One thread runs consistently through the case law: the recognition that public authorities must beware of surrendering to the dictates of unlawful pressure groups. The implications of such surrender for the rule of law can hardly be exaggerated ... Tempting though it may sometimes be for public authorities to yield too readily to threats of disruption, they must expect the courts to review any such decision with particular rigour – this is not an area where they can be permitted a wide measure of discretion. As when fundamental rights are in play, the courts will adopt a more interventionist role.

2.1.1   The courts are independent of the executive in the administration of justice

Prohibitions del Roy (Case of Prohibitions) (1607): Justice is administered in the name of the king, not by the king in person

Facts
King James VI and I (1603–25) purported to hear and decide a case himself. On appeal, it was argued that, in matters which were not covered by express legal authority, the monarch himself 'may take what causes he shall please to determine, from the determination of the judges, and may determine them himself'. This right was divinely given to the king and the judges were merely his delegates to exercise it during his pleasure.

Decision
The Court of the King's Bench held, annulling the king's determination, that matters concerning the administration of justice were solely determined in the Courts of Justice, and that no king after the Norman Conquest had assumed the right to judge any case himself. (This is not strictly correct, as a number of post-Conquest monarchs, notably John (1199–1216), regularly heard cases themselves.)

Per Lord Coke CJ:
... Then the King said that he thought the law was founded on reason, and that he and others had reason, as well as the judges: to which it was answered by me ... that God had endowed His Majesty with excellent science, and great endowments of nature: but His Majesty was not learned in the laws of his realm of England, and causes which concern the life, or inheritance, or goods, or fortunes of his subjects, are not to be decided by natural reason but by the artificial reason and judgment of the law, which law is an art which requires long study and experience, before that a man can attain to the cognisance of it ...

Liversidge v Anderson (1941) HL: Judges are under a duty to uphold the law as it is and not to favour the executive over the subject

Facts
The appellant, a senior member of the British Union of Fascists, was detained in prison under the Defence (General) Regulations 1939. Regulation 18B provided as follows:

If the Secretary of State has reasonable cause to believe any person to be of hostile origin or associations ... and that, by reason thereof, it is necessary to exercise control over him, he may make an order against that person directing that he be detained.

In the course of an action for a declaration that his detention was unlawful, and damages for false imprisonment, the appellant sought particulars of the grounds on which the Secretary of State believed him to be of hostile associations, and the grounds on which he believed it necessary to exercise control over him. Having failed at first instance and before the Court of Appeal, the appellant appealed to the House of Lords.

Decision

The Lords held, by a majority, that the appeal would be dismissed. On their true construction, the words 'has reasonable cause to believe' meant no more than that the Secretary of State should, in good faith, himself consider that he had reasonable cause.

Lord Atkin, dissenting, stated that the relevant words were capable only of meaning that the Secretary of State should objectively have good cause, and observed that, for generations, this meaning had consistently been attributed to similar expressions in the area of police powers and the wider criminal law. With regard to the opinion of the majority of their Lordships, he said:

I view with apprehension the attitude of judges who, on a mere question of construction, when face to face with claims involving the liberty of the subject, show themselves more executive-minded than the executive. Their function is to give words their natural meaning ... In England, amidst the clash of arms, the laws are not silent. They may be changed, but they speak the same language in war as in peace. It has always been one of the pillars of freedom, one of the principles of liberty for which, on recent authority, we are now fighting, that the judges are no respecters of persons, and stand between the subject and any attempted encroachments on his liberty by the executive, alert to see that any coercive action is justified in law.

Comment

Although the decision of the House of Lords upheld the approach taken by the Home Secretary, the *dicta* of Lord Atkin have been regarded ever since as the correct statement of the law.

R v Horseferry Road Magistrates' Court ex p Bennett (1993) HL: Judiciary are entitled to insist that executive bodies act within the law

Facts

The appellant, who was wanted in the UK for alleged criminal offences in connection with the raising of money, was placed in police custody in South Africa and forcibly brought to this country. There was no extradition treaty between South Africa and the UK and, although the Extradition Act 1989 provided for a special procedure in the absence of a treaty, it was not invoked. The appellant challenged the jurisdiction of the magistrates' court to hear committal proceedings against him, on the ground that the South African and British police had colluded to kidnap him. The Divisional Court rejected his application for judicial review.

Decision

The House of Lords held, on appeal, that domestic courts should take cognisance of the circumstances in which a person had been brought within the jurisdiction. Where it had been done in breach of international law, the laws of the State where the person had been found and in disregard of an available legal process, it was open to a court to stay the individual's prosecution as an abuse of process and to order his release.

Per Lord Griffiths:

Your Lordships are now invited to extend the concept of abuse of process a stage further. In the present case, there is no suggestion that the appellant cannot have a fair trial, nor could it be suggested that it would have been unfair to try him if he had been returned to this country through extradition procedures. If the court is to have the power to interfere with the prosecution in the present circumstances, it must be because the judiciary accept a responsibility for the maintenance of the rule of law that embraces a willingness to oversee executive action and to refuse to countenance behaviour that threatens either basic human rights or the rule of law ... If it comes to the attention of the court that there has been a serious abuse of power it should, in my view, express its disapproval by refusing to act upon it.

2.1.2   The powers of the executive do not exceed those known to the courts

Entick v Carrington (1765): The executive does not have powers beyond those granted by the law. In particular, it cannot claim special powers simply because it is the executive

Facts

Entick was alleged to be the author of seditious writings. Two king's messengers, purporting to act under the authority of a warrant issued not by a court but by the Secretary of State, broke into Entick's house and carried away his papers. Entick sued the messengers for trespass. The Secretary of State argued, *inter alia*, that he had the power to issue warrants, because it was essential to government that he should have it.

Decision

The Court of the King's Bench held that the warrant was illegal and void. It was incumbent upon the Secretary of State to establish what law authorised his invasion of another's rights. He had been unable to show any statute or common law to sanction the issue of the warrant. The arguments of State necessity, or of a claimed distinction between State offences and others, were of no validity.

Per Lord Camden CJ:

By the laws of England, every invasion of private property, be it ever so minute, is a trespass. No man can set his foot upon my ground without my licence, but he is liable to an action, though the damage be nothing ... If he admits the fact, he is bound to show by way of justification, that some positive law has empowered or excused him. The justification is submitted to the judges, who are to look into the books and see if such a justification can be maintained by the text of the statute law, or by the principles of common law. If no such excuse can be found or produced, the silence of the books is an authority against the defendant, and the plaintiff must have judgment.

Comment

This is a decision of vital importance in that it makes clear that the government does not have power to interfere with the rights of the subject merely because it is the government, but must show lawful authority for such interference. However, the principle only applies where positive rights are at stake – here, rights in property.

Malone v Metropolitan Police Commissioner (No 2) (1979) Ch D: Presumption of legality of executive action where no positive right applies

Facts

The plaintiff was charged with handling stolen goods. In the course of his trial, counsel for the prosecution admitted that Malone's telephone had been tapped and his conversations recorded on the authority of a warrant issued by the Home Secretary. Malone brought proceedings against the Metropolitan Police Commissioner claiming declarations, *inter alia*, that the tapping was unlawful.

Decision

The Chancery Division held that the action failed.

Per Sir Robert Megarry VC:

England, it may be said, is not a country where everything is forbidden except what is expressly permitted; it is a country where everything is permitted except what is expressly forbidden ... If the tapping of telephones by the Post Office at the request of the police can be carried out without any breach of the law, it does not require any statutory or common law power to justify it; it can lawfully be done simply because there is nothing to make it unlawful ... The reason why a search of premises which is not authorised by law is illegal is that it involves the tort of trespass to those premises; and any trespass, whether to land or goods or to the person, that is made without legal authority, is *prima facie* illegal. Telephone tapping by the Post Office, on the other hand, involves no act of trespass.

R v Inland Revenue Commissioners ex p Rossminster Ltd (1980) HL: General warrants not of themselves unlawful

Facts

Rossminster's premises were searched by officers of the Inland Revenue acting pursuant to warrants issued by the appropriate judicial authority. The warrants were drafted in broad and general terms, and did not specify the detail or types of offences which Rossminster was suspected of having committed. The Court of Appeal found in favour of Rossminster, holding that the court was under a duty to construe the legislation to ensure that it encroached as little as possible on the liberties of subjects. Unless a person knew the details of an offence of which he was suspected, he could take no steps to secure himself or his property. The warrant was therefore invalid. The Inland Revenue Commissioners appealed to the House of Lords.

Decision

The House of Lords held, allowing the appeal, that the warrant accorded sufficiently with the provisions of the legislation under which it had been issued. The courts did have a duty to supervise the legality of any exercise of a power which, as here, substantially infringed individual liberties. However, they had no right to impede the working of legislation.

Morris v Beardmore (1980) HL: A modern *Entick v Carrington*

Facts

Following an accident in which the appellant's car had been involved, police officers wished to interview him. The appellant's son let them into his house, but the appellant refused to come down from his bedroom and informed the police that they were trespassing. The police did not leave, but asked him to provide a specimen for a breath test. He refused and was charged with failure to provide the specimen. The Divisional Court, overturning the decision of the justices, held that the request for the specimen was not vitiated by the fact of the trespass. The appellant appealed to the House of Lords.

Decision

The House of Lords held, allowing the appeal, that the appellant had not validly been required to provide the specimen, since the request had come not from a police officer in the execution of his duty, but from an officer who was trespassing. It was correct to state that the relevant statute contained no provision prohibiting the action taken by the officers, but that did not establish its legality. If Parliament intended to authorise the doing of an act which otherwise would constitute a tort actionable at the suit of the person to whom the act was done, that required express provision in the statute.

2.1.3   The rule of law imposes duties upon law makers

Merkur Island Shipping Corp v Laughton (1983) **HL:** Laws should be clear and unambiguous

Facts

The International Transport Workers' Federation (ITF) adopted a practice of 'blacking' named ships – preventing them from obtaining harbour facilities – in pursuit of a campaign for better terms and conditions of employment for crews of ships flying flags of convenience. On 16 July 1982, the ITF sought to prevent a Liberian-registered ship from loading at Liverpool. The plaintiff ship owners sought an interlocutory injunction to restrain the ITF, and damages for losses caused by the blacking. The question arose whether legislation prevented the trade union from being liable for the losses. The answer involved the court in construing the relevant sections of three Acts of Parliament together (the Trade Union and Labour Relations Act 1974, the Trade Union and Labour Relations (Amendment) Act 1976 and the Employment Act 1980).

Decision

In the House of Lords, Lord Donaldson referred to the difficulty which the court had experienced and the time which had been spent in seeking to understand the statutory provisions. It was necessary to the efficacy and maintenance of the rule of law that people should be able to discover what the law required of them. When Parliament's legislation directly affected individuals, clarity and simplicity of expression ought to be given as high a priority as refinements of policy.

Per Lord Diplock:

Absence of clarity is destructive of the rule of law; it is unfair to those who wish to preserve the rule of law; it encourages those who wish to undermine it. The statutory provisions which it became necessary to piece together into a coherent whole … are drafted in a manner which, having regard to their subject matter and the persons who will be called upon to apply them, can, in my view, only be characterised as most regrettably lacking in the requisite degree of clarity.

Phillips v Eyre (1870): Presumption against retroactive effect of legislation

Facts

Following the suppression of a rebellion in Jamaica, an Indemnity Act was passed to protect local law-enforcement agencies from liability arising from their actions during the rebellion. The plaintiff sued for assault and false imprisonment.

Per Willes J:

Retrospective laws are, no doubt, *prima facie* of questionable policy, and contrary to the general principle that legislation by which the conduct of mankind is to be regulated ought, when introduced for the first time, to deal with future acts, and ought not to change the character of past transactions carried on upon the faith of the then existing law ... Accordingly, the court will not ascribe retrospective force to new laws affecting rights, unless by express words or necessary implication it appears that such was the intention of the legislature.

Waddington v Miah (1974) HL: Presumption applied

Facts

The respondent had been convicted at Grimsby Crown Court on counts of being an illegal immigrant and being in possession of a false passport, contrary to ss 24 and 26 of the Immigration Act 1971. The offences were alleged, in the indictment, to have been committed on dates before the relevant sections had come into force. The Court of Appeal quashed the convictions on the ground that the language of the 1971 Act was not apt to compel a construction according its provisions retroactive effect. The Crown appealed to the House of Lords.

Decision

The House of Lords held, dismissing the appeal, that the case was a very clear one. The 1971 Act contained no transitional provisions which would allow it to be used to prosecute offences under Acts which it had repealed. In view of the fact that the Universal Declaration of Human Rights, approved by the General Assembly of the United Nations, and the European Convention on Human Rights each effectively pronounced against the enactment of retroactive criminal legislation, it was scarcely credible that any government department would promote, or that Parliament would pass, such legislation.

Comment

For an example of retroactive criminal legislation, see the War Crimes Act 1991, though those responsible for it argued that it was not retroactive as such, since it did not create liability where none had existed, but created a mechanism to give a British court jurisdiction.

2.1.4   Retroactivity and the common law

C v Director of Public Prosecutions (1994–95) Divisional Court and HL: Courts could not make retroactive change to the common law so as to create criminal liability where none had previously existed

Facts

A rebuttable presumption of incapacity of harm applied to children aged between 10 and 13. The appellant was convicted of interfering with a motorcycle with the intent to commit theft or taking and driving away contrary to s 9(1) of the Criminal Attempts Act 1981. He was aged 12 at the time of the offence and it was therefore necessary for the prosecution to prove, in addition to the *mens rea* for the offence, that he had known that what he was doing was seriously wrong. He appealed by way of case stated on the ground that the prosecution had failed to rebut the presumption.

In the Divisional Court, Laws J held that the presumption was no longer part of English law. He recognised that since the common law had not yet developed a practice of prospective rulings, and the basis of judicial rulings was that the law had always been as was now stated, the effect of his decision would be to change the law as at the time of the appellant's offence. In many cases, this would be a powerful inhibition upon the extent to which the common law courts could justly alter the scope of the criminal law. However, this was not such a case, because if the appellant were able to complain that he had ordered his behaviour on the basis that the presumption still existed, he would conclusively have rebutted its application to his case. The appellant appealed to the House of Lords.

Decision

The House of Lords held, allowing the appeal, that the presumption continued to be part of English law. Regarding the issue of retroactivity, Lord Lowry conceded that Laws J was correct to consider that it would work no practical injustice in the appellant's case, but objectively, something which when done was not regarded as a crime would, if the Divisional Court were right, ultimately turn out to have been one.

2.1.5   The necessity for the publication of laws

Simmonds v Newell (1953) QBD: Specific defence when there has been a failure to publish

Facts

Section 3(2) of the Statutory Instruments Act 1946 reads as follows:

In any proceedings against any person for an offence consisting of a contravention of any such statutory instrument, it shall be a defence to prove that the instrument had not been issued by His Majesty's Stationery Office at the date of the alleged contravention unless it is proved that at that date reasonable steps had been taken for the purpose of bringing the purport of the instrument to the notice of the public, or of persons likely to be affected by it, or of the persons charged.

A company and its directors were prosecuted for selling steel above the maximum price permitted by the Iron and Steel Prices Order 1951 and subsequently appealed against conviction on the basis of s 3(2). The decision had been taken in the Ministry of Supply not to print the schedules to the order which specified maximum prices; the schedules were available for inspection at Steel House in London and copies of some of them were to be distributed by trade associations. The Solicitor General accepted that in this situation the Crown bore the burden of proving that s 3(2) had been satisfied.

Decision

The Divisional Court held that, since no evidence had been adduced to show that the order had been publicised, the defendants should have been acquitted.

Per Lord Goddard CJ:

... It is not desirable, in criminal matters, that people should be prosecuted for breaches of orders unless the orders can fairly be said to be known to the public.

Comment

Here, failure to publish the instrument afforded a specific defence in criminal proceedings, but the case below applies the principle more widely.

Lim Chin Aik v R (1963) PC: General principle that publication is required

Facts

An order was made under the Singapore Immigration Ordinance 1952 prohibiting the appellant from entering Singapore. He entered and was convicted under the Ordinance of entering Singapore while prohibited by an order from so doing. The relevant section of the Ordinance contained no express *mens rea* requirement, and, on his appeal against conviction, it was conceded by the Crown that the appellant had not been proved to have *mens rea* with regard to his infraction of the order.

Decision

The Judicial Committee of the Privy Council held, allowing the appeal, that the presumption that *mens rea* was required for conviction had not been overcome. In response to the Crown's argument that knowledge of the order did not need to be proved since ignorance of the law was no defence, Lord Evershed stated:

Their Lordships are unable to accept this contention. In their Lordships' opinion, even if the making of the order by the Minister be regarded as an exercise of the legislative as distinct from the executive or administrative function (as they do not concede), the maxim cannot apply to such a case as the present where it appears that there is in the State of Singapore no provision, corresponding, for example, to that contained in s 3(2) of the English Statutory Instruments Act 1946, for the publication in any form of an order of the kind made in the present case or any other provision designed to enable a man by appropriate inquiry to find out what 'the law' is.

2.1.6 The principle that laws should be stable

Practice Statement (Judicial Precedent) (1966) HL: The House of Lords might overrule its own precedents, but should not make a practice of doing so

Per Lord Gardiner LC:

Their Lordships regard the use of precedent as an indispensable foundation upon which to decide what is the law and its application to individual cases. It provides at least some degree of certainty upon which individuals can rely in the conduct of their affairs, as well as a basis for orderly development of legal rules.

Their Lordships nevertheless recognise that too rigid adherence to precedent may lead to injustice in a particular case and also unduly restrict the proper development of the law. They propose, therefore, to modify their present practice and, while treating former decisions of this House as normally binding, to depart from a previous decision when it appears right to do so.

In this connection, they will bear in mind the danger of disturbing retrospectively the basis on which contracts, settlements of property, and fiscal arrangements have been entered into and also the especial need for certainty in the criminal law.

Williams v Fawcett (1986) CA: Exceptional nature of decision to overrule

Facts
The appellant had been committed to prison for various breaches of an undertaking not to molest the respondent. He appealed against his committal on the grounds that the order to commit failed to specify the breaches, that an adjournment had wrongly been refused and that the notice to show cause why he should not be committed had been signed by the respondent's solicitor and not by the 'proper officer' (as required by rules of court).

Decision
The Court of Appeal held that the appeal would be allowed on the first two of these grounds, but not on the third. Sir John Donaldson MR reviewed four decisions of the Court of Appeal (one of them his own), which suggested that the committal should be quashed on the third ground as well. Although the Court of Appeal was normally obliged to follow its own previous decisions, it was established by *Young v Bristol Aeroplane Co Ltd* (1944) that it might depart from an earlier decision which it was satisfied had been made *per incuriam* (wrongly and carelessly). Such cases would be of the rarest occurrence. The Master of the Rolls continued:

If we are bound by these decisions, and we are unless they can be treated as having been reached *per incuriam*, they represent a very considerable change in the law for which, so far as I can see, there is absolutely no warrant. The change to which I refer is, of course, a requirement that these notices shall be signed by the proper officer. The rule of *stare decisis* is of the very greatest importance, particularly in an appellate court such as this, which sits in six or seven divisions simultaneously. But for this rule, the law would not only bifurcate; it would branch off in six or seven different directions.

2.1.7   *Judicial creativity and the stability of laws*

Duport Steels Ltd v Sirs (1980) HL: Importance of maintaining stability of laws

Facts
In the course of an industrial dispute, and in order to put pressure on the government to provide the British Steel Corporation with the funds necessary for it to make an increased pay award to its employees, a trade union called out on strike those of its members who worked for British Steel and those who worked for private employers. The private employers sought injunctions against the union. Section 13(1) of the Trade Union and Labour Relations Act 1974 conferred immunity from liability in tort

for an act done by a person 'in contemplation or furtherance of a trade dispute'. The Court of Appeal construed the relevant provisions of the Act narrowly and found for the employers. The union appealed to the House of Lords.

Decision
The Lords held, reversing the decision of the Court of Appeal, that the duty of the courts was to apply the laws made by Parliament and not to adapt them to the judicial view of what they ought to be.

Per Lord Scarman:
In our society, the judges have in some aspects of their work a discretionary power to do justice so wide that they may be regarded as law makers. The common law and equity, both of them in essence systems of private law, are fields where, subject to the increasing intrusion of statute law, society has been content to allow the judges to formulate and develop the law. The judges, even in this, their very own field of creative endeavour, have accepted, in the interests of certainty, the self-denying ordinance of *stare decisis*, the doctrine of binding precedent; and no doubt this judicially imposed limitation on judicial law making has helped to maintain confidence in the certainty and even-handedness of the law.

2.2   Equality before the law

AV Dicey: *An Introduction to the Study of the Law of the Constitution* (10th edn, 1965), pp 202–03:

It means ... equality before the law, or the equal subjection of all classes to the ordinary law of the land administered by the ordinary law courts; the 'rule of law' in this sense excludes the idea of any exemption of officials or others from the duty of obedience to the law which governs other citizens or from the jurisdiction of the ordinary tribunals; there can be with us nothing really corresponding to the 'administrative law' (*droit administratif*) or the 'administrative tribunals' (*tribuneaux administratifs*) of France. The notion which lies at the bottom of the 'administrative law' known to foreign countries is that affairs or disputes in which the government or its servants are concerned are beyond the sphere of the civil courts and must be dealt with by special and more or less official bodies. This idea is utterly unknown to the law of England, and indeed is fundamentally inconsistent with our traditions and customs.

2.2.1   The law's application to the executive
The Crown is not bound by statute except in the absence of express words and, historically, enjoyed immunity from legal action at common law. This position was modified by the Crown Proceedings Act 1947, which abolished the Crown's blanket immunity from actions in contract and tort, and decisions since then have chipped away further at the traditional immunity.

British Broadcasting Corp v Johns (Inspector of Taxes) (1964) CA: Crown is not bound by statute in absence of express words

Facts
The Corporation was established as a non-profit making body by Royal Charter. It was assessed for income tax on the surplus of its receipts of funds appropriated to it by Parliament over its expenses. The Corporation argued (*inter alia*) that, as an emanation of the Crown, it enjoyed Crown immunity from taxation because it was a

body constituted by the Crown for the purpose of executing functions required and created for the purpose of government.

Decision

The Court of Appeal held that the Corporation's contention was incorrect. The BBC was not entitled to the Crown's exemption from taxation, since broadcasting was not a function of government and the BBC was an independent body corporate which was not exercising functions required and created by the government.

Diplock LJ explained the basis of Crown immunity as follows:

> Since laws are made by rulers for subjects, a general expression in a law such as 'any person' descriptive of those on whom the law imposes obligations or restraints is not to be read as including the ruler himself. Under our more sophisticated Constitution, the question of sovereignty has in the course of history come to be treated as comprising three distinct functions of a ruler: executive, legislative and judicial ... The modern rule of construction of statutes is that the Crown, which today personifies the executive government of the country and is also a party to all the legislation, is not bound by a statute which imposes obligations or restraints on persons or in respect of property, unless the statute says so expressly or by necessary implication.

Rederiaketiebolaget Amphitrite v R (1921) QBD: Reason for Crown immunity

Facts

The suppliants were a Swedish shipping company and owners of the ship *Amphitrite*. During the First World War, when the Royal Navy operated a blockade intended to prevent munitions reaching Germany, they obtained the following undertaking from the British legation in Stockholm: 'I am instructed to say that the steamship *Amphitrite* will earn her own release and be given a coal cargo if she proceed to the United Kingdom with a full cargo consisting of at least 60% approved goods.' In the event, the ship was detained. The suppliants submitted a petition of right (an ancient procedure for obtaining a remedy as against the Crown) for damages for breach of contract.

Decision

The Queen's Bench Division held that there was no contract between the suppliants and the Crown. The government could bind itself by a commercial contract and, if it did so, it would be bound to perform its undertaking or pay damages for failure to do so. However, the statement by the British legation was merely an expression of intention to act in a particular way in a certain event, and so fell short of giving rise to a contract.

Per Rowlatt J:

> My main reason for so thinking is that it is not competent for the government to fetter its future executive action, which must necessarily be determined by the needs of the community when the question arises. It cannot by contract hamper its freedom of action in matters which concern the welfare of the State.

M v Home Office (1993) HL: Minister might be personally liable for contempt of court, though minister and court were both emanations of Crown

Facts

Following the rejection of his application for asylum, M was ordered to be removed from the UK by 6.30 pm on 1 May 1991. At 5.20 pm on that day, M made a new application for judicial review of the refusal of asylum, based on new grounds. Garland J, to whom the application was made in chambers, obtained an undertaking from counsel for the Home Office that M's removal would be postponed. As a result of confusion, it was not postponed and M was not removed from the plane taking him to Zaire during a stopover in Paris. At 11.20 pm, Garland J made an *ex parte* order requiring the Home Secretary to procure M's return to the UK.

On 2 May, the Home Secretary cancelled arrangements for M's return on the grounds that the original decision to refuse M's asylum application had been correct, and that the court lacked jurisdiction to make an *ex parte* order against a Minister of the Crown. Garland J subsequently set aside his order of 1 May. An action alleging contempt of court for breach of the undertaking and the order was then brought on M's behalf against the Home Office and the Home Secretary. At first instance, the action was dismissed, on the basis that s 21 of the Crown Proceedings Act 1947 protected government departments and ministers from proceedings for contempt of court. The Court of Appeal held that the order of Garland J, although made without jurisdiction, was binding until set aside. Government departments and ministers were protected from liability by the Act, since, for these purposes, they lacked legal personality, but Kenneth Baker, the Home Secretary, was personally guilty of contempt of court.

The Home Secretary appealed and the applicant cross-appealed on his application against the Home Office.

Decision

The House of Lords held that the courts below had erred in holding that there was no jurisdiction in these circumstances for the ordering of an injunction or the finding of contempt. Injunctive power was to be inferred from s 31 of the Supreme Court Act 1981. The power to make a finding of contempt existed as a matter of principle and necessity, albeit only against a minister or department, and not directly against the Crown. However, since the Home Secretary had acted throughout on advice, and since his error was understandable, it was not proper to find him personally in contempt of court.

Per Lord Templeman:

... The argument that there is no power to enforce the law by injunction or contempt proceedings against a minister in his personal capacity would, if upheld, establish the proposition that the executive obey the law as a matter of grace and not as a matter of necessity, a proposition which would reverse the result of the Civil War.

Comment

Here, the House of Lords used the doctrine of the separation of powers to create a distinction between the Crown as executive and the Crown as monarch, which allowed a remedy to be granted against a minister.

2.3   Rights are declared by the common law

AV Dicey: *An Introduction to the Study of the Law of the Constitution* (10th edn, 1965), pp 195, 203:

We may say that the Constitution is pervaded by the rule of law on the ground that the general principles of the Constitution (as, for example, the right to personal liberty, or the right of public meeting) are ... the result of judicial decisions determining the rights of private persons in particular cases brought before the courts; whereas under many foreign constitutions the security (such as it is) given to the rights of individuals results, or appears to result, from the general principles of the Constitution ... In short, the principles of private law have with us been by the action of the courts and Parliament so extended as to determine the position of the Crown and of its servants; thus, the Constitution is the result of the ordinary law of the land.

2.3.1   The principle is in the keeping of the courts

Harman v Secretary of State for the Home Department (1983) HL: Courts must balance good of society in general and rights of individual

Facts

The appellant (Harriet Harman, currently a government minister) was a solicitor. In the course of an action brought by her client against the Home Office, she obtained discovery of quantities of documents and gave an undertaking that she would not use them other than for the purposes of the instant action. After extracts from some of the documents had been read out in open court, the appellant allowed a journalist to have access to those documents. The journalist wrote and published an article based on the documents. The Home Office applied for an order that the appellant was in contempt of court.

At first instance and in the Court of Appeal, the contempt was found proved. The appellant appealed to the House of Lords.

Decision

The House of Lords held by a majority, dismissing the appeal, that the appellant had correctly been held to be in contempt of court.

Per Lord Scarman (dissenting):

A balance has to be struck between two interests of the law; on the one hand, the protection of a litigant's private right to keep his documents to himself notwithstanding his duty to disclose them to the other side in the litigation, and, on the other, the protection of the right, which the law recognises, subject to certain exceptions, as the right of everyone, to speak freely, and to impart information and ideas, upon matters of public knowledge.

CHAPTER 3

SEPARATION OF POWERS

3.1   The doctrine

John Locke: *Second Treatise of Civil Government*, Ch XII, para 143:

It may be too great a temptation to human frailty, apt to grasp at power, for the same persons who have the power of making laws, to have also in their hands the power to execute them.

The doctrine of the Separation of Powers is a political and philosophical model, not a statement of reality, but it has exercised great influence on constitutional thinking and judicial attitudes. In particular, the US constitution is a practical embodiment of the Separation of Powers, with its clear distinction of both function and personnel between executive, legislature and judiciary and system of checks and balances between them. In the UK, it is used extensively by the judiciary in upholding its traditional independence from the government, and, along with the rule of law, forms the philosophical basis for judicial review of executive action.

   In his book, *De L'Esprit des Lois* of 1731, Montesquieu first classifies the functions of government as 'legislative', making law; 'executive', operating and applying law; and 'judicial', interpreting and defining law. He went on to state that these three functions should be performed by three separate and equal agencies of government, as the concentration of more than one function in any single agency of government is a threat to individual liberty.

Montesquieu: *De l'Esprit des Lois*, Book XI, Ch 6:

Political liberty is to be found only when there is no abuse of power. But constant experience shows us that every man invested with power is liable to abuse it, and to carry his authority as far as it will go ... To prevent this abuse, it is necessary from the nature of things that one power should be a check on another ... When the legislative and executive powers are united in the same person or in the same body of magistrates, there can be no liberty ... Again there is no liberty if the power of judging is not separated from the legislative and executive. If it were joined with the executive, the life and liberty of the subject would be exposed to arbitrary control; for the judge would then be the legislator. If it were joined with the executive power, the judge might behave with violence and oppression. There would be an end to everything if the same man, or the same body, whether of the nobles or of the people, were to exercise those three powers, that of enacting laws, of executing public affairs and that of trying crimes or individual causes.

3.2   Application of the doctrine in the courts

M v Home Office (1993) HL: One emanation of the Crown could be in contempt of another

Facts
See 2.2.1 above.

Decision
At first instance (upheld by Court of Appeal and House of Lords), Simon Brown J used the 'constitutional fiction' of Separation of Powers to dispose of the Home Office argument that the Home Secretary and the courts were both manifestations of the Crown, and the Crown could not be in contempt of itself.

Per Simon Brown J:
The Crown's submissions overlook ... the constitutional realities of today: Parliament, the executive and the judiciary ... have long been recognised as three distinct elements of a single State, each exercising their separate powers, their relation to each other controlled by convention and the rule of law ... The mere fact that the contempt jurisdiction emanates from the Crown cannot of itself decide the issue whether a separate institution of the State is amenable to that jurisdiction.

3.3   Concept of judicial independence

3.3.1   The view of the judiciary
It has been emphasised over and over again in judgments that the courts should not usurp the power of Parliament to legislate by, for example, casting doubt on the legality of legislation or by placing an interpretation on a statute which the words will not reasonably bear, nor should the judiciary involve itself in political matters or the merits of decisions taken by executive bodies.

Duport Steels v Sirs (1980) HL: Importance of separation of judiciary from legislature

Facts
See 2.1.7 above.

Per Lord Diplock:
At a time when more and more cases involve the application of legislation which gives effect to policies which are the subject of bitter public and parliamentary controversy, it cannot be too strongly emphasised that the British Constitution, though largely unwritten, is firmly based on the Separation of Powers: Parliament makes the laws, the judiciary interpret them.

The Constitution's Separation of Powers, or more accurately, functions, must be observed if judicial independence is not to be put at risk. For if people and Parliament come to think that judicial power is to be confined by nothing other than the judge's sense of what is right ... confidence in the legal system will be replaced by fear of it ... Society will then be ready for Parliament to cut the power of the judges.

Comment
It may be argued that the judiciary's espousal of the Separation of Powers is part of a self-denying ordinance to keep them out of political matters and to avoid giving the

executive, via Parliament, a reason to reduce their powers. The British Constitution is kept in its present balance by unwritten and largely unenforceable rules of practice.

R v Secretary of State for the Home Department ex p Brind (1991): Need for the judiciary to avoid involving itself in the merits of executive decisions

Facts

This was a judicial review of the Home Secretary's decision to use his powers under s 29 of the Broadcasting Act 1981 to prohibit live broadcasts by representatives of terrorist organisations linked with Northern Ireland. There was no question that the Home Secretary had power to impose the ban; the issue was whether he had used his power properly; in particular whether the decision was '*Wednesbury* unreasonable' – so unreasonable that no reasonable authority, properly directing itself, could ever have come to it. See further Chapter 14 below.

Per Lord Ackner:

This standard of unreasonableness ... has been criticised as being too high. But it has to be expressed in terms that confine the jurisdiction exercised by the judiciary to a supervisory, as opposed to an appellate, jurisdiction. Where Parliament has given to a minister or other person or body a discretion, the court's jurisdiction is limited, in the absence of a statutory right of appeal, to the supervision of the exercise of that discretionary power, so as to ensure that it has been exercised lawfully ...

R v Her Majesty's Treasury ex p Smedley (1985) CA: Courts must move with extreme care in dealing with matters relating, even directly, to internal workings of Parliament

Facts

The appellant sought an order of certiorari to quash the decision of the Chancellor of the Exchequer to operate a procedure provided by s 1(2) of the European Communities Act 1972, in order to confer the status of Community Treaty on a financial undertaking given by the government to the Community. The procedure entitled the Treasury to give effect to the undertaking upon an affirmative resolution of both Houses of Parliament, without needing to introduce legislation for the purpose.

Decision

The Court of Appeal held that the legitimacy of the proposed action by the Treasury depended upon there being a sufficiently close connection between the undertaking and the Treaties. Here, sufficient connection did exist and the appeal would therefore be dismissed. Where an administrative order or regulation was required by statute to be approved by resolution of both Houses of Parliament, the court could, in an appropriate case, intervene by using judicial review to examine the governmental exercise of the discretion to operate that procedure before both Houses had given their approval. However, the jurisdiction to do so was to be exercised with great circumspection in order to avoid encroaching on the functions of Parliament.

Per Sir John Donaldson MR:

Although the UK has no written constitution, it is a constitutional convention of the highest importance that the legislature and the judicature are separate and independent of one another, subject to certain ultimate rights of Parliament over the judicature which are immaterial for present purposes. It therefore behoves the courts to be ever sensitive to the paramount need to refrain from trespassing upon the province of Parliament or, so far as this can be avoided, even appearing to do so.

R v Secretary of State for the Home Department ex p Fire Brigades Union (1995) HL: Court could not require a minister to make delegated legislation, but could ensure that he kept the question of whether to legislate under review

Facts

The Criminal Injuries Compensation Board was set up in 1964 under prerogative powers in order to compensate the victims of crime. Compensation under the scheme was assessed on the same basis as damages at common law. Sections 108–17 of and Scheds 6 and 7 to the Criminal Justice Act 1988 substantially gave statutory enactment to the scheme. Section 171 provided that '... this Act shall come into force on such day as the Secretary of State may by order made by statutory instrument appoint and different days may be appointed ... for different provisions'.

No order had been made under the section to bring the statutory scheme into force and the original scheme was still in operation. In a White Paper, published in December 1993, the government proposed to introduce a tariff system of compensation for criminal injuries, using prerogative powers. It was common ground that in several cases payments under the tariff scheme would be less than those under the old or the statutory systems of compensation. They will accordingly be repealed when a suitable legislative opportunity occurs. The applicants argued that, although s 177 gave the Secretary of State a discretion as to when the statutory scheme might be implemented, it equally imposed on him a duty to implement it at some time. The Court of Appeal upheld the application by a majority.

Decision

The House of Lords held, by a majority, that the Secretary of State's appeal should be dismissed. Although the court could not intervene in the legislative process by requiring the Secretary of State to introduce the statutory scheme, it did not follow that he had an absolute and unfettered discretion whether or not to bring it into effect. He was under a duty to keep its introduction under consideration and not to procure events to take place and then rely on those events as grounds for not introducing the statutory scheme. In claiming that the introduction of the tariff scheme under the prerogative rendered undesirable the implementation of the statutory scheme, the Secretary of State had abused his discretion and had acted unlawfully.

In the view of the minority, the Secretary of State was answerable to Parliament for any failure in his responsibilities, and that was the only place for any possible failure to be called into question. In the absence of a written constitution, sensitivity was required of the parliamentarian, the administrator and the judge alike if the delicate balance of the unwritten rules of the Constitution was not to be disturbed and all recent advances undone. The Secretary of State's decision in the present case was quite unsuitable to be the subject of review by a court of law.

CHAPTER 4

PARLIAMENT AND THE COURTS

Introduction

This area is often referred to as parliamentary privilege, since it involves the independence of Parliament and its members from external control, something which Parliament has jealously guarded since the 17th century. This doctrine has a number of consequences, not least in defining the limits of parliamentary privilege, since the courts have shrunk from adjudicating in areas where Parliament has claimed exclusive jurisdiction.

4.1   The relationship of Parliament and the courts

4.1.1   The consequences of conflict

Jay and Topham's Case (1689): Courts have no jurisdiction in the internal affairs of Parliament

Facts

Serjeant Topham, Serjeant at Arms of the House of Commons (responsible for security and discipline within the House), arrested various individuals for breach of privileges of the House. Those arrested brought actions for assault and battery and false imprisonment against him. Before the Court of King's Bench, Topham pleaded that he had acted in obedience to the House of Commons and that the court therefore had no jurisdiction over him. This plea was rejected by the judges and judgment was given against him.

The Committee of Privileges reported to the House that the judgment of the court was itself a breach of the privileges of Parliament. The House ordered three of the King's Bench judges to attend before it. After hearing an explanation for their failure to accede to Serjeant Topham's arguments, the House resolved that they had acted in breach of privilege and committed them to the custody of the Serjeant at Arms.

Comment

The main reason in practice that the courts are considered to have no jurisdiction in the internal affairs of Parliament is that when conflict has arisen between the two, the courts have ultimately backed down. Contrast *Stockdale v Hansard* and *The Sheriff of Middlesex's Case* below.

4.1.2   The judicial view of parliamentary claims to privilege

R v Paty (1705): Commons is the sole judge of its own privileges

Facts

Five residents of Aylesbury began a legal action against the constables of that constituency on the ground that they had wrongly refused to permit them to vote. The Speaker of the House of Commons committed the residents to Newgate Prison for contempt of the jurisdiction and breach of the known privileges of the House of Commons. They applied for writs of habeas corpus to the Court of Queen's Bench. (Application for a writ of habeas corpus is an ancient procedure by which a person may require the courts to rule on the legality of his detention and order his release if the detention is unlawful.)

Decision

The court held, by a majority, that the House of Commons was the proper judge of its own privileges. Dissenting, Holt CJ denied that the commencing and prosecuting of an action was a breach of privilege, and stated that when the House of Commons exceeded its legal bounds and authority, its acts were wrongful and could not be more justified than the acts of ordinary men. The authority of the House of Commons was from the law and, as it was circumscribed, so it might be exceeded.

Stockdale v Hansard (1839): Parliament as a whole is guardian of its privileges, not Commons alone

Facts

A report by two inspectors of prisons described an illustrated anatomical textbook found in the possession of a prisoner in Newgate Prison as 'disgusting and obscene'. By order of the House of Commons, Hansard printed and sold the report. The plaintiff, who was the book's publisher, brought an action for libel against Hansard. The defendants contended that they had acted solely in obedience to the order of the House and that the report was to be regarded as part of the proceedings of the Commons (and therefore protected by parliamentary privilege under Art 9 of the Bill of Rights 1689), since it had been presented to and laid before the House. The House had resolved that the power of publishing its proceedings was an essential incident of its constitutional functions. The plaintiff replied that a resolution of the House of Commons could not alter the law of the land.

Decision

The court held that the defence pleaded was not known to the law. The defendants were seeking to assert an arbitrary and absolute power overriding the law. The mere resolution of one chamber of Parliament could confer no such power. The House of Commons undoubtedly enjoyed necessary and important privileges, but the courts and not the Commons were the arbiters of the extent of such privileges. The judgment of the House of Commons on a matter within its jurisdiction would be beyond the scrutiny of the courts, but the courts were bound to inquire whether a matter before them did indeed fall within the jurisdiction of the House. The defendants had argued on the grounds of necessity, custom and universal acquiescence for the existence of a privilege to protect the publication of libellous material. The defendants had failed to establish the first two grounds and the third was irrelevant to the legality of the privilege claimed.

Comment

Section 1 of the Parliamentary Papers Act 1840, passed as a result of this case, stays either criminal or civil proceedings against persons for the publication of papers or reports certified to have been printed by the authority of either House of Parliament.

4.1.3   The judicial view of Parliament's right to punish contempt

The Sheriff of Middlesex's Case (1840): The court backs down in face of claim of privilege

Facts

Hansard failed to enter a defence to a further action arising from the same facts as *Stockdale v Hansard* (above). Acting pursuant to a writ of the Court of Queen's Bench, the Sheriff of Middlesex levied execution upon Hansard's property. The House of Commons committed the Sheriff for contempt of the House. In response to a writ of habeas corpus, the Serjeant at Arms of the House produced the Speaker's warrant of commitment. The warrant did not specify the contempt alleged. A motion was brought for the Sheriff's discharge from custody.

Decision

The court held that it had no jurisdiction to interfere in the Sheriff's detention. A warrant for commitment, which alleged a general contempt of the House, could be inquired into no further by the court. It constituted a complete answer to the writ of habeas corpus. Conversely, the court would act, as justice might require, where a warrant had been issued which purported to commit not for contempt, but for some arbitrary and unjust cause.

4.1.4   The courts and the proceedings of the House

Bradlaugh v Gossett (1884): House of Commons absolutely entitled to determine its own composition

Facts

The plaintiff, an atheist, was duly elected as Member of Parliament for Northampton. The House took the view that, as an atheist, he could not sit or vote in the Commons, since he could not properly take the oath as required by statute. He was therefore prevented by a resolution of the House of Commons from taking the oath. The defendant, the Serjeant at Arms, had forcibly ejected the plaintiff when he sought to enter the House. The plaintiff sought an injunction to prevent the defendant from enforcing the order of the House, and a declaration that the order was void. The defendant asserted that the statement of claim disclosed no cause of action.

Decision

The court held, dismissing the plaintiff's action, that, even if the House had misinterpreted the provisions of the Parliamentary Oaths Act 1866, the matter remained outside the court's jurisdiction. Where statute determined rights to be exercised within the House, the House alone had jurisdiction to interpret that statute. Conversely, statutory rights exercisable out of the House were in the sole keeping of the courts. The officers of the House would be subject to the sanctions of the ordinary law for crimes committed in the House, and Parliament had never sought to suggest otherwise. However, the Serjeant at Arms was entitled to use reasonable force to eject the plaintiff from the House.

Comment
The following case suggests that the House of Commons may in the future take a less rigid view of its jurisdiction vis à vis the courts.

Attorney General v Jones (1999): Courts may deal with matters relating to composition of Parliament at Parliament's request

Facts
Fiona Jones, Labour MP for Newark, was convicted of knowingly making a false declaration as to her election expenses during the 1997 election campaign, contrary to s 82(6) of the Representation of the People Act 1983. Section 160(4) of the Act provides:

A candidate ... reported by an election court personally guilty of a corrupt practice shall for five years from the date of the report be incapable:
(a) Of being registered as an elector or voting at any parliamentary election in the United Kingdom ... and
(b) Of being elected to and sitting in the House of Commons, and
(c) Of holding any public or judicial office, and, if already elected to the House of Commons or holding such office, shall from that date vacate that seat or office.

The seat was consequently declared vacant by the Speaker. When the defendant's conviction was quashed by the Court of Appeal, the Attorney General, acting on behalf of the Commons, sought a declaration that she was entitled to resume her seat.

Decision
The Queen's Bench Division granted the declaration, basing their decision on the proper construction of the statute.

4.2   Privileges of Parliament

4.2.1   Freedom from civil arrest

Members of either House have freedom from arrest in civil matters only, peers at all times, MPs while Parliament is sitting and for 40 days before and after sittings.

Stourton v Stourton (1963): Privilege applies in matters unconnected with parliamentary duties

Facts
Baron Mowbray, Segrave and Stourton was a peer of the realm and entitled to sit in the House of Lords. In the course of proceedings brought against him by his wife under the Married Women's Property Act 1882, he breached a court order. Lady

Mowbray applied for a writ of attachment with a power of arrest against him. Lord Mowbray claimed parliamentary privilege against civil arrest.

Decision

The Probate, Divorce and Admiralty Division held that, since the parliamentary privilege from arrest clearly applied only to arrest in connection with civil matters and not to criminal arrest, it was necessary in each case to ascertain whether the arrest in question was merely designed to compel compliance with civil law or was truly punitive in nature. The power of arrest sought in the present case was civil, not criminal. To grant it would lead the court and the court's officers into an invasion of the privilege of Parliament.

4.2.2   Freedom of speech in Parliament

Freedom of speech in debates and proceedings in Parliament is guaranteed by Art 9 of the Bill of Rights 1689, so that no action in defamation may be brought against a member on the basis of utterances in circumstances covered by Art 9.

Church of Scientology of California v Johnson-Smith (1972): Words used in Parliament cannot be used as evidence in defamation proceedings

Facts

In the course of a defamation action against the defendant, a Member of Parliament, for remarks made by him in a television interview, for which he claimed qualified privilege, the plaintiffs sought to prove the defendant's actual malice by adducing evidence of what he had said in Parliament. Counsel for the defendant suggested that admission of the evidence might involve the court in a breach of parliamentary privilege.

Decision

The court held that the evidence would be excluded. It was clear that no action for defamation could be maintained on the basis of what was said in Parliament. It would equally be a breach of privilege to permit reference to *Hansard*'s reports of parliamentary proceedings as evidence to support a cause of action arising outside Parliament. Extracts from *Hansard* could be read in court without further comment in order to establish matters of fact, but it was not proper to draw further inferences from them. The law on this aspect of parliamentary privilege derived from Art 9 of the Bill of Rights (1689), which provided:

That the freedome of speech and debates or proceedings in Parlyament ought not to be impeached or questioned in any court or place out of Parlyament.

Rost v Edwards (1990) QBD: Exclusive jurisdiction of Parliament in this area

Facts

The plaintiff sought damages for libel in respect of an article said to allege that he had misused his position as a member of the House of Commons Select Committee on Energy for personal gain. At the trial of the action, he wished to call evidence to establish that the article had adversely affected his chances of being appointed chairman of the Select Committee and had resulted in his deselection from the Standing Committee on the Energy Bill. When it became clear that questions of parliamentary privilege might be involved, the case was adjourned pending the court's resolution of possible conflict between the privilege secured by Art 9 of the Bill of Rights and the plaintiff's right freely to present his case in court.

Decision

The Queen's Bench Division held that, if the plaintiff wished to call evidence to support his account of the consequences of the alleged libel, it would be necessary for him to petition the House of Commons for its consent, since the common law established that the use intended by the plaintiff to be made of the material which he sought to adduce would amount to a questioning of parliamentary proceedings. Popplewell J stated that, had the authorities been less insistent, the court might have been prepared to hold that the 'questioning' forbidden by the Bill of Rights was only that which involved some allegation of improper motive. After observing the constitutional need for comity between Parliament and the courts, he continued:

I hope ... I may be permitted to say this, that the effect of this judgment if the House declines the petition may (and I emphasise the word may) be to deprive a litigant of his proper rights. This has particular importance in a case where, as far as one can see, neither freedom of speech nor the dignity of the House will have been affected. No question, as I understand it, arises of questioning the validity of any decision of the House or its Committee or making any suggestion of improper motive. Accordingly, in so far as it is appropriate for me to make any comment on the exercise of the House's judgment about a matter over which they have exclusive jurisdiction ... I express the hope that they will approach the matter sympathetically.

Prebble v Television New Zealand Ltd (1994) PC: MP cannot waive privilege, as it is privilege of Parliament rather than of individual members

Facts

The defendant company broadcast a television programme in which it alleged that the plaintiff, a minister in the New Zealand Government, had abused his position by conspiring to assist certain business interests during a privatisation in return for party political donations. In response to the plaintiff's action for libel, the defendant pleaded (*inter alia*) justification, relying on particulars of proceedings in the New Zealand Parliament. The plaintiff applied to strike out these particulars on the ground that they infringed parliamentary privilege and succeeded at first instance.

The New Zealand Court of Appeal upheld the judge's ruling and additionally held that, in light of the defendant's resulting disadvantage in the litigation, the action should be stayed pending the waiver of privilege by Parliament. The plaintiff appealed against the stay of proceedings to the Privy Council, which addressed the questions whether the defendant's particulars infringed Art 9 and, if so, whether the New Zealand Court of Appeal had been correct to order a stay. The defendant submitted either that privilege only operated to prevent examination of a statement which was itself said to give rise to legal liability, or alternatively that privilege did not operate to protect the maker himself of a parliamentary statement against a defendant's challenge to his veracity or *bona fides*.

Decision

The Privy Council held, allowing the appeal in part, that the defendant's case did involve a breach of Art 9, but that, since the greater part of it rested on matters not subject to privilege, there had been insufficient reason to grant a stay, effectively preventing the plaintiff from vindicating his reputation. Such a stay was to be granted only in extreme circumstances. Both the defendant's submissions were rejected. The defendant had relied on the Australian case of *Wright and Advertiser Newspapers Ltd v Lewis* (1990) in support of the second submission. Lord Browne-Wilkinson cited that case and continued:

Although their Lordships are sympathetic with the concern felt by the South Australian Supreme Court, they cannot accept that the fact that the maker of the statement is the initiator of the court proceedings can affect the question whether Art 9 is infringed. The privilege protected by Art 9 is the privilege of Parliament itself. The actions of any individual Member of Parliament, even if he has an individual privilege of his own, cannot determine whether or not the privilege of Parliament is to apply.

Comment

Section 13 of the Defamation Act 1996 overrules this aspect of *Prebble's* case in relation to the UK Parliament, allowing individual Members of Parliament to waive parliamentary privilege. This change was strongly criticised during debates on the Defamation Bill, since it allowed an MP to opt in and out of privilege as it suited him.

Hamilton v Al Fayed (1999) CA: Parliamentary investigation of conduct of MP was a proceeding in Parliament and could not be the subject of court proceedings, but legal action based on facts investigated by Parliament might go ahead

Facts

The plaintiff, a former Member of Parliament, waived his parliamentary privilege pursuant to s 13 of the Defamation Act 1996 and began defamation proceedings against the defendant in respect of the defendant's allegations that the plaintiff had taken money from him as payment for asking questions in Parliament. The plaintiff's conduct had been criticised in a report by the Parliamentary Commissioner for Standards. The Commons Committee on Standards and Privileges had prepared a confirmatory report on the matter, which was approved by resolution of the House itself. The defendant sought to strike out the plaintiff's claim as an abuse of the process of the court on the grounds that:

(1) the matter had been fully and fairly litigated in another court of competent jurisdiction;

(2) the plaintiff's action would involve questioning proceedings in Parliament in contravention of Art 9 of the Bill of Rights 1689; and/or

(3) the action would constitute a collateral attack upon Parliament's investigation of the plaintiff's conduct.

At first instance, Popplewell J refused the defendant's application, making criticisms of the parliamentary investigation. The defendant appealed.

Decision

The Court of Appeal held, dismissing the appeal, that it was not open to the court to decide whether the plaintiff's action was an abuse of process, since the answer to that question required scrutiny of the procedural fairness of a proceeding in Parliament in contravention of Art 9. Judicial criticism at first instance of the parliamentary investigation had been impermissible for the same reason. Provided the plaintiff's action did not raise similar criticisms, there was no reason for it not to proceed. In so far as the court seised of the plaintiff's claim might reach a conclusion at variance with that of the Commissioner, it should only adopt that as a reason for declining the claim if persuaded that the effect of the difference would be to undermine the authority of Parliament. This effect could not be deduced from the possibility of the difference itself, but would be predicated upon the facts and circumstances of the particular case.

4.2.3   Can the courts refer to debates in Parliament as an aid to the construction of legislation?

Beswick v Beswick (1967) HL: Reasons why a court should not use the record of debates for this purpose

Facts

The respondent argued that s 56(1) of the Law of Property Act 1925 allowed her to sue in her personal capacity on a contract to which she was not party.

The House of Lords held that the contention was incorrect (though the respondent was permitted to maintain an action as administratrix of her late husband's estate). The 1925 Act was a consolidating Act and it was quite certain that those responsible for the legislation must have believed and intended that s 56 would make no substantial change in earlier law.

Per Lord Reid:

In construing any Act of Parliament, we are seeking the intention of Parliament ... For purely practical reasons, we do not permit debates in either House to be cited: it would add greatly to the time and expense involved in preparing cases involving the construction of a statute if counsel were expected to read all the debates in Hansard, and it would often be impractical for counsel to get access to at least the older reports of debates in select committees of the House of Commons; moreover, in a very large proportion of cases such a search, even if practicable, would throw no light on the question before the court.

Davis v Johnson (1978) HL: Record of debates is not reliable indicator of intention of Parliament

Facts

On appeal from the grant of an ouster injunction, the question arose whether s 1 of the Domestic Violence and Matrimonial Proceedings Act 1976 did or did not confer jurisdiction on a county court to exclude a person from premises in which he had a proprietary interest.

Decision

The House of Lords held, dismissing the appeal, that the power conferred by s 1 was exercisable irrespective of the proprietary rights with which it might conflict. The House of Lords reached this conclusion without reference to *Hansard*.

Per Lord Scarman:

There are two good reasons why the courts should refuse to have regard to what is said in Parliament or by ministers as aids to the interpretation of a statute. First, such material is an unreliable guide to the meaning of what is enacted. It promotes confusion, not clarity. The cut and thrust of debate and the pressures of executive responsibility, essential features of open and responsible government, are not always conducive to a clear and unbiased explanation of the meaning of statutory language. And the volume of parliamentary and ministerial utterances can confuse by its very size. Secondly, counsel are not permitted to refer to Hansard in argument. So long as this rule is maintained by Parliament (it is not the creation of the judges), it must be wrong for the judge to make any judicial use of proceedings in Parliament for the purpose of interpreting statutes ...

Pepper (Inspector of Taxes) v Hart (1993) HL: Exception to the general principle

Facts

The appellants, who were members of staff at an independent school, had received a taxable benefit – the education of their sons at concessionary fees at that school. Under s 61(1) of the Finance Act 1976, they were to be taxed on the 'cash equivalent' of that benefit. Section 63 of the Act defined 'cash equivalent' as 'an amount equal to the cost of the benefit', and defined that amount as 'the amount of any expense incurred in or in connection with its provision'. The Crown contended that the amount in question was the ordinary cost of an education at the school (the 'average cost'). The appellants argued that the cost of the benefit was to be regarded as the actual cost of its provision to the school, which was negligible (the 'marginal cost'). To support their contention, the appellants sought to refer the House to *Hansard*'s report of the proceedings in Parliament, which had led to the passage of the 1976 Act.

Decision

The House of Lords held, by a majority, that the rule prohibiting reference to *Hansard* in the construction of legislation should be relaxed. The arguments against so doing were that:

(1)   the rule reflected and preserved the proper roles of Parliament and the courts;

(2)   relaxation of the rule would expose litigants to the practical difficulty of the expense involved in researching parliamentary material;

(3)   the citizen ought to have access to a known and defined legal text which regulated his legal rights; and

(4)   *Hansard* was an improbable source of helpful guidance as to the proper construction of legislation.

In favour of relaxation, it was desirable that where ambiguity or obscurity attended the legislatively expressed will of Parliament, the courts should not blind themselves to a clear indication of what Parliament intended by its choice of words. The Attorney General had submitted that the courts' use of parliamentary material would infringe

Art 9, but consultation of such material in the view of the House would not amount to the 'impeachment' or 'questioning' of the freedom of speech or debate in Parliament.

Reference to parliamentary material would therefore be permitted where legislation was ambiguous or obscure, or tended to lead to an absurdity; where the material relied upon consisted of one or more statements by a minister or other promoter of the Bill, together, if necessary, with such other parliamentary material as was necessary to understand such statements and their effect; and the statements relied on were clear. These requirements were satisfied in the present case and statements made to Parliament by the Financial Secretary to the Treasury made it clear that s 63 of the Act was intended to have the meaning argued for by the appellants.

4.2.4   Unauthorised reports of proceedings in Parliament attract common law qualified privilege

Official publications of either House attract absolute privilege under s 1 of the Parliamentary Papers Act 1840, but the reporting of Parliament by the press is covered by the ordinary law of qualified privilege.

Wason v Walter (1868): Public have an interest in receiving reports of debates

Facts
The plaintiff sued one of the proprietors of *The Times* for libel. The newspaper had published a report of a debate in the House of Lords in which the plaintiff considered himself to have been defamed.

Decision
The court held that the English law of defamation was based upon the concept of malice. In the majority of cases, it was not necessary to prove actual malice; it would be presumed as a matter of law to have accompanied the defendant's wrongful act. However, there were circumstances in which the presumption of malice would not arise, and in such a case it would be necessary for the plaintiff to prove actual malice, if he could. Reports of proceedings in Parliament were such an example. The rationale for extending qualified privilege to them was explained by Cockburn CJ to be the same as that which underlay the privileged status of the reports of the proceedings of courts of justice:

The presumption of malice is negatived in the one case, as in the other, by the fact that the publication has in view the instruction and advantage of the public, and has no particular reference to the party concerned. There is in the one case, as in the other, a preponderance of general good over partial and occasional evil.

4.2.5   The right to control internal proceedings

Bradlaugh v Gossett (1884): Internal proceedings of Parliament are matter for Parliament alone

Facts
See 4.1.4 above.

Per Stephen J:

The House of Commons is not a court of justice, but the effect of its privilege to regulate its own internal concerns practically invests it with a judicial character when it has to apply to particular cases the provisions of Acts of Parliament. We must presume that it discharges this function properly and with due regard to the laws, in the making of which it has so great a share. If its determination is not in accordance with the law, this resembles the case of an error by a judge whose decision is not subject to appeal.

Rost v Edwards (1990) QBD: What is a 'proceeding in Parliament'?

Facts

See 4.2.2 above. The plaintiff wished to put before the jury an explanation what the Register of Members' Interests was, what the criteria for registration were, what he was therefore required to disclose and what in fact he did disclose. Counsel for the defendants concurred with the plaintiff in submitting that the Register was not a 'proceeding in Parliament'. The Solicitor General argued that it was, submitting that it embraced the whole process by which either House reaches a decision in a particular debate, together with things said or done by a Member of Parliament in the exercise of his function as a member in a committee in either House, and everything said or done in either House in the transaction of parliamentary business.

Decision

The Queen's Bench Division held that the Register was not a 'proceeding in Parliament'. The plaintiff and defendants would therefore be permitted to make use of it in the trial.

Per Popplewell J:

There are clearly cases where Parliament is to be the sole judge of its affairs. Equally, there are clear cases where the courts are to have exclusive jurisdiction. In a case which may be described as a grey area a court ... should not be astute to find a reason for ousting the jurisdiction of the courts or even defeating a proper claim by a party to litigation before it. If Parliament wishes to cover a particular area with privilege, it has the ability to do so by passing an Act of Parliament giving itself the right to exclusive jurisdiction. Ousting the jurisdiction of the courts has always been regarded as requiring the clearest possible words. Nothing in the authorities ... in any way covers the instant situation ...

4.3   Maintaining the constitutional balance between legislature and judicature

Duport Steels Ltd v Sirs (1980) HL

See 2.1.7 and 3.3.1 above.

R v Her Majesty's Treasury ex p Smedley (1985) CA

See 3.3.1 above.

CHAPTER 5

THE LEGISLATIVE SOVEREIGNTY OF PARLIAMENT

Introduction

The doctrine of parliamentary sovereignty, or parliamentary supremacy, is a product of the constitutional settlement at the end of the 17th century. It has two elements: that Parliament may make or unmake any law; and that a parliamentary statute is the highest law known in the UK, and may not be set aside except by Parliament itself.

5.1   Statute overrides international law

Mortensen v Peters (1906): Parliament may legislate contrary to international law by express words

Facts

The appellant was the captain of a Norwegian trawler. He was convicted by a Scottish sheriff court of fishing with an otter trawl within the Moray Firth, contrary to a bylaw made under the Herring Fishery (Scotland) Act 1889, which prohibited the use of such equipment anywhere within the Moray Firth, and applied even outside the three mile limit of British territorial waters. He appealed on the ground that, since he was not a British subject and had not been fishing within territorial waters, he was not subject to the jurisdiction of the Scottish court.

Decision

The court held, dismissing the appeal, that the question was purely one of construction. If the appellant's conduct fell within the terms of the Act, the court was bound to give effect to the Act. There was a presumption that Parliament would not seek to exceed what an international tribunal might hold to be its proper sphere of legislative competence, but if by express words or plain implication Parliament had done so, the presumption would have no further effect.

Comment

Though Mortensen's conviction was upheld, his sentence was nevertheless reduced to a purely nominal level.

Cheney v Conn (1968): UK courts must give priority to UK statutes

Facts

The plaintiff taxpayer challenged assessments of income tax and surtax raised under the Finance Act 1964 on the ground that a part of the tax raised was used to fund the construction of nuclear weapons. He contended, *inter alia*, that this purpose was contrary to international law, which was part of the law of England.

Decision

The Chancery Division held, dismissing the appeal by way of case stated, that while it was correct that international law formed part of the law of England, where a statute is unambiguous, its provisions must be followed even if they are contrary to international law.

Per Ungoed-Thomas J:

What the statute itself enacts cannot be unlawful, because what the statute says and provides is itself the law, and the highest form of law that is known to this country. It is the law which prevails over every other form of law, and it is not for the court to say that a parliamentary enactment, the highest law in this country, is illegal.

5.2   Statute overrides political fact

Madzimbamuto v Lardner-Burke (1969) PC

See 1.2 above.

5.3   The courts and the legislative sovereignty of Parliament

5.3.1   Challenge to the content of Acts of Parliament

R v Jordan (1967): Courts cannot question validity of an Act of Parliament

Facts

The defendant was sentenced to 18 months' imprisonment for offences under the Race Relations Act 1965. He applied for legal aid to seek a writ of habeas corpus on the ground that the Act was invalid as being a curtailment of his rights of free speech.

Decision

The Queen's Bench Divisional Court held, dismissing the application, that Parliament was supreme and there was no power in the courts to question the validity of an Act of Parliament. The ground of the application was completely unarguable.

Comment

Since the Human Rights Act 1998 came into force in October 2000, it has been possible to obtain a 'declaration of incompatibility' between a statute and the provisions of the European Convention on Human Rights, but this does not render the Act concerned void or unenforceable. See 21.5 below.

5.3.2   Challenge to the manner in which an Act has been passed

Edinburgh and Dalkeith Railway Co v Wauchope (1842) HL: Courts cannot look at the manner in which an Act has been passed

Facts

The respondent, a landowner, had argued in the Court of Session that a private Act of Parliament authorising the construction of a railway should be disapplied because its promoters had failed to give notice as required by House of Commons standing orders to persons affected by its provisions. The argument was abandoned in the House of Lords, but Lord Campbell commented:

My Lords, I think it right to say a word or two before I sit down, upon the point that has been raised with regard to an Act of Parliament being held inoperative by a court of justice because the forms, in respect of an Act of Parliament, have not been complied with … It seems to me there is no foundation for it whatever; all that a court of justice can look to is the parliamentary roll; they see that an Act has passed both Houses of Parliament, and that it has received the royal assent, and no court of justice can inquire into the manner in which it was introduced into Parliament, what was done previously to its being introduced, or what passed in Parliament during the various stages of its progress through both Houses of Parliament …

Lee v Bude and Torrington Junction Railway Co (1871)

The facts, so far as they are material, are sufficiently given in the passage cited below.

Per Willes J:

It is further urged that the company was a mere nonentity, and that there never were any shares or shareholders. That resolves itself into this, that Parliament was induced by fraudulent recitals (introduced, it is said, by the plaintiffs) to pass the Act which formed the company. I would observe, as to these Acts of Parliament, that they are the law of this land; and we do not sit here as a court of appeal from Parliament … If an Act of Parliament has been obtained improperly, it is for the legislature to correct it by repealing it: but, so long as it exists as law, the courts are bound to obey it. The proceedings here are judicial, not autocratic, which they would be if we could make laws instead of administering them.

Pickin v British Railways Board (1974) HL: Court could not inquire into whether Parliament's rules of procedure had been followed

Facts

The respondent, a railway enthusiast, owned land adjoining an abandoned railway line. Relying on a private Act of Parliament of 1836, he argued that the strip of land over which an abandoned track passed vested in the owners of the land to either side of the track. The Board claimed that by a further private Act, the British Railways Act 1968, it retained ownership of the land. In reply, Pickin alleged that the 1968 Act was invalid, since its passage through Parliament had been obtained by fraud. The Bill had been represented as unopposed, whereas notice had not been given to affected landowners as the rules of parliamentary procedure required. Furthermore, the Bill had falsely stated that a list of landowners was deposited with the clerk of the county council.

Decision

The House of Lords held, allowing the Board's appeal, that Pickin depended upon proof that the Board's fraud caused the passing of the 1968 Act. Proof of that, in turn, required examination of the manner in which the officers of Parliament dealt with the Bill's passage. There was no authority to permit such an investigation. If an Act had been obtained in breach of parliamentary procedure, it was for Parliament, and not the courts, to investigate the matter.

Comment

Both the above cases concern private Acts, that is, Acts dealing only with specified individuals or organisations which are subject to a special parliamentary procedure. The same principle, however, applies to public Acts.

***Manuel v Attorney General* (1983) Ch D and CA:** Compliance with requirements as to outward forms was all that was necessary

Facts

At the request of the Senate and the House of Commons of Canada, the UK Parliament passed the Canada Act 1982, whereby it terminated its competence to legislate for Canada. The plaintiffs, who were Indian chiefs, argued that the Act was *ultra vires* Parliament. They submitted that, by the Statute of Westminster 1931, Parliament had deprived itself of all power to legislate for Canada, save in accordance with s 4 of that Act, which required the prior consent of the Canadian Parliament, the provincial legislatures and the Indian nations. They claimed that the proper consents had not been obtained. The Attorney General moved that the statement of claim be struck out as disclosing no reasonable cause of action.

Decision

The Chancery Division held that the case was covered by the authority of *Pickin v British Railways Board* (above). It made no difference that the Act in that case had been purely domestic legislation, while the present Act purported to apply outside the UK.

The Court of Appeal held, dismissing the plaintiffs' appeal, that on the true construction of the 1931 Act, all that was required was a declaration of the Dominion's request for and consent to the legislation. Actual consent was not required. If compliance with s 4 was legally required, then it was present by reason of the conforming declaration contained in the preamble to the 1982 Act. For the purposes of the appeal, it was assumed that Parliament could restrict the form of subsequent legislation, although the proposition appeared to be contrary to *Ellen Street Estates Ltd v Minister of Health* (see below). The court emphasised that it was not purporting to decide the issue.

5.4   The doctrine of implied repeal

One of the elements of parliamentary sovereignty is that Parliament may make or unmake any law. This includes the doctrine of implied repeal, which states that, even in the absence of express provision for repeal, a later Act repeals inconsistent provisions of an earlier Act to the extent of the inconsistency.

5.4.1   Conflicting Acts of Parliament

Ellen Street Estates Ltd v Minister of Health (1934) CA

Facts

Section 2 of the Acquisition of Land (Assessment of Compensation) Act 1919 enacted rules governing the quantum of compensation to be paid in respect of land compulsorily acquired. Section 46 of the Housing Act 1925 created rules for the assessment of compensation which differed from those of the earlier Act, and were less favourable to the appellant. Section 7(1) of the 1919 Act stated:

The provisions of the Act or order by which the land is authorised to be acquired, or of any Act incorporated herewith, shall in relation to the matters dealt with in this Act, have effect subject to this Act, and so far as inconsistent with this Act those provisions shall cease to have or shall not have effect …

Section 46 of the 1925 Act included the words:

Subject as aforesaid, the compensation to be paid for such land shall be assessed in accordance with [the 1919 Act].

The appellant argued that compensation should be assessed in accordance with the 1919 provisions.

Decision

The Court of Appeal held that, in so far as the 1925 provisions were inconsistent with the 1919 provisions, the 1925 provisions alone applied. Parliament could alter an Act previously passed either by expressly modifying or repealing it, or, as here, by enacting provisions inconsistent with it. The latter provisions would impliedly repeal inconsistent previous enactments.

Per Maugham LJ:

The legislature cannot, according to our Constitution, bind itself as to the form of subsequent legislation, and it is impossible for Parliament to enact that in a subsequent statute dealing with the same subject matter there can be no implied repeal.

Manuel v Attorney General (1983) Ch D and CA

See 5.3.2 above.

5.5   'Manner and form' limitations

Can Parliament limit the manner and form in which legislation is made, that is, ordain that a special procedure must be followed before legislation of a particular type may be passed? For instance, s 1 of the Northern Ireland (Constitution) Act 1973 provides that Northern Ireland shall not cease to be part of the UK save with the consent of a majority of its population in a referendum held for that purpose. Is that procedural requirement enforceable, so that a court would be able to declare an Act void which removed Northern Ireland from the UK without a preliminary referendum or in defiance of the result of such a referendum? There is no specific UK case law dealing with this issue, but there has been much discussion based partly on case law from other jurisdictions. The orthodox view draws on *Pickin v British Railways Board* and *Manuel v Attorney General* to state that all that is necessary to render an Act valid is compliance with outward forms – a statement on the face of the Act that a referendum has taken place and the majority of voters supported the change will suffice.

5.5.1   Derivative legislatures

Both the cases below involve non-sovereign legislatures, whose powers were circumscribed by some form of 'higher law' which does not exist within the UK Constitution.

Attorney General for New South Wales v Trethowan and Others (1932) PC: Failure to comply with an entrenched procedural requirement did render a measure void

Facts

Section 5 of the Colonial Laws Validity Act 1865 (an Act of the Westminster Parliament) gave the legislature of New South Wales (NSW) power to make laws altering its Constitution: 'provided that such laws shall have been passed in such manner and form as may from time to time be required by any Act of Parliament … or colonial law …' Section 7A of the Constitution Act (an Act of the NSW legislature) provided that no Bill abolishing the Legislative Council (the upper house of the NSW legislature) should be presented to the Governor for royal assent unless approved by a majority of electors voting in a referendum, and s 7A was protected from repeal by an equivalent provision. In 1930, the NSW government intended to present to the Governor a Bill to abolish the Legislative Council and another Bill to repeal s 7A. Neither measure had been approved in a referendum. The plaintiffs, who were members of the Legislative Council, sought a declaration that presentation of the Bills would be unlawful, and injunctions restraining the presentation of the Bills.

Decision

The Privy Council held that s 7A was a colonial law within the meaning of s 5 of the 1865 Act. The procedural condition created by s 7A (the referendum requirement) was binding on the NSW legislature by virtue of s 5 of the 1865 Act. It would therefore be unlawful to present the Bills to the governor unless they had first received the referendum approval required by s 7A. If the Bills received the royal assent, but did not have referendum approval, they would not be valid Acts of the NSW legislature.

Bribery Commissioner v Ranasinghe (1965) PC: Procedural requirement entrenched by constitution

Facts

By virtue of the Constitution of Ceylon, the Ceylon Parliament had power to amend or repeal the Constitution provided that a Bill for that purpose was certified by the Speaker as having obtained the requisite parliamentary majority. A provision of the Ceylon Bribery Amendment Act 1958, governing the appointment of tribunal members, conflicted with the Constitution of Ceylon. The 1958 Act had not been certified by the Speaker. The Supreme Court of Ceylon held the respondent's conviction for a bribery offence to be null and void on the ground that the appointment of members of the Bribery Tribunal was unlawful since the enabling provision of the 1958 Act had not been properly enacted. The Bribery Commissioner appealed to the Privy Council.

Decision

The Privy Council held, dismissing the appeal, that, in the case of amendment and repeal of the Constitution, the Speaker's certificate was a necessary part of the legislative process. A Bill which did not bear the certificate would be invalid, even after it had received royal assent. The court would inquire whether the Speaker's certificate was endorsed on the original copy of the Bill. It was true that a narrow view had been taken in England of the court's power to look behind an authentic copy of an Act. However, there had never been any need in the UK for courts to look into the law making process, since there was never a governing instrument which prescribed law making powers.

Per Lord Pearce:

The court has a duty to see that the Constitution is not infringed and to preserve it inviolate. Unless, therefore, there is some very cogent reason for doing so, the court must not decline to open its eyes to the truth.

5.6 The status and powers of Parliament under the 1707 Union legislation

Scottish academics have long argued that the powers of the Westminster Parliament are circumscribed by the Acts of Union of 1707, which dissolved the separate English and Scottish Parliaments and replaced them with a Parliament of Great Britain. The Acts of Union are underpinned by a Treaty of Union negotiated by commissioners representing the two Parliaments, and guarantees protection to Scottish interests in specified spheres (particularly the continuance of the separate Scottish legal system). The Treaty contains no provisions for its own amendment and, since the dissolution of the two Parliaments, there is no body with jurisdiction to amend it. However, case law shows the Scottish courts consider such matters outside their jurisdiction and so avoid pronouncements on the compatibility of legislation with the Treaty.

MacCormick v The Lord Advocate (1953) **Court of Session:** Issue left open by courts

Facts

The petitioners sought a declarator that a proclamation by which the Queen took the title 'Elizabeth the Second of the United Kingdom of Great Britain' was contrary to Art I of the Treaty and Acts of Union of 1707, as no previous Queen Elizabeth had reigned over Scotland. The Acts, passed by the Parliaments of England and Scotland, had extinguished those Parliaments and established the Parliament of Great Britain as their successor. The petitioners argued, *inter alia*, that Parliament had no power to alter those provisions in the Treaty and Acts of Union, which were declared to be fundamental and unalterable since the legislative authority from which they derived was anterior to Parliament.

Decision

The Inner House of the Court of Session (equivalent to the Court of Appeal) held, dismissing the appeal, that the petitioners had raised no issue which they could show to be justiciable by the court.

Per Lord President Cooper:

The Treaty and the associated legislation ... contain some clauses which expressly reserve to the Parliament of Great Britain powers of subsequent modification, and other clauses which either contain no such power or emphatically exclude subsequent alteration ... I have never been able to understand how it is possible to reconcile with elementary canons of construction the adoption by the English constitutional theorists of the same attitude to these markedly different types of provisions ...

I have not found in the Union legislation any provision that the Parliament of Great Britain should be 'absolutely sovereign' in the sense that Parliament should be free to alter the Treaty at will ... It is of little avail to ask whether the Parliament of Great Britain 'can' do this thing or that, without going on to inquire who can stop them if they do ... This at least is plain, that there is neither precedent nor authority of any kind for the view that the domestic courts of either Scotland or England have jurisdiction to determine whether a governmental act of the type here in controversy is or is not conform to the provisions of a treaty ...

Gibson v The Lord Advocate (1975) Court of Session: Court held issue before it to be non-justifiable

Facts

Article XVIII of the Act of Union 1707 authorised Parliament to alter certain aspects of Scots law, but provided 'that no alteration be made in laws which concern private right except for evident utility of the subjects within Scotland'. A Scots fisherman sought a declarator that the opening of Scottish coastal waters to nationals of other Community States under EEC Regulations (directly applicable by the European Communities Act 1972) was contrary to Art XVIII.

Decision

The Court held, dismissing the appeal, that the issue was outside the sphere of private rights.

Per Lord Keith (*obiter*):

... The question whether a particular Act of the UK Parliament altering a particular aspect of Scots private law is or is not 'for the evident utility' of the subjects within Scotland is not a justiciable issue in this court.

Lord Keith added, however, that he expressed no view on what the position would be:

... if the UK Parliament passed an Act purporting to abolish the Court of Session or the Church of Scotland or to substitute English law for the whole body of Scots private law.

Pringle (1991)

Facts

The Abolition of Domestic Rates, etc (Scotland) Act 1987 introduced the community charge (poll tax) legislation in Scotland one year earlier than it was due to be introduced in England and Wales. The petitioner argued that it accordingly infringed Art IV of the Scots Act of Union which, he claimed, required that there should be no difference in the rights, privileges and advantages enjoyed by citizens in Great Britain, unless expressly provided for in the Act of Union. The petitioner did not directly allege that the 1987 Act was invalid, but sought relief from his own liability to pay the poll tax.

Decision

The court held, dismissing the petition, that the court had no jurisdiction to grant the remedy claimed. Reaching no conclusion on the compatibility of the 1987 Act and Art IV of the Act of Union, the Lord President Lord Hope rejected the respondent's submission that the issue as a whole was not justiciable, but stated that much more detailed inquiry would be needed before he would be persuaded of the alleged incompatibility.

5.7 Challenge in the courts to subordinate legislation

5.7.1 Bylaws

Bylaws are a form of delegated legislation having effect within a specified geographical area only, and are made by bodies such as local authorities under powers granted by statute.

Kruse v Johnson (1898): The court has jurisdiction to consider validity of bylaws

Facts

Kruse, a minister of religion, was conducting an open-air service within 50 yards of a dwelling house in a village in Kent. He continued to sing a hymn after he had been asked by a police constable to stop. A bylaw made by Kent county council read as follows:

No person shall sound or play upon any musical or noisy instrument or sing in any public place or highway within 50 yards of any dwelling house after being required by a constable or by an inmate of such house personally or by his or her servant, to desist.

Johnson, a police superintendent, preferred an information against Kruse, who was convicted by the magistrates under the bylaw. He appealed by way of case stated to the Divisional Court, contending that the bylaw was invalid for unreasonableness, since it was not on its face limited to acts which were a nuisance, and because it might be put into operation by a policeman independently of judicial process.

Decision

The Divisional Court held, by a majority, that the conviction would be confirmed. Lord Russell of Killowen CJ considered the nature of a bylaw, and said:

A bylaw of the class we are considering I take to be an ordinance affecting the public or some portion of the public, imposed by some authority clothed with statutory powers, ordering something to be done or not to be done, and accompanied by some sanction or penalty for its non-observance. It necessarily involves restriction of liberty of action by persons who come under its operation as to acts which, but for the bylaw, they would be free to do or not to do as they pleased. Further, it involves this consequence – that, if validly made, it has the force of law within the sphere of its legitimate operation – see *Edmund v Watermen's Co* (1855) ... We thus find that Parliament has thought fit to delegate to representative public bodies ... the power of exercising their own judgment as to what are the bylaws which to them seem proper to be made for good rule and government in their own localities. But that power is accompanied by certain safeguards; there must be antecedent publication of the bylaw, with a view, I presume, of eliciting the public opinion of the locality upon it, and such bylaws shall have no force until after they have been forwarded to the Secretary of State.

However, the presence of the safeguards did not prevent the court from examining the validity of bylaws when they were brought into question. The court would be less vigilant to examine the bylaws of representative public bodies than it would be in the case of bylaws made by railway companies and similar undertakings. They ought to be 'benevolently' interpreted, and credit given to those who were to administer them that they would be reasonably administered. The court might find bylaws to be unreasonable if they were partial in their operation, as between different classes, manifestly unjust, made in bad faith or oppressive. In any of these cases, it would be possible to say that Parliament never intended to give authority to make such rules.

The bylaw in the present case could not be said to be unreasonable; annoyance was a subjective concept, and a policeman was a responsible person in whom it was not improper to vest the power of putting the bylaw into operation against an individual.

5.7.2   *Statutory instruments*

Statutory instruments are legislative measures made by ministers on the basis of powers delegated by statute. They are subject to challenge in the courts on grounds, *inter alia*, that an instrument is *ultra vires* its enabling Act, or that procedural requirements have not been followed.

R v Sheer Metalcraft Ltd (1954): Consideration of validity of statutory instruments

Facts
See *Simmonds v Newell* (2.1.5 above).

The defendants argued at trial that the Iron and Steel Prices Order was not a valid statutory instrument, since the schedules setting out the maximum prices had not been printed with it and the minister had not certified under reg 7 of the 1947 Statutory Instruments Regulations that this was unnecessary.

Decision
The court held that the order was valid. The making of a statutory instrument and its issue were different procedures. The making of a valid instrument was complete when it had been made by the minister concerned and laid before Parliament. At that stage, it entered into force and was capable of being contravened. Where the remaining procedures relating to its issue had not been complied with, the burden was upon the Crown to prove that the instrument had nevertheless been brought to the attention of the public or of persons likely to be affected by it, or of the defendants themselves, for

the purposes of the defence to prosecution provided by s 3(2) of the Statutory Instruments Act 1946.

Hoffman-La Roche AG v Secretary of State for Trade and Industry (1975) HL: Principles on which court will act

Facts

The Secretary of State applied for an injunction to compel certain pharmaceutical companies to reduce the price of various products in accordance with a statutory instrument made for that purpose. The companies alleged that the statutory instrument had been made in breach of aspects of natural justice required by statute to be observed as a precondition to the valid making of subordinate legislation in the area. They refused to reduce their prices, and issued a writ, claiming that the statutory instrument was *ultra vires* and void.

Decision

The House of Lords held, granting the injunction sought by the Secretary of State, that the companies had failed to show a sufficiently strong *prima facie* case that the statutory instrument was *ultra vires*.

Per Lord Diplock:

My Lords, in constitutional law, a clear distinction can be drawn between an Act of Parliament and subordinate legislation, even though the latter is contained in an order made by statutory instrument approved by resolutions of both Houses of Parliament ... I entertain no doubt that the courts have jurisdiction to declare it to be invalid if they are satisfied that in making it the Minister who did so acted outwith the legislative powers conferred on him by the previous Act of Parliament under which the order purported to be made; and this is so whether the order is *ultra vires* by reason of its contents (patent defects) or by reason of defects in the procedure followed prior to its being made (latent defects).

R v Secretary of State for Social Security ex p Joint Council for the Welfare of Immigrants (1997) CA: A statutory instrument may be *ultra vires* on the basis of breach of human rights

Facts

Pursuant to powers purportedly conferred by the Social Security and Contributions Act 1992, the Secretary of State made the Social Security (Persons from Abroad) Miscellaneous Amendment Regulations 1996. The effect of the Regulations was to remove statutory entitlement to income-related benefit from asylum seekers who did not apply for asylum immediately upon reaching the UK, or whose asylum claims were pending appeal following rejection by the Home Secretary. The Regulations were intended to deter economic migrants from making spurious asylum claims, to speed up the asylum application process and to save public money. The Divisional Court refused a declaration that the Regulations were *ultra vires* the Act of 1992, and the Council appealed to the Court of Appeal.

Decision

The Court of Appeal held, allowing the appeal by a majority, that the effect of the Regulations would be either to oblige some genuine asylum seekers to abandon their claim and return to the country from which they had fled, or to force them into penury and thus to jeopardise their ability to pursue their claims. Despite the fact that Parliament had been closely involved in the making of the Regulations, they were *ultra vires*. Only primary and not subordinate legislation could effectively put the statutory right to claim refugee status beyond the reach of those intended to have it. The human rights at issue were so basic that there was no need to refer to the European Convention on Human Rights to show their violation; Simon Brown LJ cited with approval Lord Ellenborough CJ's observation in *R v Inhabitants of Eastbourne* (1803) that, in the absence of positive law, the law of humanity obliged the provision of relief to poor immigrants to save them from starving.

CHAPTER 6

THE CONSEQUENCES OF MEMBERSHIP OF THE EUROPEAN UNION FOR THE LEGISLATIVE SOVEREIGNTY OF PARLIAMENT

Introduction

The UK entered the then European Economic Community, European Coal and Steel Community and EURATOM on 1 January 1973 under the terms of the European Communities Act (ECA) 1972, which ratified the earlier Treaty of Accession and made provision for the incorporation of EC law into national law.

6.1 EC law overrides subsequent inconsistent domestic legislation

6.1.1 The European view

Costa v ENEL Case 6/64 (1964) ECJ: EC law has priority over later national law

Facts
The plaintiff sought to avoid paying his electricity bill on the basis that Italian legislation nationalising the Italian electricity industry breached Arts 102, 93, 53 and 37 of the EC Treaty. The magistrate sought a preliminary ruling from the European Court of Justice (ECJ) under Art 177 (now Art 234). The Italian Government argued that the magistrate's request for a preliminary ruling under Art 177 was 'absolutely inadmissible', since the Italian court was bound to apply Italian domestic law. The Italian court held that subsequent national laws could not override EC legislation, and that the request for a preliminary ruling on the interpretation of EC Treaty law was therefore appropriate.

Decision
On the relative status of EC and domestic law, the ECJ said as follows:

The precedence of Community law is confirmed by Art 189, whereby a regulation 'shall be binding' and 'directly applicable in all Member States'. This provision, which is subject to no reservation, would be quite meaningless if a State could unilaterally nullify its effects by means of a legislative measure which could prevail over Community law …

The transfer by the States from their domestic legal system to the Community legal system of the rights and obligations arising under the Treaty carries with it a permanent limitation of their sovereign rights, against which a subsequent unilateral act incompatible with the concept of the Community cannot prevail.

6.1.2　The view of the English courts

The view of the English courts is more restrictive: on its proper construction, s 2(4) of the ECA provides that all directly applicable and directly effective EC legislation – that is, legislation which does not require express incorporation into the national law of Member States, and that which confers rights on individuals which are enforceable in the national courts of Member States – is part of English law and has priority over inconsistent national law. However, this does not apply to EC law (principally unimplemented directives) which is neither directly applicable nor directly effective.

R v Secretary of State for Transport ex p Factortame Ltd (No 2) (1990) ECJ and HL: By virtue of s 2(4) of the ECA 1972, directly applicable EC legislation overrides inconsistent UK legislation, and a litigant must be given a remedy for breach of the EC legislation even though this involves breach of a principle of the UK Constitution

Facts

The applicants, which were companies incorporated under UK law, owned deep sea fishing vessels registered as British under the Merchant Shipping Act 1894. Most of the applicants' directors and shareholders were Spanish nationals. The Merchant Shipping Act 1988 required all vessels to be re-registered. Under the 1988 Act and regulations issued pursuant to it, the applicants' connections with Spain would disqualify their vessels from registration as British. The applicants sought to challenge the legality of the relevant provisions of the Act and the regulations by judicial review, on the grounds that the legislation contravened the EC Treaty and the ECA 1972 by depriving them of enforceable Community rights.

The Divisional Court sought a preliminary ruling from the ECJ on the nature and extent of the Community rights said to be infringed by the Act, and granted interim relief in the form of an injunction to disapply the Act, pending final judgment in the case. The Court of Appeal set aside the Divisional Court's order. The House of Lords upheld the ruling of the Court of Appeal, holding that the English courts had no jurisdiction to grant an injunction against the Crown, or to disapply an English Act of Parliament, in advance of any decision of the ECJ that the Act contravened Community law.

Decision

The ECJ ruled:

... The reply to the question raised should be that Community law must be interpreted as meaning that a national court which, in a case before it concerning Community law, considers that the sole obstacle which precludes it from granting interim relief is a rule of national law must set aside that rule.

The House of Lords held, *per* Lord Bridge:

... Whatever limitation of its sovereignty Parliament accepted when it enacted the European Communities Act 1972 was entirely voluntary. Under the terms of the Act of 1972, it has always been clear that it was the duty of a UK court, when delivering final judgment, to override any rule of national law found to be in conflict with any directly enforceable rule of Community law ... There is nothing in any way novel in according supremacy to rules of Community law in those areas to which they apply, and to insist that ... national courts must not be inhibited by rules of national law from granting interim relief in appropriate cases is no more than a logical recognition of that supremacy.

Comment
Lord Bridge follows the *dicta* of Lord Denning MR in *Macarthys v Smith* (1979) (see 6.2.2 below).

6.2   The obligation to construe domestic legislation to achieve conformity with the EC Treaty

6.2.1   The original European view

Von Colson and Kamann v Land Nordrhein-Westfalen Case 14/83 (1984) ECJ: Domestic courts must construe national legislation in conformity with the EC Treaty

Facts
The applicants established before a German court that they had been refused jobs on the grounds of their sex. The only remedy available under German law was the reimbursement of travel expenses incurred by the applicants in attending the job interviews. The applicants claimed that this was contrary to Art 6 of the Equal Treatment Directive (76/207/EEC). The Directive left it to Member States to put in place effective remedies in order to achieve the object of the Directive. An Art 177 (now Art 234) preliminary reference was made to the European Court.

Decision
The ECJ held that the Directive, although it left Member States free to choose remedies for breach of the prohibition against sex discrimination, required that remedies chosen should constitute an effective deterrent and that compensation should, therefore, be adequate in relation to the damage sustained. The national court therefore came under a duty:

... to interpret and apply the legislation adopted for the implementation of the Directive in conformity with the requirements of Community law, *in so far as it is given discretion to do so under national law.*

6.2.2   The view of the English courts

Macarthys v Smith (1979) CA: Lord Denning postulates the approach of national courts to conflicts between UK and EC law

Facts
The respondent, Mrs Smith, was appointed to a position formerly occupied by a male employee. Her duties were the same as his had been, but she received less pay. She claimed that she was entitled to be paid at the same rate for the same work. Her claim succeeded before the industrial tribunal and the Employment Appeal Tribunal. The

Equal Pay Act appeared to be restricted in its operation to a case where the male and the female employees were employed at the same time. Her employer appealed.

Decision
The Court of Appeal held, by a majority, that an Art 177 reference to the European Court was appropriate.

Per Lord Denning MR:
In construing our statute, we are entitled to look to the Treaty as an aid to its construction, and even more, not only as an aid but also as an overriding force. If in close investigation it should appear that our legislation is deficient ... then it is our bounden duty to give priority to Community law. Such is the result of s 2(1) and (4) of the European Communities Act 1972.

... Thus far, I have assumed that our Parliament, whenever it passes legislation, intends to fulfil its obligations under the Treaty. If the time should come when our Parliament deliberately passes an Act – with the intention of repudiating the Treaty or any provision in it – or intentionally of acting inconsistently with it – and says so in express terms – then I should have thought it would be the duty of our courts to follow the statute of our Parliament. I do not, however, envisage any such situation ... Unless there is an intentional and express repudiation of the Treaty, it is our duty to give priority to the Treaty. In the present case, I assume that the UK intended to fulfil its obligations under Art 119.

6.2.3   Purposive construction not applicable to legislation not introduced in order to comply with Treaty obligations

Duke v GEC Reliance Systems Ltd (1988) HL: Approach set out in *Macarthy* is not applicable to domestic legislation which pre-dates the incompatible provision of EC law

Facts
The appellant was dismissed by her employer when she was between the ages of 60 and 65, pursuant to the employer's policy that female employees were to be retired at 60 and male employees at 65. The appellant alleged that this constituted sex discrimination. She sought to bring an action under s 6(4) of the Sex Discrimination Act 1975. She argued, in the alternative, that, if on a plain reading, s 6(4) preserved the lawfulness of discriminatory retirement ages for men and women, it should nevertheless be construed in a manner to give effect to the Equal Treatment Directive (76/207/EEC) adopted by the Council of Ministers on 9 February 1976.

Decision
The court held, dismissing the appeal, that the Sex Discrimination Act 1975 was not passed in order to give effect to the Equal Treatment Directive (which post-dated it), but had been intended (until its amendment in 1986) to preserve discriminatory retirement ages. Section 2(4) of the European Communities Act 1972 did not enable or constrain a British court to distort the meaning of a British statute to achieve the equivalent of direct effect between individuals.

Per Lord Templeman:
The *Von Colson* case is no authority for the proposition that the German court was bound to invent a German law of adequate compensation if no such law existed and no authority for the

proposition that a court of a Member State must distort the meaning of a domestic statute so as to conform with Community law which is not directly applicable.

6.2.4   Purposive construction applicable to legislation introduced in order to comply with Treaty obligations

Litster v Forth Dry Dock & Engineering Co Ltd (1990) HL: Purposive construction applicable to national law which post-dates the relevant provision of EC law on the assumption that the former was passed in order to give effect to the latter

Facts
Directive 77/187/EEC provided safeguards for employees where a business was transferred between owners. The Transfer of Undertakings (Protection of Employment) Regulations 1981 were made to implement the Directive. The Regulations permitted employees to pursue actions against the new employer provided they had been in the employment of the former owner 'immediately before' the transfer. A company became insolvent and went into receivership. The employees were made redundant one hour before the transfer of the business. An appeal by the employer to the Court of Session from tribunal judgments favourable to the employees was successful. The employees appealed to the House of Lords, contending that the relevant part of the Regulations should not be interpreted narrowly, but should be given a purposive construction in order to conform to the object of the Directive.

Decision
The House of Lords held, allowing the appeal, that the UK courts were under a duty to follow the practice of the European Court of Justice by giving a purposive construction to Directives and to regulations issued for the purpose of complying with Directives.

Per Lord Oliver:
... *Pickstone v Freemans plc* (1989) has established that the greater flexibility available to the court in applying a purposive construction to legislation designed to give effect to the UK's Treaty obligations to the Community enables the court, where necessary, to supply by implication words appropriate to comply with those obligations ... Having regard to the manifest purpose of the regulations, I do not, for my part, feel inhibited from making such an implication in the instant case.

6.3   The current European view

Marleasing SA v La Comercial Internacional Case C-196/89 (1992): National courts must adopt the purposive approach in all cases, irrespective of which legislation came first

Facts
Marleasing sought a declaration that the contracts setting up the defendant companies were void as sham transactions intended for the defrauding of creditors, and that the companies were therefore nullities. This involved pleading 'lack of cause'.

Directive 68/151/EEC listed the exclusive grounds on which nullity could be invoked, but did not include lack of cause. The Directive was unimplemented in Spain and the deadline for implementation had passed. The Spanish court made an Art 177) now Art 234) reference on the status of the Directive.

Decision

The ECJ held that, although a directive could not impose obligations on individuals (and consequently a provision of a directive could not be relied upon against a private party), the Spanish court was nevertheless under an obligation to interpret national law in the light of the wording and the purpose of the Directive. In so stating, the Court broadened the doctrine of *Von Colson*:

... In applying national law, whether the provisions in question were adopted before or after the Directive, the national court called upon to interpret it is required to do so, *as far as possible*, in the light of the wording and the purpose of the Directive in order to achieve the result pursued by the latter and thereby comply with the third paragraph of Art 189 of the Treaty. [Emphasis added.]

6.4   Fundamental principles of Community law in the domestic courts

R v Ministry of Agriculture, Fisheries and Food ex p First City Trading (1996): Definition of 'fundamental principle' of EC law

Facts

The applicant sought to review the beef stocks transfer scheme which had been designed by the Ministry to give financial aid to certain exporters affected by the European Community's decision to prohibit the export of beef slaughtered in the UK. The applicant argued that the scheme discriminated without objective justification in favour of exporters with slaughtering and cutting-up facilities, and that it therefore breached the fundamental Community law principles of equal treatment or non-discrimination.

Decision

The court held that, in deciding whether fundamental principles of Community law applied to a domestic measure, distinctions were to be drawn between:
(a)   those measures taken solely by virtue of domestic law, and those authorised or obliged to be taken by virtue of substantive Community law (for instance, the passing of domestic legislation in order to give effect to a directive); and
(b)   principles of law developed by the European Court within its limited jurisdiction, and Community Treaty provisions which had sovereign legislative force. The principles of Community law as developed by the European Court applied only to measures taken pursuant to powers or duties conferred or imposed by substantive Community law. The government's scheme was within the first category of measure. It could not therefore be challenged by reference to the Community principle of equal treatment, and the application accordingly failed.

CHAPTER 7

THE PREROGATIVE POWERS OF THE CROWN

7.1   Definitions

Sir William Blackstone: *Commentaries on the Laws of England* (8th edn, 1778), Book 1, p 239:

By the word 'prerogative', we usually understand that special pre-eminence, which the king hath, over and above all other persons, and out of the ordinary course of the common law, in right of his regal dignity. It signifies, in its etymology (from *prae* and *rogo*), something which is required or demanded before, or in preference to, all others. And hence it follows that it must be in its nature singular and eccentrical; that it can only be applied to those rights and capacities which the king enjoys alone, in contradistinction to others, and not to those which he enjoys in common with any of his subjects: for if once any prerogative of the Crown could be held in common with the subject, it would cease to be prerogative any longer.

AV Dicey: *An Introduction to the Study of the Law of the Constitution* (10th edn, 1959), pp 424–25:

The prerogative appears to be both historically and as a matter of actual fact nothing else than the residue of discretionary or arbitrary authority, which at any given time is legally left in the hands of the Crown ... From the time of the Norman Conquest down to the Revolution of 1688, the Crown possessed in reality many of the attributes of sovereignty. The prerogative is the name for the remaining portion of the Crown's original authority ... Every act which the executive government can lawfully do without the authority of the Act of Parliament is done in virtue of this prerogative.

Essentially, the prerogative comprises the non-statutory powers of the Crown which are unique to the Crown. It survives from the period in which the monarch ruled as well as reigned. Examples of prerogative powers are defence of the realm (against both external and internal enemies), the making of treaties (and conduct of foreign policy generally) and the granting of honours.

Today, the great bulk of prerogative powers are exercised by ministers, or by the monarch only on the advice of ministers. A major area of conflict between Crown and Parliament during the 17th century was the extent to which the monarch might rely on prerogative powers to rule independently of Parliament. By the Bill of Rights 1689 the most contentious prerogatives claimed by Charles I (1625–49) and James II (1685–88) (the so-called suspending and dispensing powers, and any power to raise revenue for the use of the Crown without parliamentary approval) were formally abolished. It thus became established law that a prerogative could be abolished or placed in abeyance by statute.

7.2   Prerogative powers conflicting with law

In a number of cases in the 17th century, the courts began to consider the nature and extent of the prerogative.

Case of Monopolies (Darcy v Allein) (1602): Court rules the exercise of a prerogative unlawful

Facts
In the 16th and early 17th centuries, the grant of monopolies was used by the Crown as a means of raising revenue. The plaintiff had received the grant of a sole licence for 21 years to import, manufacture and sell playing cards from Queen Elizabeth I (1558–1603), in return for a payment of 100 marks (£66 13s 4d). The plaintiff brought an action against the defendant for infringement of the monopoly.

Decision
The court held that the grant of the monopoly to the plaintiff was contrary to common law and statute, and therefore void.

Comment
Here the court was prepared to rule an exercise of the prerogative unlawful, but this practice did not continue after 1689.

7.3   Prerogative powers unauthorised by law

Case of Proclamations (1610): Royal proclamations did not make law

Facts
King James VI of Scotland and I of England (1603–25) sought, by proclamation, to declare the building of new houses in London and the making of wheat starch to be offences (in order that he could raise money by levying fines upon offenders).

Decision
The court held that the king had no prerogative power to declare new offences by proclamation. The law of England was divided into three parts – common law, statute and custom – but the king's proclamation was no part of the law. The king enjoyed no prerogative powers except those which the law of the land allowed him. The most he might do by proclamation to prevent offending was to admonish his subjects to keep the law upon pain of punishment inflicted according to the law.

British Broadcasting Corp v Johns (Inspector of Taxes) (1964) CA: No new prerogatives may be created

Facts
See 2.2.1 above.

Decision
Counsel for the Corporation also argued that the Crown had a prerogative right to a monopoly of the use of wireless telegraphy and telephony, since they were (at the relevant time) new inventions, and that it had chosen to exercise this monopoly through the Corporation. Rejecting this submission, Diplock LJ said:

This contention involves adopting what [counsel for the BBC] describes as a modern, and I as a 17th century, view of the scope of the prerogative. But it is 350 years and a civil war too late for the Queen's courts to broaden the prerogative. The limits within which the executive government may impose obligations or restraints on citizens of the United Kingdom without any statutory authority are now well settled and incapable of extension.

7.4   The relationship between prerogative and statute

7.4.1   The prerogative is abridged or placed in abeyance by statute

Attorney General v De Keyser's Royal Hotel Ltd (1920) HL: The general principle

Facts

The War Office took possession of De Keyser's Royal Hotel to provide billets for troops. The lessees of the hotel claimed compensation as of right for loss of profit. The Crown argued that the hotel had been possessed under the Defence of the Realm Regulations or by a *de facto* exercise of the prerogative, and that the exercise of neither power obliged the Crown to pay compensation. The lessees argued that the taking of the hotel was authorised by the Defence Act 1842, which made the payment of compensation mandatory.

Decision

The House of Lords held, dismissing the Crown's appeal, that, where power was conferred on the Crown by legislation, the Crown would be taken to act under those powers, and not under equivalent pre-existing prerogative powers.

Per Lord Atkinson:

… When such a statute expressing the will and intention of the King and of the three estates of the realm [monarch, Lords and Commons] is passed, it abridges the royal prerogative while it is in force to the extent that the Crown can only do the particular thing under and in accordance with the statutory provisions, and that its prerogative power to do that thing is in abeyance.

Per Lord Sumner:

… If there is adequate power to do all that is required by proceeding under the statute, where is the emergency and public necessity which is the foundation for resort to the prerogative?

Laker Airways v Department of Trade (1977) CA: A more recent application of the principle

Facts

In 1972, the Civil Aviation Authority granted Laker Airways, the first budget airline, a licence pursuant to the Civil Aviation Act 1971 to enable it to operate a cut-price service between London and New York. The following year, the government designated Laker Airways as a scheduled carrier under the Bermuda Agreement on international air travel, with the result that the US authorities then became bound to give Laker landing rights in New York. Following a change of government in the UK and the institution of a policy calculated to protect British Airways from competition on the London–New York route, a new Secretary of State issued guidance causing the Civil Aviation Authority to withdraw Laker's licence. The Secretary of State also revoked Laker's designation under the Bermuda Agreement. Laker challenged both actions. The Secretary of State claimed that the revocation of the designation was a prerogative act relating to the government's conduct of international affairs, which was not justiciable by the courts.

Decision

The Court of Appeal held that the Secretary of State was effectively claiming the right to frustrate the statutory grant of the licence to Laker by prerogative powers. The question for the court was whether he might withdraw the designation while the licence remained in force. The Attorney General had argued that the Secretary of State was free to do so because the Civil Aviation Act 1971 did not curb the prerogative powers of the Crown. However, *Walker v Baird* (see 7.7.2 below) made it clear that prerogative powers could not be used in this way to take away the rights of citizens. The 1971 Act was intended by Parliament to govern the rights and duties of British citizens in all aspects of civil aviation. The Act made provision for revocation of a licence and should be taken to regulate all aspects of revocation. The Secretary of State had used the prerogative power unlawfully.

7.4.2   Where prerogative powers are directed towards the protection of the individual

The authorities above show that, generally, the prerogative is placed in abeyance where a statute gives similar powers. However, the following case defined an exception to this principle.

R v Secretary of State for the Home Department ex p Northumbria Police Authority (1989) CA: Exception to the general principle

Facts

The Home Secretary issued a circular stating that all police requirements for plastic baton rounds and CS gas for dealing with riots were to be met from a central store. Local police authorities were to be notified of the provision of such equipment. The Northumbria Police Authority sought a declaration that the Home Secretary had no power to issue the equipment without the consent of the local police authority, save in a grave emergency. The Authority contended that the Police Act 1964 constituted a complete and comprehensive code defining and limiting the functions of local police authorities, chief constables and the Home Secretary with regard to the provision of equipment to police forces. The Act gave the Home Secretary no power to provide equipment without the consent of the local police authorities, but the Home Secretary argued that he enjoyed further prerogative powers to supply equipment without the consent of local police authorities. The Divisional Court accepted both arguments. The Authority appealed and the Home Secretary cross-appealed.

Decision

The Court of Appeal held, allowing the cross-appeal, that the 1964 Act imposed no requirement on the Home Secretary to supply equipment *only* with the consent of local police authorities. Therefore, the supply as made was lawful under the Act. The appeal would therefore be dismissed. Further, although it had been the invariable practice to leave the maintenance of public order to the police, the Crown retained a prerogative power to preserve the peace.

Per Nourse LJ:
At all events, there being no decision to the contrary, I decline to hold that a power so valuable to the common good no longer exists ... I therefore conclude that, if the necessary power had not been available under s 41 of the 1964 Act, the terms and implementation of para 4 of the Home Office circular would have been within the prerogative powers of the Crown.

Per Purchas LJ:
It is well established that the courts will intervene to prevent executive action under prerogative powers in violation of property or other rights of the individual where this is inconsistent with statutory provisions providing for the same executive action. Where the executive action is directed towards the benefit or protection of the individual, it is unlikely that its use will attract the intervention of the courts. In my judgment, before the courts will hold that such executive action is contrary to legislation, express and unequivocal terms must be found in the statute which deprive the individual from receiving the benefit or protection intended by the exercise of prerogative power ...

Comment
For police powers and duties in relation to public order, see Chapter 25.

7.4.3   The prerogative may not be used to frustrate the will of Parliament

R v Secretary of State for the Home Department ex p Fire Brigades Union (1995) HL: Limits on exercise of prerogative power when statute is not yet in force

Facts
See 3.3.1 above.

Decision
The House of Lords held, by a majority, that the Secretary of State's appeal should be dismissed. Although the court could not intervene in the legislative process by requiring the Secretary of State to introduce the statutory scheme, it did not follow that he had an absolute and unfettered discretion whether or not to bring it into effect. He was under a duty to keep its introduction under consideration, and not to procure events to take place and then rely on those events as grounds for not introducing the statutory scheme. In claiming that the introduction of the tariff scheme under the prerogative rendered undesirable the implementation of the statutory scheme, the Secretary of State had abused his discretion and had acted unlawfully.

7.5   Legal challenge to the exercise of prerogative power

From the *Case of Proclamations* onwards, the courts have exercised a jurisdiction to determine whether a particular power existed as a prerogative, and the nature and extent of any claimed prerogative. After 1689 they made no claim to power to adjudicate on the *exercise* of prerogative power until recent times, though by the 1960s they had developed in judicial review a jurisdiction to adjudicate on the exercise by public bodies of their *statutory* powers.

Burmah Oil Co Ltd v Lord Advocate (1965) HL: Exercise of a particular prerogative is lawful only when compensation is payable for consequent loss to subjects

Facts
During the Japanese invasion of Burma in 1942, the appellant's oil installations were destroyed on the order of the commander of the British forces in order to prevent them from falling into enemy hands. The appellant sought compensation and appealed to the House of Lords on the preliminary finding in the lower courts that, in the circumstances, compensation was not payable.

Decision
The House of Lords held, allowing the appeal (by a majority), that, although the prerogative power to wage war had been recognised for centuries, the authorities disclosed no rule that private property might be taken by the Crown, even in times of war or imminent danger, without any payment being made for it.

Comment
The effect of this decision was reversed by the passing of the War Damage Act 1965, which retrospectively cancelled the Crown's liability to pay compensation for war damage lawfully caused.

Blackburn v Attorney General (1971) CA: Courts cannot rule on legality of exercise of any prerogative

Facts
The appellant applied for declarations that, by signing the Treaty of Rome, the government would permanently surrender in part the sovereignty of the Crown in Parliament and in so doing would act contrary to the law. At first instance, the appellant's statement of claim was struck out as disclosing no reasonable cause of action.

Decision
The Court of Appeal held, dismissing the appeal, that, when ministers of the Crown negotiate and sign a treaty, their actions cannot be challenged or questioned in the courts. Lord Denning MR added that no treaty had yet been signed. If a treaty was to be signed and incorporated into English law, the courts would take such notice of it as Parliament instructed.

Council of Civil Service Unions v Minister for the Civil Service (1985) HL (GCHQ case): No distinction in principle between prerogative power and any other, but exercise of certain prerogatives held non-justiciable

Facts
The Government Communications Headquarters (GCHQ) was responsible for the provision of intelligence to the government, and for the security of military and official communications. Since the establishment of GCHQ in 1947, its staff had been

permitted to belong to civil service trade unions, and GCHQ management had regularly consulted with the unions. Following industrial action at GCHQ, the Prime Minister, in her capacity as minister for the Civil Service, and acting under prerogative powers whose exercise had been delegated to her by Order in Council (a form of delegated legislation), sought to curtail staff rights of trade union membership. The Council of Civil Service Unions sought a declaration that the Minister had acted unfairly in removing staff rights of trade union membership without consultation. The Minister argued that consultation would have provoked the very disruption and endangering of national security which her instruction was intended to terminate.

Decision

In the House of Lords, the minority considered the exercise of a delegated prerogative power to be justiciable. The majority were of the view that what was important was not the source of the power, but the nature of the power. The traditional distinction between statutory and prerogative powers was artificial, since the latter were no longer exercised by the monarch directly, but by public authorities, such as ministers, in the same way as the former.

Per Lord Roskill:

I am unable to see, subject to what I shall say later, that there is any logical reason why the fact that the source of the power is the prerogative and not statute should today deprive the citizen of that right of challenge to the manner of its exercise which he would possess were the source of the power statutory …

But I do not think that that right of challenge can be unqualified. It must, I think, depend upon the subject matter of the prerogative power which is exercised … Prerogative powers such as those relating to the making of treaties, the defence of the realm, the prerogative of mercy, the grant of honours, the dissolution of Parliament and the appointment of ministers as well as others are not, I think, subject to judicial review because their nature and subject matter are not such as to be amenable to the judicial process. The courts are not the place where to determine whether a treaty should be concluded or the armed forces disposed in a particular manner or Parliament dissolved on one date rather than another.

7.6 Particular prerogative powers

7.6.1 Defence of the realm

'Defence of the realm' is a broad concept and includes not only defence of British territory against external and internal enemies, but also deployment and operations of British troops anywhere in the world.

Burmah Oil Co Ltd v Lord Advocate (1965) HL

See 7.5 above.

7.6.2 The prerogative power of keeping the peace

The king's peace is an ancient concept based on the traditional role of the monarch as protector of his people. Prerogative powers relating to keeping the peace remain of importance in relation to prevention and detection of crime and maintaining public order.

R v Secretary of State for the Home Department ex p Northumbria Police Authority (1989) CA

See 7.4.2 above.

7.6.3   The treaty making power of the Crown

Blackburn v Attorney General (1971) CA

See 7.5 above.

Ex p Molyneaux and Others (1986): Making of treaties not susceptible to judicial review

Facts

The Anglo–Irish agreement, concluded by the governments of the Irish Republic and the UK in 1985, provided for the establishment of an Inter-Governmental Conference concerned with Northern Ireland and its relations with the Irish Republic. The applicants were members and officers of the Ulster Unionist Council. They sought a declaration by way of judicial review that it would be contrary to law for the UK Government to implement the agreement by use of the prerogative without the authority of new legislation. In support of this, they argued that:

(1)   the agreement and its implementation would impose fetters on the statutory powers and duties of the Secretary of State for Northern Ireland;

(2)   the agreement would contravene Art 6 of the Union with Ireland Act 1800, since it would remove parity of privilege and status as between the people of Northern Ireland and those of Great Britain; and

(3)   the prerogative power on which the government had purported to rely in entering the agreement had in fact been delegated in its entirety to the Northern Ireland executive authority by the Northern Ireland Constitution Act 1973.

Decision

The court held that the application disclosed no arguable case and would accordingly be dismissed. The applicants' second contention was wrong, because there could be no contravention of Art 6, save by a treaty with a foreign power, and the Ireland Act 1949 provided that the Republic was not to have that status in law.

The third argument failed because the delegation of the prerogative by the 1973 Act had been only partial, and an Act of the following year had in any event returned the delegated power to the Secretary of State. With respect to the first contention, the court denied that the agreement would constitute a fetter on the discretion of the Secretary of State. The establishment of the Inter-Governmental Conference would not therefore contravene any statute, any rule of common law or any constitutional convention. Nor would it amount, as the applicants had originally claimed, to the establishment in the UK of a new standing body for the purpose of influencing the conduct of the government without the authority of the Queen in Parliament. It would establish nothing in the UK because it existed only in the field of international relations.

Per Taylor J:

It is akin to a treaty. It concerns relations between the UK and another sovereign State and it is not the function of this court to inquire into the exercise of the prerogative in entering into such an agreement or by way of anticipation to decide whether the method proposed of implementing the agreement is appropriate.

R v Secretary of State for Foreign and Commonwealth Affairs ex p Rees-Mogg (1994): Non-justiciability of treaty-making powers is subject to exceptions in so far as provided by statute

Facts

The applicant sought, *inter alia*, a declaration that, by ratifying Title V of the Treaty on European Union signed at Maastricht on 7 February 1992, the government would be transferring part of the prerogative powers to conduct foreign and security policy to Community institutions without statutory authority.

Decision

The Court of Appeal held, dismissing the application, that Title V did not entail a transfer of prerogative powers, but an exercise of them. The applicant's arguments would be rejected either on the grounds that the questions raised were not justiciable or, if they were, that they failed on the merits. After citing *Blackburn* and *Molyneaux* as authorities for the proposition that the court had no jurisdiction to consider the question raised by the applicant, Lloyd LJ stated that it would be possible for the court to accept that argument and to go no further. However, counsel for the applicant had pointed out that the principle of non-justiciability was not universal and absolute, but subject to exceptions. Section 6 of the European Parliamentary Elections Act 1978 created such an exception, obliging a court, if so required, to consider whether any treaty which the government proposed to ratify involved an increase in the powers of the European Parliament. Lloyd LJ stated that, although that exception was not in issue in the present case, he was prepared to assume that he was entitled to consider the applicant's assertions.

7.6.4　The prerogative of mercy

The prerogative of mercy, today exercised by the Home Secretary, is a power to pardon persons convicted of criminal offences. A royal pardon preserves the conviction but removes or reduces the sentence passed by the court. The power to substitute a sentence of life imprisonment in the case of persons sentenced to death is also an exercise of the prerogative of mercy.

de Freitas v Benny (1975) PC: Exercise of prerogative of mercy is not susceptible to review

Facts

The appellant was convicted of murder and sentenced to death by the Supreme Court of Trinidad and Tobago. After exhausting all his rights of appeal against conviction, he applied to court claiming that:

(1)　the execution upon him of the death sentence would infringe his rights to life as secured by the Constitution of Trinidad and Tobago, since it amounted either

per se or because of delay to 'cruel and unusual punishment', prohibited by the
Constitution; and

(2)   before advice was tendered to the Governor General regarding the exercise of the
prerogative of mercy, the appellant was entitled to be shown the material placed
before the Advisory Committee on the prerogative of mercy, and entitled to be
heard and legally represented before the Committee.

Decision

The Privy Council held, dismissing the appeal, that death was made a mandatory
penalty for murder by the law of Trinidad and Tobago, so that the prohibition against
cruel and unusual punishment did not apply to it. The appellant's arguments
concerning delay were rejected. The claimed rights to notice and a hearing in
connection with the decision on the prerogative of mercy did not exist.

Per Lord Diplock:

Except in so far as it may have been altered by the Constitution, the legal nature of the exercise
of the royal prerogative of mercy in Trinidad and Tobago remains the same as it was in England
at common law. At common law, this has always been a matter which lies solely in the discretion
of the sovereign, who by constitutional convention exercises it in respect of England on the
advice of the Home Secretary to whom Her Majesty delegates the discretion. Mercy is not the
subject of legal rights. It begins where legal rights end. A convicted person has no legal right
even to have his case considered by the Home Secretary in connection with the exercise of the
prerogative of mercy.

Since that case the courts have adopted a more interventionist approach.

R v Secretary of State for the Home Department ex p Bentley (1994) QBD: Prerogative of mercy reviewable in limited circumstances

Facts

The applicant was the sister of Derek Bentley, who was hanged in 1953 for his part in
the murder of a police officer. The fatal shot had been fired by Bentley's accomplice,
who was too young to be subject to the death penalty, and was sentenced instead to
life imprisonment. Despite a recommendation from the jury and the advice of Home
Office officials that Bentley should not be subject to capital punishment in these
circumstances, the then Home Secretary, Sir David Maxwell Fyfe, refused to commute
his sentence. In 1992, the Home Secretary declined to recommend a posthumous
pardon for Bentley on the grounds that, although he personally agreed that Bentley
should not have been hanged, it had been the policy of successive Home Secretaries
not to recommend the exercise of the royal prerogative for the grant of a free pardon
unless satisfied that the person concerned was both morally and technically innocent
of any crime. The applicant alleged that the grant of a free pardon did not entail
recognition that Bentley was wrongly convicted, and that the Home Secretary had
erred in law in considering that it did.

Decision

The court held, making no order but inviting the Home Secretary to reconsider his
decision, that the *GCHQ* case (see 7.5 above) made it clear that the powers of the
court could not be ousted merely by invoking the word 'prerogative'. The question in

each case was whether the nature and subject matter of the decision was amenable to the judicial process. The formulation of criteria for the exercise of the prerogative of granting a free pardon was a matter of policy which was not justiciable. However, the prerogative might have been exercised by the grant of a conditional pardon, whereby the penalty first imposed would be (notionally) replaced by a lesser sentence. The Home Secretary had not properly considered that possibility and should now do so.

Comment

Here the judge (Watkins LJ) was effectively reviewing the exercise of a non-justiciable prerogative power while claiming not to be. He used the established practice of considering the nature and extent of a prerogative power (cf *Burmah Oil v Lord Advocate*) to conclude that the Home Secretary had been mistaken as to the scope of his powers, in order to invite him to reconsider his decision, though no formal declaration was granted. Watkins LJ also stated *obiter* that a decision would be reviewable if it had been made on unlawful grounds – involving, for example, racial or sexual discrimination.

Reckley v Minister of Public Safety (No 2) (1996) PC: Limitation of the principle in *ex p Bentley*

Facts

The appellant was convicted of murder and sentenced to death by a Bahamian court. Articles 91 and 92 of the Constitution of The Bahamas provided for non-binding advice on the exercise of the prerogative of mercy to be given by an Advisory Committee to a designated minister. The decision to grant or withhold mercy would be taken by the Governor General, acting on the Minister's advice. The appellant, having exhausted all other forms of recourse, argued (*inter alia*) that the execution upon him of the death sentence would contravene his constitutional rights since he had not been permitted either to see material placed before the Advisory Committee, or to make representations to the Committee.

Decision

The Privy Council held, dismissing the appeal, that Lord Diplock's analysis of the position in *de Freitas v Benny* (above) was determinative of the point. It was reinforced by the facts that:

(1) the Advisory Committee's consideration of death sentence cases was legally enjoined and was not dependent on the taking of any initiative by the prisoner;

(2) the Minister was not bound to accept the Committee's advice, so that the discretion he retained was clearly of a purely personal character; and

(3) the Minister's constitutional discretion to determine the material placed before the Committee was inconsistent with the appellant's claimed right to make representations to the Committee. Thus, the exercise of the prerogative of mercy under the Bahamian Constitution was not justiciable. The decision in *Bentley* (above) was based on exceptional facts and had no bearing on the present appeal, since it had not been directly concerned with the prerogative of mercy in a death sentence case.

The appellant had relied on *Doody v Secretary of State for the Home Department* (see 18.2 below) as the source of a right in fairness to make representations, but there Lord Mustill had distinguished the situation before him from one in which, as here, the prisoner was 'essentially in mercy' so that there was 'no ground to ascribe to him the rights which fairness might otherwise demand'. Lord Goff, having earlier described the Advisory Committee as 'a reputable and impartial source', stated that the existence of the Advisory Committee, whose members were selected by the Governor General, provided an important constitutional safeguard, which dealt with any difficulty created by the absence of supervision by the courts.

7.6.5   The issue of a passport

R v Secretary of State for Foreign and Commonwealth Affairs ex p Everett (1989) CA: Refusal of a passport is susceptible to judicial review

Facts

The applicant, a British passport holder living in Spain, applied to the British Embassy for a new passport. His request was refused on the grounds that a warrant for his arrest had been issued in the UK (ironically, for passport fraud), and it was the policy of the Secretary of State not to issue new passports to persons who were wanted by the police in connection with serious crime. The applicant sought an order of certiorari to quash the decision on the basis that no details of the warrant had been given to him. Details were provided to him before the date of the hearing. At first instance, the court held that the Secretary of State had failed to consider whether the applicant's case was one in which an exception should be made to the policy governing the issue of passports. The Secretary of State appealed, claiming that passports were issued pursuant to prerogative powers which were not justiciable by the courts.

Decision

The Court of Appeal held that the appeal would be allowed. The Secretary of State was under a duty to give reasons where he refused a passport, to give details of the warrant extant and to consider whether an exception to his policy relating to the issue of passports should be made in the circumstances of the applicant's case. Since the information had become available to the applicant, and since there were no exceptional factors in his case, there were no grounds for granting relief. The court accepted the Secretary of State's submission that the issue of passports was an exercise of prerogative power, but rejected his contention that it was therefore not justiciable. As a matter of common sense, the court should be able to inquire into a refusal to issue a passport. The power was not to be compared with plainly non-justiciable exercises of prerogative powers, such as the conduct of foreign affairs or the signing of treaties.

Comment

The power to issue a passport remains a prerogative power by accident of history and, unlike the majority of prerogative powers, is intimately linked with the rights and freedom of the individual – in this case to move outside the UK and to return to the UK from elsewhere – hence the view of the court that its exercise should be justiciable.

7.7 Acts of State

The term 'act of State' is often used of acts of the British Crown in foreign affairs. As noted above, much of British foreign policy is conducted under prerogative powers, but 'act of State' is used to denote acts of the Crown towards foreign States and subjects of foreign States when outside the domains of the Crown. ECS Wade defined an act of State as 'an act of the Executive as a matter of policy performed in the course of its relations with another state, including its relations with subjects of that state, unless they are temporarily within the allegiance of the Crown [by being 'friendly aliens' resident within the domains of the Crown]' ((1934) British Yearbook of International Law 98, p 103). Proof of act of State is a complete defence to legal action against the Crown, but case law shows that the concept is now narrowly treated by the courts, such that it is only applicable to actions in relation to persons who are not British subjects, which take place outside British territory.

7.7.1 The attitude of the courts to acts of State

Salaman v Secretary of State for India (1906) PC: Proof of act of State ousts jurisdiction of courts, although the court may inquire into a claim of act of State

Facts
The Secretary of State was appointed the successor to the East India Company by the Government of India Act 1858. In the 1840s, the Company had entered into an agreement with the regents of the then infant Maharajah of the Punjab, Duleep Singh, by which the Company assumed sovereignty over the Punjab, took possession of all State property, and in return was to pay a pension to the Maharajah. The appellant was the trustee in bankruptcy of the Maharajah's residuary legatee. He alleged that the Company, and subsequently the Secretary of State, was trustee of the pension and, therefore, liable to account to the appellant for arrears.

Decision
The Privy Council held that the Company's actions amounted to acts of State done by the East India Company as trustees for the Crown.

Per Fletcher Moulton LJ:
An act of State is essentially an exercise of sovereign power, and hence cannot be challenged, controlled, or interfered with by municipal courts ... But it may and often must be part of their duty to take cognisance of it. For instance, if an act is relied upon as being an act of State, and thus as affording an answer to claims made by a subject, the courts must decide whether it was in truth an act of State, and what was its nature and extent ... But, in such an inquiry, the court must confine itself to ascertaining what the act of State in fact was, and not what in their opinion it ought to have been ...

7.7.2   British subjects on British territory and the defence of act of State

Walker v Baird (1892) PC: Acts in relation to British subjects on British territory cannot be acts of State

Facts
With the authority of the government, officers of the Crown seized a lobster fishery in Newfoundland. They claimed to be acting under instruction to enforce an agreement on lobster fishing made between the Crown and the French Government. An action was begun against the officers in the Newfoundland courts. The Superior Court of Newfoundland held that the defence of act of State could not be pleaded against British subjects for a trespass within British territory in time of peace. The officers appealed to the Privy Council.

Decision
The Privy Council held that the appeal would be dismissed. The suggestions that the appellants' acts could be justified as acts of State, or that the court was not competent to inquire into the construction of treaties or other acts of State, were wholly untenable.

7.7.3   Aliens on British territory and the defence of act of State

Johnstone v Pedlar (1921) HL: Acts in relation to friendly aliens on British soil are not acts of State

Facts
The respondent, Pedlar, was a naturalised citizen of the US. He was arrested and convicted of an offence in Dublin. He brought an action against Johnstone, the Chief Commissioner of the Dublin Metropolitan Police, seeking the return of a cheque and sums of money which had been found in his possession at the time of his arrest. Johnstone maintained that these items were the property of an illegal association (the IRA) and were in the respondent's possession for the illegal purposes of that association. He further maintained that the respondent was an alien and that the property had been taken from him and detained by an officer of the Crown at the direction of the Crown as an act of State for the defence of the realm and the prevention of crime. In support of this claim, he produced a certificate signed by the Chief Secretary for Ireland.

The Irish Court of Appeal found for Pedlar. The allegations concerning the illegal purpose for which Pedlar had had the property were held not to have been proved. Johnstone appealed to the House of Lords.

Decision
The Lords held, dismissing the appeal, that the respondent had been in British territory at the time of his arrest. He was not a subject of the British Crown, but it was correct to say that, as a 'friendly alien' resident within the domains of the Crown, as Ireland was at this time, he had to be treated as if he were. The subject of a State at peace with the Crown, while permitted to reside in this country, was under the Crown's protection in the same way as a British subject, and owed the Crown a duty of

local allegiance. It was for this reason that, in cases dealing with the defence of act of State, it had been said that the act should have been carried out abroad as well as against a foreigner in order that the defence should succeed. If it were otherwise (*per* Viscount Finlay):

> … Aliens in this country, instead of having the protection of British law, would be at the mercy of any department entitled to use the name of the Crown for an 'act of State'. It would have effects upon aliens in the country of a far reaching nature as to person and property.

7.7.4 British subjects outside British territory and the defence of act of State

Nissan v Attorney General (1970) HL: Acts in relation to a British subject outside British territory are not acts of State

Facts
Nissan, a British subject and citizen of the UK and Colonies, who owned a hotel in Cyprus, brought an action against the Crown claiming a declaration that he was entitled to compensation in respect of damage by British forces to his hotel and the destruction of stores. The hotel had been occupied by the British forces in Cyprus in the course of an attempt to restore peace between the opposing Greek and Turkish populations on the island. The involvement of the British forces was pursuant to an agreement between the Crown and the government of Cyprus. Nissan claimed that the occupation of the hotel was a lawful exercise of the prerogative and that compensation was accordingly payable. The Court of Appeal held that compensation was payable. The Attorney General appealed to the House of Lords.

Decision
The House of Lords held that the appeal would be dismissed. In the opinion of the majority, the occupation of the hotel did not have the character of an act of State. The agreement between the Crown and the government of Cyprus was an act of State, but the occupation of the hotel was not sufficiently closely connected with it to qualify for the same description. Lord Wilberforce, Lord Morris and Lord Pearson declined to decide the question whether there were circumstances in which an act done outside the realm could ever be an act of State in relation to a British subject. *Walker v Baird* (see 7.7.2 above) was inconclusive on this point, since the plaintiff had not only been a British subject, but had been on British territory. In the opinion of Lord Reid, the authorities contained *dicta* favouring both views, but he was not prepared to hold that the description 'act of State' would in any event oust the jurisdiction of the court:

> If I thought that any act done against the person or property of a British subject wherever situated could be an act of State in the sense that he was deprived of all right to apply to an English court for redress, then I would think that the taking of this hotel was an act of State. But … I am of opinion that a British subject – at least if he is also a citizen of the UK and Colonies – can never be deprived of his legal right to redress by any assertion by the Crown or decision of the court that the acts of which he complains were acts of State. It seems to me that no useful purpose is served by inquiring whether an act in respect of which a British subject claims legal redress is or is not an act of State, because a decision of that question can make no difference to the result.

CHAPTER 8

JUDICIAL REVIEW UNDER ORDER 53

Introduction

Judicial review is a practical application of the rule of law and the doctrine of the separation of powers. The judiciary ensure that the executive act within the limits of their powers, and that they use those powers for proper purposes and in a proper manner. It is perhaps the principal check and balance which exists within the British constitutional system. It is not concerned with the merits of a decision, but rather with its legality, and therefore is not an appeal.

As with many elements of the British Constitution and legal system, judicial review emerged in a piecemeal fashion, from precedents and practices developed through applications for the ancient 'prerogative orders' of certiorari, mandamus and prohibition (see below 8.4) and for declarations as to the state of the law in a particular area. In 1977 a formal procedure for judicial review was created under Order 53 of the Rules of the Supreme Court.

Judicial review is available in respect of the actions of public bodies in exercising public powers – that is, the powers available to them as organs of the executive, rather than powers which are available equally to individuals and non-executive bodies.

8.1   The nature of the inquiry

R v Somerset County Council ex p Fewings (1995) CA: Review not appeal

Facts

The council resolved to ban the hunting of deer with hounds on a common which it owned. A paper circulated to councillors before the meeting at which the ban was imposed stated that a decision would have to be reached 'largely on the grounds of ethics, animal welfare and social considerations'. It was later agreed between the parties that the council's powers of management were to be found in s 120(1)(b) of the Local Government Act 1972, which permitted the council to acquire land for 'the benefit, improvement or development of their area'.

At first instance, Laws J quashed the ban on the ground that the council had taken into account an irrelevant consideration by basing its decision chiefly on a free-standing distaste for the alleged cruelty of hunting. The council appealed to the Court of Appeal.

Decision

The Court of Appeal held (Simon Brown LJ dissenting) that the judgment of Laws J would be upheld. There was a fundamental difference between the rights of private and public landowners: the former might do as they wished within the law, whereas the latter could act only with positive legal justification. The 'cruelty argument' was not necessarily an irrelevant consideration, but the evidence showed that the limited scope of the council's powers of management had never been drawn to its attention. A relevant consideration had therefore been overlooked, and the council could not be said to have exercised its power to further the object prescribed by the statute.

Per Laws J:
Although judicial review is an area of the law which is increasingly, and rightly, exposed to a good deal of media publicity, one of its most important characteristics is not, I think, generally very clearly understood. It is that, in most cases, the judicial review court is not concerned with the merits of the decision under review. The court does not ask itself the question, 'Is this decision right or wrong?' Far less does the judge ask himself whether he would himself have arrived at the decision in question.

8.2 Which bodies are susceptible to judicial review?

Judicial review is available where a public body is exercising public powers. Initially, this mainly involved bodies which had been created by statute and the powers granted to them by statute. However, the jurisdiction has evolved to embrace, first, powers available under the royal prerogative, provided they are 'justiciable' in nature (see the *GCHQ* case, at 7.5 above), and, more generally, powers considered to be 'public' in nature.

8.2.1 The jurisdiction as formerly defined

R v Electricity Commissioners ex p London Electricity Joint Committee Co (1924) CA: Jurisdiction goes beyond bodies exercising judicial powers

Facts
The committee sought orders of certiorari and prohibition against the Electricity Commissioners in relation to a proposed scheme for the improvement of the existing organisation of the supply of electricity in the London and Home Counties Electricity District. On appeal, the question arose whether the Commissioners were a body against which the prerogative orders would lie.

Decision
The Court of Appeal held, *per* Atkin LJ:

… The operation of the writs [of prohibition and certiorari] has extended to control the proceedings of bodies which do not claim to be, and would not be recognised as courts of justice. Wherever any body of persons having legal authority to determine questions affecting the rights of subjects, and having the duty to act judicially, act in excess of their legal authority, they are subject to the controlling jurisdiction of the King's Bench Division exercised in these writs.

8.2.2   The source of the respondent's powers

8.2.2.1   Prerogative powers

R v Criminal Injuries Compensation Board ex p Lain (1967): Jurisdiction encompasses certain bodies exercising prerogative powers

Facts

The Criminal Injuries Compensation Board was a non-statutory body set up by the government in 1964 under prerogative powers. The applicant was the widow of a police constable who had applied to the board for compensation after sustaining serious injury. The Board decided that National Insurance and police pension fund payments to the widow should be deducted from its award, and therefore made no payment. Counsel for the Board argued that it fell outside Atkin LJ's definition of the court's supervisory jurisdiction in *Ex p London Electricity Joint Committee Co* in that:

(1)   the Board was not a body of persons having 'legal authority', in the sense of having statutory authority; and

(2)   the Board did not 'determine the rights of subjects', since its decisions gave rise to no enforceable rights.

The applicant sought an order of certiorari to quash the Board's decision.

Decision

The Divisional Court held, refusing the application, that the Board's decision disclosed no error of law. The question which first arose was whether the Board's decisions were amenable to the court's supervisory jurisdiction. In answer to the Board's first argument (*per* Lord Parker CJ):

> ... The writ of certiorari has been issued not only to courts set up by statute but also to courts whose authority was derived, *inter alia*, from the prerogative. Once the jurisdiction is extended, as it clearly has been, to tribunals as opposed to courts, there is no reason why the remedy by way of certiorari cannot be invoked to a body of persons set up under the prerogative.

Further, the Board had been recognised by Parliament in debate, and received its funding from Parliament. Rejecting the Board's second argument, Lord Parker said that Atkin LJ had not intended to confine his principle to cases in which the determination affected rights in the sense of enforceable rights. He added:

> ... The exact limits of the ancient remedy of certiorari have never been, and ought not to be, specifically defined ... We have, as it seems to me, reached the position when the ambit of certiorari can be said to cover every case in which a body of persons, of a public as opposed to a purely private or domestic character, has to determine matters affecting subjects provided always that it has a duty to act judicially.

8.2.2.2   Self-conferred powers

R v Panel on Takeovers and Mergers ex p Datafin (1987) CA: Jurisdiction may extend to bodies which have taken power on themselves

Facts

The Panel was an institution in the City of London which devised and operated a code of conduct to be observed in the takeovers of listed public companies. It was a self-regulating, unincorporated association which had not been established by any recognised external authority, and it performed its functions 'without visible means of legal support' (*per* Lord Donaldson MR). The applicants were engaged in a battle with a rival firm to take over a third company. They complained to the Panel that their rivals had been engaged in improper dealings with the third company. The Panel decided to reject their complaint. The applicants sought orders of certiorari, prohibition and mandamus, and an injunction. The Panel argued that the supervisory jurisdiction of the court was confined to bodies whose power derived solely from legislation or the exercise of the prerogative.

Decision

The Court of Appeal held that the Panel had made its decision properly and judicial review would therefore be refused. However, it was subject to the court's jurisdiction. Lord Donaldson MR approved the approach taken by the court in *ex p Lain*, and said:

In all the reports, it is possible to find enumerations of factors giving rise to the jurisdiction, but it is a fatal error to regard the presence of all those factors as essential or as being exclusive of other factors. Possibly the only essential elements are what can be described as a public element, which can take many different forms, and the exclusion from the jurisdiction of bodies whose sole source of power is a consensual submission to its [*sic*] jurisdiction.

Regard was to be had not only to the source of the Panel's powers, but also to the fact that it operated as an integral part of a system which had a public law character and performed public law functions. The government had made the Panel the centrepiece of its legislation in the field of takeovers and mergers. Given that it remained self-regulating, it was more and not less appropriate that it should be subject to the supervisory jurisdiction of the court.

Comment

Here Lord Donaldson MR drew on the *GCHQ* case as authority for the proposition that what is important is not the source of the power but the nature of the power. Case law since, although accepting this proposition, has taken a narrower view of the concept of power which is 'public' in nature.

R v Advertising Standards Authority Ltd ex p The Insurance Service (1990): *Datafin* principle confirmed

Facts

The applicant, a motor insurance company, sought judicial review of the Authority's decision to uphold a complaint about the accuracy of one of its promotional leaflets. The Authority was a company limited by guarantee which, under its Memorandum of Association, undertook: 'The promotion and enforcement throughout the United Kingdom of the highest standards of advertising in all media ...' The Misleading Advertisements Regulations 1988, drawn up to implement an EC Directive, made the Director General of Fair Trading subject to a duty to consider complaints brought against advertisements. It appeared from the Regulations that the Director General would use his powers only if satisfied that a complaint to the Authority had failed to produce a satisfactory result.

Decision

The court held that the Authority was subject to judicial review. Like the Panel on Takeovers and Mergers, the Authority had no powers granted to it by statute or at common law, nor any contractual relationship with the advertisers whom it controlled. Nevertheless, it was clearly exercising public law functions which, if the Authority did not exist, would undoubtedly be exercised by the Director General of Fair Trading. In the present case, the Authority had failed to take into account a material consideration in determining the applicant's case, and its decision would therefore be quashed.

R v Chief Rabbi ex p Wachmann (1992): *Datafin* principle restricted

Facts

The applicant was the Orthodox rabbi of a synagogue belonging to the United Hebrew Congregations of Great Britain and the Commonwealth, the spiritual head of which was the Chief Rabbi. Allegations of conduct unbecoming a rabbi (adultery with a member of his congregation) were made against the applicant and confirmed by a commission of inquiry appointed by the Chief Rabbi. The Chief Rabbi notified the president of the synagogue that he regarded the applicant as unfit to continue in office. In the light of the Chief Rabbi's decision, the executive and council of the synagogue terminated the applicant's employment. The applicant sought leave to move for judicial review of the Chief Rabbi's decision that he was unfit to hold office.

Decision

The Court of Appeal held that the Chief Rabbi was not subject to judicial review. To attract the court's supervisory jurisdiction, there had to be not merely a public but potentially a governmental interest in the respondent's decision making power. The Chief Rabbi's functions were essentially intimate, spiritual and religious; there would be no intervention by Parliament, the government or the court in this area.

However, dealing with a point made in *Datafin*, it was wrong to regard the applicant's submission to the jurisdiction of the Chief Rabbi as merely consensual. Rather, the applicant was pursuing a vocation in an area governed exclusively by the Chief Rabbi and therefore had no choice but to accept his jurisdiction.

Comment

This case suggests that the proper test of whether a power is public in nature is whether it is governmental – that is, if the body exercising the power did not exist, the government would create a statutory body to exercise that power. The powers of the Chief Rabbi were not governmental because they were spiritual. It was further held that it was not appropriate for a secular court to intervene in a spiritual sphere.

R v Disciplinary Committee of the Jockey Club ex p Aga Khan (1993) CA: What is 'governmental' power?

Facts

The Jockey Club controlled and regulated horse racing in Great Britain. Owners who wished to race their horses entered into contractual relations with the Club, expressly submitting to the disciplinary jurisdiction of the committee. One of the applicant's horses failed a routine drugs test and was disqualified following an inquiry by the Committee. The applicant sought judicial review of the Committee's decision. The Jockey Club contended that it was not subject to judicial review since it was independent of government in origin, constitution and function, and its relation with the applicant was essentially one of private law.

Decision

The Court of Appeal held that, in the circumstances, the Committee's decision was not susceptible to judicial review. The issue was to be determined in the light of all the facts of the case; no single feature or test was decisive. Although the Jockey Club effectively regulated a significant national activity of which it had *de facto* control and exercised powers of a public character, it was not in origin a public body and its powers were not governmental in nature. Furthermore, the applicant's contractual relationship with the Club allowed him sufficient remedy against it in private law.

Comment

Arguably, the crucial factor in this case was that the applicant had a potential remedy at private law. It would seem that the main reason why it was concluded that the Jockey Club's powers were not governmental was that the Club exercised power so effectively that there had never been any question of government intervention – a somewhat narrow application of the test. There is, however, a suggestion in some of the *dicta* that, although the Jockey Club's relationship with the Aga Khan was governed by private law, certain of its functions, including the licensing of persons involved in the racing industry and the management of racecourses, might properly be considered matters of public law and so susceptible to judicial review.

R v Legal Aid Board ex p Donn & Co (1996): The current test

Facts

The Legal Aid Board was established by the Legal Aid Act 1988. Section 4 of the Act empowered the Board to do anything which was calculated to facilitate the discharge of its functions. By s 4(4), this included entering into contracts, provided and solely to the extent that the Lord Chancellor directed. The applicants, a firm of solicitors, submitted a tender to an area office of the respondents seeking a contract to undertake multi-party litigation on behalf of hundreds of sufferers of 'Gulf War Syndrome'. The respondent's office suspected that the presence of a Territorial Army officer among the applicant's advisers could give rise to a conflict of interest, and this was among the grounds on which a rival firm's tender was preferred.

The applicants alleged that the respondents' investigation of the matter had been procedurally flawed and unfair, and submitted that the Board was susceptible to judicial review either because it was statutorily underpinned by the Act, or because the tendering process involved a sufficient public law element. At the invitation of Ognall J, the applicants developed only the second of these submissions.

Decision

The court held that the question for the court was whether, in the absence of statutory underpinning, the Board might be subject to judicial review in administering the tendering process. In answering this question, it was appropriate to consider both the nature and purpose of the selection procedure, and the consequences to which the procedure would give rise. There could be no universal test of a sufficient public law element, and the answer would be one of impression and degree. In light of the amounts of public money being allocated by the Board on behalf of potential litigants who could afford no other means of vindicating their rights, the public interest in the proper outcome of the process was clear. Further, the Board was the sole and final arbiter of the tendering process. Even if some private law remedy were available to the applicants, the public dimensions of the matter were sufficient to render it justiciable in public law. On the facts, the applicants' complaints about the tendering process were made out, and the application accordingly succeeded.

Comment
This ruling seems to return to the broad approach found in *Datafin*.

8.2.2.3 *Bodies whose powers derive from contract*

R v Lord Chancellor's Department ex p Nangle (1991): Judicial review not available where body derives power from contract

Facts
The applicant held a clerical post in the Civil Service. His appointment was stated to be at the pleasure of the Crown, and was governed by the Civil Service Pay and Conditions of Service Code. The Code stated that the relationship between civil servants was technically based not on contract but on the prerogative. The applicant was disciplined for misbehaviour by being transferred to another department and losing salary increment rights. He applied for judicial review. The respondent department argued that the applicant had a contract of employment with the Crown.

Decision
The Divisional Court held, dismissing the application for judicial review, that all the incidents of a contract of employment were present in the applicant's relation with the Crown. There had been offer, acceptance, consideration and an intention to create legal relations at the inception of the applicant's employment. The Civil Service Code set out in detail the matters which would normally be covered by a contract of employment. The statement that the prerogative, rather than contract, was to govern the relationship did not suffice to make its conditions voluntary. It followed that the parties must have intended their relationship to be governed by private rather than public law. Accordingly, the applicant should have issued a writ claiming damages for breach of contract.

8.2.2.4 *Bodies whose jurisdiction is exercised consensually*

Law v National Greyhound Racing Club (1983): Judicial review not available where body derives power from consensual submission

Facts
The plaintiff was a greyhound trainer whose licence was suspended because his greyhound had traces of prohibited substances in its tissues. The Club moved to strike

out the plaintiff's action on the grounds that he was seeking public law remedies and should therefore have applied for judicial review under Order 53.

Decision

The court held that the Club's argument was incorrect; the plaintiff was correct to proceed in private law. The plaintiff had a contract with the Club, and thus the Club's decision was made in private, not public, law. A steward's inquiry under the Club's rules of racing concerned only those who voluntarily submitted themselves to the stewards' jurisdiction. Lawton LJ conceded that the public might well have an interest in the way in which the stewards' powers were exercised, and that the exercise of those powers might affect the rights of individuals. However, such consequences might equally flow from the decisions of many other domestic tribunals and were insufficient to make a domestic, consensually appointed tribunal into a public body.

Comment

By contrast, the Court of Appeal in the *Aga Khan* case accepted that the Jockey Club's powers extended to persons with whom it did not have either a contractual relationship or a relationship deriving from consensual submission, since it has power to 'warn off' any person – that is, forbid him from entering any premises connected with horse racing.

8.3   Special bars to judicial review

R v Chief Rabbi ex p Wachmann (1992)

See 8.2.2.2 above.

R v Parliamentary Commissioner for Standards ex p Al Fayed (1998)
CA: Judicial review not available against Parliamentary Commissioner for Standards

Facts

The applicant sought leave to apply for judicial review of a decision of the Parliamentary Commissioner for Standards, alleging that he had acted beyond his power in rejecting the applicant's complaint that a minister of the Crown had corruptly received a payment. The Commissioner, in his report, had concluded that the minister had no case to answer. The application for leave was rejected at first instance and renewed before the Court of Appeal.

Decision

The Court of Appeal held, refusing the application, that responsibility for the supervision of the Commissioner had been placed by Parliament, through its standing orders, on the Committee of Standards and Privileges of the House, and not on the courts. The Commissioner, in fact, was one of the means by which the Committee carried out its functions; it was conceded that the Committee's functions were part of the proceedings of the House and, therefore, protected from the scrutiny of a court by Art 9 of the Bill of Rights 1688. The Commissioner's role differed from that of the ombudsman, who had been held in *R v Parliamentary Commissioner for Administration ex p Dyer* (1994) to be reviewable, because the ombudsman's function was to investigate the activities of government, while the Commissioner for Standards was concerned with the propriety of the activities of those engaged within Parliament. In exercise of what Sedley J at first instance had referred to as the 'mutuality of respect between two sovereignties', the court:

... would not seek to encroach upon the parliamentarian ... The only question for the judge is whether the decision taken by the body under review was one which it was legally permitted to take in the way that it did.

8.4   Remedies available under Order 53

8.4.1   The Prerogative Orders

8.4.1.1   Certiorari

An order of certiorari (Latin for 'to be certified') quashes a decision already taken and refers the matter back to the original decision maker for reconsideration. It is the most common form of order made in judicial review. The decision maker is not prevented from reaching the same decision a second time.

Notes to Order 53, para 14/19, state as follows:

Certiorari is an order which brings up into the High Court a decision of an inferior court or tribunal or of a public authority for it to be quashed ... Where the court quashes a decision, it has power to remit the matter to the court, tribunal or authority concerned with a direction to reconsider it and to reach a decision in accordance with the judgment given by the court in the judicial review proceedings ...

Attorney General for Hong Kong v Ng Yuen Shiu (1983) PC: Nature of certiorari

Facts

The government of Hong Kong announced that it was terminating its policy of not repatriating illegal immigrants from China who had reached the urban area of Hong Kong. The applicant and others, illegal immigrants of Chinese origin from Macau, sought to clarify their position. They were told by the Secretary for Security that they would be interviewed and that each case would be treated on its own merits. A removal order was made against the applicant.

Decision

The Privy Council held that the conditional order of prohibition made by the Court of Appeal would be replaced by an order of certiorari to quash the removal order which had been made against the respondent.

Per Lord Fraser:

That order of certiorari is of course entirely without prejudice to the making of a fresh removal order by the Director of Immigration after a fair inquiry has been held at which the respondent has been given an opportunity to make such representations as he may see fit as to why he should not be removed.

8.4.1.2 Prohibition

Orders of prohibition are uncommon for two reasons. First, the order is pre-emptive, in that it prevents a particular decision or action in the future, and application for judicial review is in practice usually made after the decision. Secondly, the courts are reluctant to interfere with the executive in the exercise of its discretion.

Notes to Order 53, para 14/20, state as follows:

Prohibition is an order restraining an inferior court or tribunal or a public authority from acting outside its jurisdiction. Thus where, for example, a tribunal is proposing to adjudicate upon some matter which is not within its jurisdiction judicial review will lie and the court can make an order of prohibition.

R v Kent Police Authority ex p Godden (1971) CA: Availability of prohibition

Facts

The applicant, a police chief inspector, was placed on sick leave after the Chief Medical Officer of the force, Dr Crosbie Brown, certified that he was unfit for police duty on the ground that he was suffering from a mental disorder. The applicant's own doctor sent him to a consultant psychiatrist, who reported that he was in good mental and physical health. The police authority took steps compulsorily to retire the applicant, and notified him that they had selected Dr Crosbie Brown as their 'duly qualified practitioner' to determine whether the applicant was permanently disabled within the meaning of the Police Pensions Regulations 1971. The applicant sought orders of prohibition and mandamus.

Decision

The Court of Appeal held, granting both orders, that the rule against bias (see Chapter 16 below) disqualified Dr Crosbie Brown from acting. The doctor had already put his own medical opinion of the applicant on affidavit, and so had committed himself to his view. He would be disqualified either because he could not bring a completely impartial judgment to bear, or because it could not appear to the applicant that he could do so.

Comment

Here prohibition was appropriate as a means of disqualifying Dr Crosbie Brown from acting, since he was not in a position to make a judgment which was both impartial and seen to be impartial.

8.4.1.3 Mandamus

An order of mandamus (Latin for 'we command') is the prerogative order least frequently made, due to the courts' reluctance to interfere with the discretion of executive bodies.

Notes to Order 53, para 14/21, state as follows:

Mandamus is an order requiring an inferior court or tribunal or person or body of persons charged with a public duty to carry out its judicial or other public duty. An order of mandamus ... will lie against an officer of the Crown who is obliged by statute to do some ministerial or administrative act which affects the rights or interests of the applicant.

R v Inland Revenue Commissioners ex p National Federation of Self-Employed and Small Businesses Ltd (1982) HL: Nature of mandamus

Facts

In order to avoid tax, casual workers in the newspaper industry were in the habit of giving false names when drawing their pay. The Inland Revenue Commissioners (IRC) decided to offer them an amnesty in respect of past tax avoidance in return for their co-operation in the future. The Federation sought a declaration that the IRC's decision to grant the amnesty was unlawful, and mandamus to compel the IRC to assess and collect all arrears of tax.

Decision

The Lords held that the Federation did not have *locus standi* to bring the action (see Chapter 10 below) but Lord Scarman commented generally on the nature of mandamus:

Mandamus is the most elusive of the prerogative writs and orders. The nature of the interest an applicant must show, the nature of the duty which it is available to enforce, and the persons or bodies to whom it may issue have varied from time to time in its development. It is, of course, a judicial remedy; it is equally clear that it is a remedy to compel performance of a public legal duty, that it does not go to the Crown itself and that it is only available if the applicant shows a sufficient interest.

Chief Constable of the North Wales Police v Evans (1982) HL: Exceptional nature of mandamus

Facts

The respondent, a probationary police constable, was informed by the Chief Constable of his force that, if he did not resign, he would be discharged. The Chief Constable had decided to dispense with the respondent's services on the basis of rumours about his private life, but the respondent was at no stage told of the matters alleged against him, or given an opportunity to be heard in response to them. At first instance and in the Court of Appeal, the Chief Constable's decision was held to be in breach of the principles of natural justice (see Chapter 16). He appealed to the House of Lords, seeking substantive relief in the form of an order of mandamus to compel his reinstatement. The Chief Constable cross-appealed.

Decision

The House of Lords held, dismissing the Chief Constable's appeal, that the treatment meted out to the respondent had been little short of outrageous. However, the grant of an order of mandamus would border on a usurpation of the Chief Constable's powers, and a declaration stating the rights of the respondent would be granted in its place. The statement of Lord Denning MR in the Court of Appeal, to the effect that the respondent was entitled not only to a fair hearing, but also to a fair and reasonable decision by the Chief Constable, was disapproved.

8.4.2   Other remedies

The three prerogative orders are all available only in public law matters and exclusively by way of application for judicial review. Two other remedies, declaration and injunction, are creations of the ordinary common law and equally available in private law proceedings.

8.4.2.1   Declaration

A declaration is simply a statement of the law; it is not a remedy as such. After a declaration has been made, it is up to the applicant to seek a remedy via private law proceedings in contract or tort as appropriate. In *Chief Constable of North Wales v Evans*, for example, the court issued a declaration that the enforced resignation was a nullity, allowing the plaintiff to seek a remedy in damages.

Dyson v Attorney General (1911) CA: Availability of declaration

Facts

The appellant brought an action for a declaration that he was not obliged to answer certain questions on a form issued to him by the IRC. He proceeded against the Attorney General as a representative of the interest of the Crown. His action was disallowed at first instance on the ground that the only procedure available in such a case was the preferment of a petition of right.

Decision

The Court of Appeal held, allowing the appeal, that the appellant might properly seek a declaration of his rights against the Attorney General as representative of the Crown.

Per Cozens-Hardy MR:

The power to make declaratory decrees was first granted to the Court of Chancery in 1852 by s 50 of 15 and 16 Vict c 87 … The jurisdiction is, however, now enlarged, for by Ord 25 r 5: 'No action or proceeding shall be open to objection, on the ground that a merely declaratory judgment or order is sought thereby, and the court may make binding declarations of right whether any consequential relief is or could be claimed or not.' I can see no reason why this section should not apply to an action in which the Attorney General, as representing the Crown, is a party. The court is not bound to make a mere declaratory judgment, and in the exercise of its discretion will have regard to all the circumstances of the case.

Equal Opportunities Commission and Another v Secretary of State for Employment (1994) HL: Availability of declaration not affected by Order 53

Facts

Under the Employment Protection Consolidation Act 1978, full-time workers qualified for unfair dismissal and redundancy payments after two years, while part-time workers qualified only after five years. The majority of full-time workers in the UK were men; the majority of part-time workers were women. The Equal Opportunities Commission (EOC) considered that this situation resulted in indirect discrimination against women, contrary to the UK's obligations under European law. In a letter sent to the EOC, the Secretary of State declined to accept that this was the case. The EOC and Mrs Day, a part-time worker made redundant after less than five years' employment, sought, *inter alia*, a declaration that the UK was in breach of its Treaty obligations. The Court of Appeal dismissed Mrs Day's claim on the grounds that it should have been brought in private law before an industrial tribunal. It held against the EOC on the grounds that the Secretary of State had made no 'decision' capable of review, that no justiciable issue had been raised, and that the EOC had no *locus standi* to seek judicial review against the Secretary of State. The EOC and Mrs Day appealed to the House of Lords.

Decision
The House of Lords held that Mrs Day's claim would be dismissed for the reasons given by the Court of Appeal. The differential provisions of the 1978 Act were incompatible with European law. There was no decision by the Secretary of State which could be the subject of a prerogative order of the court, but the EOC was not seeking to enforce the UK's Treaty obligations by order of the court. A declaration that the UK was in breach of them would be sufficient for the EOC's purposes; the court had jurisdiction to grant it, and would do so. The EOC did have *locus standi* to bring the proceedings (so held by a majority). On the question whether the court had jurisdiction to grant a declaration in circumstances in which it could not grant one of the prerogative orders, Lord Browne-Wilkinson noted that Order 53, r 1(2) did not say that declarations were available only in lieu of prerogative orders. The right to seek a declaratory judgment had previously been available in purely civil actions where there could be no question of the grant of a prerogative order. The institution of the Order 53 judicial review procedure was not to be taken to have restricted the availability of a declaration.

8.4.2.2   Injunction and damages
Order 53, rr 1 and 7, state as follows:

1 (1)   An application for ...
   (b)   An injunction under s 30 of the Supreme Court Act 1981 restraining a person from acting in any office in which he is not entitled to act, shall be made by way of an application for judicial review in accordance with the provisions of this Order.
  (2)   An application for ... an injunction (not being an injunction mentioned in para (1)(b)) may be made by way of an application for judicial review ...

7 (1)   On an application for judicial review the court may, subject to para (2), award damages to the applicant if:
   (a)   he has included in the statement in support of his application for leave under r 3 a claim for damages arising from any matter to which the application relates; and
   (b)   the court is satisfied that, if the claim had been made in an action begun by the applicant at the time of making his application, he could have been awarded damages.

CHAPTER 9

THE AVAILABILITY OF JUDICIAL REVIEW

Introduction

One of a number of differences between judicial review and actions at private law is that there are procedural hurdles to be surmounted before an application is permitted to proceed. An applicant for judicial review must demonstrate, *inter alia*, that he has 'sufficient interest' in the decision at issue and that his application has sufficient merit to be permitted to proceed. He must also comply with a strict time limit for applications.

9.1 The requirement of leave

Judicial review is a two-stage process, in that a single judge first considers whether the application should be permitted to proceed ('the leave stage'). If leave is granted, the substantive issues will be dealt with by two judges sitting in the Divisional Court of the Queen's Bench (normally a Lord Justice of Appeal together with a High Court judge).

Order 53, r 3(1) of the Rules of the Supreme Court states as follows:

3 (1) No application for judicial review shall be made unless leave of the court has been obtained in accordance with this rule.

Notes to the Rules of the Supreme Court, para 14/30, states as follows:

Leave to apply for judicial review
The application for leave to move for judicial review must be made *ex parte* to a single judge, whether in term time or vacation ...
The purpose of the requirement of leave is:
(a) to eliminate at an early stage any applications which are either frivolous, vexatious or hopeless; and
(b) to ensure that an applicant is only allowed to proceed to a substantive hearing if the court is satisfied that there is a case fit for further consideration ...

R v Inland Revenue Commissioners ex p National Federation of Self-Employed and Small Businesses Ltd (1982) HL: Purpose of leave requirement

Facts
See 8.4.1.3 above.

The IRC opposed the application on the ground, *inter alia*, that the Federation did not have sufficient interest within the terms of RSC Order 53, r 3(5). The rule provided that: 'The court shall not grant leave unless it considers that the applicant has a sufficient interest in the matter to which the application relates.' Leave was refused on these grounds by the Divisional Court but granted by a majority in the Court of Appeal. The IRC appealed to the House of Lords.

Decision

The House of Lords held, allowing the appeal, that the rule required the applicant to show a sufficient interest in the matter to which the application relates. In all but the simplest cases, it was therefore necessary first to determine the nature of the matter in question at the substantive hearing and only then to judge the sufficiency of the applicant's interest in it. Lord Diplock stated that the purpose of the leave requirement was:

> ... to prevent the time of the court being wasted by busybodies with misguided or trivial complaints of administrative error, and to remove the uncertainty in which public officers and authorities might be left as to whether they could safely proceed with administrative action while proceedings for judicial review of it were actually pending even though misconceived.

9.2   Time limits governing applications for judicial review

Order 53, r 4 of the Rules of the Supreme Court states as follows:

(1)   An application for judicial review shall be made promptly and in any event within three months from the date when grounds for the application first arose unless the court considers that there is good reason for extending the period within which the application shall be made.

(2)   Where the relief sought is an order of certiorari in respect of any judgment, order, conviction or other proceeding, the date when grounds for the application first arose shall be taken to be the date of that judgment, order, conviction or proceeding.

(3)   Paragraph (1) is without prejudice to any statutory provision which has the effect of limiting the time within which an application for judicial review may be made.

Notes to the Rules of the Supreme Court, para 14/31, states as follows:

Delay in applying for relief
Application for leave to move for judicial review must be made promptly, which in this context means as soon as practicable or as soon as the circumstances of the case will allow, and in any event such application must be made within three months from the date when grounds for the application first arose ... It is sometimes thought that an applicant for judicial review is always allowed three months in which to make his application for leave, and provided that he lodges it within that period leave cannot be refused on the grounds of delay. That is not so. The primary requirement laid down by the rules (r 4(1)) is that the application must be made 'promptly', followed by the secondary provision '... and in any event within three months ...'. Thus, there can be cases where, even though the application for leave was made within the three month period, leave might be refused because, on the facts, the application had not been made promptly ...

R v Independent Television Commission ex p TV NI Ltd (1991) CA: 'Undue delay' may occur even where application is made within three month limit

Facts

The applicant, a regional television company, bid unsuccessfully for a licence to provide a television service. On 16 October, the Independent Television Commission

(ITC) announced the names of the companies to which licences would be granted. The applicant did not apply for leave for judicial review, because it was known that another disappointed bidder had already applied and been refused leave. On 4 December, the ITC granted licences to the companies named earlier. The applicant now sought leave, was refused it at first instance, and renewed the application before the Court of Appeal.

Decision

The Court of Appeal held, refusing leave, that, after 4 December, the new licence holders were entitled to begin to invest in the setting up of the service which they had been chosen to provide, and it therefore became improper to put a licence in doubt by granting leave to question a competitor's failure to get it. Applicants in such matters, which could affect good administration through their impact on third party rights, had to act with the utmost promptitude. The present applicants had not done so.

R v Stratford-on-Avon District Council ex p Jackson (1985) CA: 'Delay' timed from date application is made

Facts

The applicant sought to challenge a planning decision of the local authority permitting construction of a supermarket. Planning permission was granted in August 1984, but the applicant failed to lodge her application for leave until May 1985. The delay was due to difficulties in obtaining legal aid, for which the applicant was not to blame. Leave to apply was granted, but subsequently set aside. The applicant renewed her application for leave to the Court of Appeal. The respondent argued that the three month period referred to in Order 53, r 4 limited the time in which the substantive application, and not merely the application for leave, should be made. The applicant submitted that when leave had been granted, it would no longer be open to the court at the substantive hearing to refuse a remedy on the ground of delay.

Decision

The Court of Appeal held, granting leave, that the applicant's difficulties in obtaining legal aid constituted sufficient explanation for the delay. She had not been to blame for this, and had shown a proper sense of urgency despite it. The court would use its discretion to extend the time period. Where delay was in question, the authorities relating to civil suits involving private law actions would not be relevant since, in judicial review proceedings, there was no true *lis inter partes*. The period in which application was to be made referred to the application for leave; if it were otherwise, the applicant's ability to observe the time limit could depend on the state of the court lists. The grant of leave in a case of delay did not prevent the respondent from raising the matter at the substantive hearing, or fetter the judge's discretion to refuse a remedy on that ground.

Per Ackner LJ:

The essential requirement of the rule is that the application must be made 'promptly'. The fact that an application has been made within three months from the date when the grounds for the application first arose does not necessarily mean that it has been made promptly. Thus, there can well be cases where a court may have to consider whether or not to extend the time for making the application, even though the application has been made within the three month period.

R v Dairy Produce Quota Tribunal for England and Wales ex p Caswell (1989) CA: Court may consider that delay does not prevent hearing of application but makes grant of remedy inappropriate

Facts

The applicants challenged the decision of the Tribunal to fix their dairy produce quota pursuant to a misconstruction (as they alleged) of the relevant regulations. At the substantive hearing, the court accepted their arguments and granted a declaration, but refused substantive relief under s 31(6) of the Supreme Court Act 1981 on the grounds that the applicants' two year delay in applying amounted to undue delay, and the grant of relief in the circumstances would be prejudicial to good administration. The applicants appealed to the Court of Appeal.

Decision

The Court of Appeal held, following *Jackson* (above), that the grant of leave to apply for judicial review where good reason for delay had been shown was without prejudice to the power of the court hearing the substantive application to refuse relief under s 31(6) of the Supreme Court Act 1981, that it would cause substantial hardship to, or substantially prejudice the rights of, any person, or would be detrimental to good administration. The court did not find it possible or desirable to define detriment to good administration, but indicated that it would amount to positive harm, affirmatively established by or capable of being inferred from evidence, and that in determining whether the foreseen consequences would be harmful, it was permissible to look not only at the particular instance, but also at the effect of the particular instance on other potential applicants, and the consequence if their applications were successful. Here, there had been undue delay since the application had not been made in time, and there was a likelihood of detriment to good administration since the grant of relief to the applicants would either entail the re-opening of numerous other claims, or alternatively secure the applicants an unfair advantage over others who had been treated similarly. The appeal was dismissed.

Comment

Remedies in judicial review are discretionary, not only in terms of the form of remedy, but under s 31(6), whether a remedy should be granted at all.

R v Criminal Injuries Compensation Board ex p A (1999) HL: Issue of delay and appropriateness of grant of remedy considered in more detail

Facts

The appellant applied for leave to move for judicial review of a decision of the Board, on the ground that evidence relevant to her claim had not been considered. The application was made 10 months after the Board's decision. Leave to apply was granted by Carnwath J, though he did not expressly extend the period for the making of the application, and he appeared to consider that the issue of delay might be raised again at the substantive hearing. The substantive application for review was heard by Popplewell J, who found no hardship, prejudice or detriment to good administration on which to base the refusal of relief, but rejected the application on the ground that the grant of leave to apply had in effect been conditional, and no good reason for extending the time period had been shown. The appellant appealed unsuccessfully to the Court of Appeal and appealed further to the House of Lords.

Decision

The House of Lords held, allowing the appeal, that the matter of delay had been decided at the leave hearing before Carnwath J. The merits of the decision to extend the period for application were not to be re-argued at the substantive hearing. Where hardship, prejudice or detriment to good administration was taken into account at the substantive hearing, that matter went to the decision of whether to grant relief, and not to the decision on the grant of leave, which had already been made in the applicant's favour.

9.3   The existence of other remedies

Generally speaking, judicial review is not available where the applicant has other potential remedies.

R v Epping and Harlow General Commissioners ex p Goldstraw (1983) CA: The general principle

Facts

In the absence of income tax returns, the applicant was assessed for tax and appealed. The appeal was adjourned at the applicant's request, but, at the re-listed date, he did not appear and was not represented. The appeal was determined by the Commissioners in the applicant's absence, although on the basis of figures put forward by his accountant. Two months later, the applicant sought to re-open the appeal. The Commissioners declined to allow this. The applicant sought judicial review of their decision, alleging that the Commissioners had acted on advice given maliciously by their clerk to the effect that they had no power to do what the applicant asked.

Decision

The Court of Appeal held that the clerk's advice was correct, so that no question of his alleged malice was legally relevant. Furthermore, the applicant, after failing to attend the appeal hearing, could have applied within 30 days to the Commissioners asking them to state a case for the opinion of the High Court, raising as a question of law the way in which the appeal had been conducted. He had not availed himself of that remedy. It was a cardinal principle that, save in the most exceptional circumstances, the residual supervisory jurisdiction of the court would not be exercised where other remedies were available and had not been used.

Preston v Inland Revenue Commissioners (1985) HL: Principle confirmed by House of Lords and exceptions considered

Facts

The appellant acquired and later sold shares in a company. An Inland Revenue inspector sought details of the share transactions. The appellant provided bare details and subsequently sought and obtained the Inland Revenue's assurance that in return for his abandoning claims to tax relief, no further inquiries would be made into the share transactions. At a later stage, when it had become too late for the appellant to make his tax relief claims, the Inland Revenue sought further information about the transactions and in consequence of the information supplied by the appellant, it issued a notice cancelling a tax advantage gained in connection with the transactions.

The appellant applied for judicial review of the Inland Revenue's action and at first instance succeeded on the grounds that it had been unfair and unreasonable. The Inland Revenue successfully appealed to the Court of Appeal, which held that its decision was merely managerial and therefore not open to review, and that it had not been unreasonable. The appellant appealed to the House of Lords.

Decision

The House of Lords held that the appeal would be dismissed on the ground that there had been no abuse of power by the Inland Revenue.

Per Lord Scarman:

... A remedy by way of judicial review is not to be made available where an alternative remedy exists ... But cases for judicial review can arise even where appeal procedures are provided by Parliament ... I accept that the court cannot in the absence of special circumstances decide by way of judicial review to be unfair that which the Commissioners by taking action against the taxpayer have determined to be fair. But circumstances can arise when it would be unjust, because it would be unfair to the taxpayer, even to initiate action under Pt XVII of the 1970 Act [to counteract a tax advantage]. For instance ... judicial review should in principle be available where the conduct of the Commissioners in initiating such action would have been equivalent, had they not been a public authority, to a breach of contract or a breach of a representation giving rise to an estoppel. Such a decision would be an abuse of power; whether it was or not and whether in the circumstances the court would in its discretion intervene would, of course, be questions for the court to decide.

R v Chief Constable of the Merseyside Police ex p Calveley (1986) CA: Circumstances in which exception might be made

Facts

The appellants were police officers against whom complaints had been made in consequence of their conduct during an arrest. An investigation into the complaints was instituted. The Police (Discipline) Regulations 1977 required officers subject to investigation to be informed 'as soon as is practicable' of the complaints or allegations made, and to be warned that statements made by them might be used in subsequent disciplinary proceedings. The appellants were not so informed for almost two and a half years. Their argument that the delay was so prejudicial as to render disciplinary proceedings against them unfair was rejected by the Chief Constable. They were found guilty of the charges brought against them and gave notice of intention to appeal against the Chief Constable's decision under s 37 of the Police Act 1964, but, before the hearing of the appeal, they sought an order of certiorari by means of judicial review. The Divisional Court rejected their application on the ground that they had not yet exhausted the internal remedies available to them. The officers appealed to the Court of Appeal.

Decision

The Court of Appeal held that the appeal would be allowed. In deciding whether judicial review would be permitted where an alternative statutory remedy subsisted, it would be appropriate to contrast the speed of the respective procedures and to consider whether the statutory remedy would resolve the question at issue fully and directly, and whether the appeal tribunal would be in a position to bring particular or technical knowledge to bear. The appeal procedure here was not speedy and although the appeal tribunal had specialised expertise, it would be wrong to overlook the fact that a police officer's submission to police disciplinary procedures was not unconditional, and he was not to be put in peril of them unless there had been substantial compliance with police disciplinary regulations. Here there had been so serious a departure from them that the court would in its discretion grant judicial review.

9.4   Public and private law

Prior to 1977, when the unified judicial review procedure under Order 53 was introduced, it was common practice to seek the non-prerogative remedies of declaration or injunction in public law matters by way of actions begun under private law, in order to circumvent the procedural restrictions associated with judicial review before that date. With the new Order 53 in place, the question arose as to whether this practice would be permitted to continue.

O'Reilly v Mackman (1983) HL: Public law matters should only be dealt with by way of application for judicial review

Facts

The appellants were prisoners who sought to challenge the validity of decisions of the Board of Visitors of Hull Prison to impose penalties on them following their involvement in a prison riot. The appellants proceeded by writ at private law, seeking a declaration that the decisions had been taken in breach of the principles of natural justice.

Decision

The House of Lords held, dismissing the appeals, that the proceedings were an abuse of process. If the matters alleged in the appellants' statements of claim were true, then it was beyond dispute that they would have a public law remedy by way of judicial review under RSC Order 53. However, the appellants had no private law rights against the Prison Board of Visitors. Although the remedy which they sought was equally available in private as in public law and, under Order 53, r 9(5), the court had power, in an application for judicial review, to order the proceedings to continue as if they had been begun by writ, the converse power did not exist.

It would generally be wrong as a matter of principle to allow the vindication of public law rights by private action, since the new Order 53, as ratified by s 31 of the Supreme Court Act 1981, created procedural safeguards in public law for public authorities whose decisions were challenged in public law. Chief among these were the stringent time limits and the requirement of leave to apply for judicial review. Litigants should not be permitted to deprive public authorities of those safeguards. There might be exceptions to that general rule, particularly where the vindication of a public right arose as an issue strictly collateral to private litigation. The question whether there were other exceptions would be left to be developed on a case by case basis.

Cocks v Thanet District Council (1983) HL

Facts

The respondent was homeless. He instituted a private law proceeding in the county court claiming that the local housing authority had a duty to house him and was in breach of that duty, and sought a declaration to that effect, consequential mandatory injunctions and damages. It appeared that the authority had decided that he had become homeless intentionally, so that he would be owed no more than a limited duty to provide him with temporary accommodation. In order to obtain the substantive relief sought, the respondent was obliged to impugn that decision. The question whether the respondent was entitled to a declaration against the decision by proceeding in private law was ordered to be tried as a preliminary issue, and was determined in his favour. The housing authority appealed to the House of Lords.

Decision

The House of Lords held, allowing the appeal, that the respondent was not entitled to continue the proceedings or to seek any of the relief which he claimed otherwise than by an application for judicial review in public law. *O'Reilly v Mackman* had decided that, as a general rule, it would be contrary to public policy to permit a person seeking to establish that a decision of a public authority infringed rights to which he was entitled to protection under public law, to proceed by way of an ordinary (private) action. The same general rule applied where the decision which the litigant wished to impugn was not alleged to infringe any existing right but was one which, being adverse to him, prevented him from establishing a necessary condition precedent to the statutory private law right which he wished to enforce.

Comment

The two cases above were decided on the same day by an identically constituted House of Lords and set out the 'exclusivity principle', by which matters of public law ought only to be brought before the courts by way of application for judicial review. However, this narrow approach almost immediately began to break down as exceptions were developed, and it is now debatable whether the principle survives at all.

Davy v Spelthorne Borough Council (1984) HL: Exceptions begin to emerge

Facts

The respondent alleged that he had agreed with the council not to exercise his right of appeal against an enforcement notice under the Town and Country Planning Acts in return for a suspension of the notice for three years. He said he had entered into this agreement on the advice of council officers and, in pursuance of the agreement, had refrained from appealing against the enforcement notice. His private law actions for an injunction to prevent enforcement of the notice and an order setting it aside were struck out by the Court of Appeal on the grounds that they could be pursued only by way of judicial review. He also issued a writ claiming damages for negligent advice from the council. The council appealed against the Court of Appeal's refusal to strike out that claim as an abuse of process.

Decision

The House of Lords held, dismissing the appeal, that the claim in negligence was a straightforward private action in tort. Unlike the appellant in *Cocks*, the respondent was not seeking to impugn the enforcement notice; his entire case rested on the fact that he had lost the opportunity to impugn it. Essentially, the public law issue was peripheral. The expressions 'private law' and 'public law' were convenient expressions for descriptive purposes, but, *per* Lord Wilberforce:

We have not yet reached the point at which mere characterisation of a claim as a claim in public law is sufficient to exclude it from consideration by the ordinary courts: to permit this would be to create a dual system of law with the rigidity and procedural hardship for plaintiffs which it was the purpose of the recent reforms to remove.

Wandsworth London Borough Council v Winder (1985) HL: Exceptions become wider

Facts

The respondent was a tenant of Wandsworth Council. The council raised his rent to a level which he claimed was unreasonable. He paid his original rent and added to it a sum representing a 'reasonable' increase. The council sued the respondent for arrears of rent and for possession of his flat. The respondent's defence was that the decision to increase the rent was void for unreasonableness. The council argued that this challenge to the validity of its decision could be made only by way of public law under Order 53.

Decision

The House of Lords held, dismissing the council's appeal, that the present case was distinguishable from *O'Reilly v Mackman* on two grounds: first, the present respondent could arguably claim an infringement of a contractual right in private law and, secondly, he had not himself initiated the action. The case could be distinguished on the same grounds from *Cocks*. The new Order 53 had been a procedural reform, not intended to extend or diminish the substantive law. The respondent was seeking only to defend an action against him on the ground that he was not liable for the whole sum claimed, and should be entitled to do so.

Roy v Kensington and Chelsea Family Practitioner Committee (1992) HL: The principle under attack

Facts

The respondent was a general medical practitioner. Under the Statement of Fees and Allowances made by the Secretary of State, a practitioner was not eligible for the full rate of the basic practice allowance (his salary in all but name) unless his local Family Practitioner Committee considered that he was devoting a substantial amount of time to National Health Service practice. The Committee decided on these grounds to reduce the respondent's allowance. The respondent brought an action claiming, *inter alia*, payment of the sums allegedly due and a declaration that the Committee was in breach of its contract with him. The Committee applied to strike out the claim as an abuse of process on the ground that challenge to its decision should have been brought by way of judicial review under Order 53 and not by writ.

Decision

The House of Lords held, dismissing the appeal, that the respondent had private law rights against the Committee. He was entitled to assert or to defend those rights by way of action brought by writ, even if that action could incidentally involve the examination of a public law issue. The respondent's private law rights dominated the proceedings; he could not obtain repayment of moneys due by way of judicial review and his action should not be made dependent on the grant of leave or of remedies which were discretionary.

Per Lord Lowry:

... Unless the procedure adopted by the moving party is ill-suited to dispose of the question at issue, there is much to be said in favour of the proposition that a court having jurisdiction ought to let a case be heard rather than entertain a debate concerning the form of the proceedings.

R v Wicks (1997) HL: Application of principle to criminal matters

Facts

An enforcement notice requiring the dismantling of a building alleged to have been erected in breach of planning controls was served on the appellant by the local planning authority under s 87 of the Town and Country Planning Act 1971. The appellant's appeal against the notice was refused by the Secretary of State and a summons was issued against him for non-compliance with the notice under s 179(1) of the Act. He elected to be tried on indictment and sought to challenge the notice in the course of the trial on the ground that the planning authority had issued it in bad faith and upon irrelevant considerations. The judge ruled that the challenge should have been brought by way of judicial review, whereupon the appellant changed his plea to guilty. He appealed unsuccessfully against conviction to the Court of Appeal and appealed further to the House of Lords.

Decision

The House of Lords held, dismissing the appeal, that the question whether an administrative decision could be challenged in criminal proceedings depended upon construction of the statute under which the prosecution was brought, rather than on the distinction between 'procedural' and 'substantive' invalidity of administrative acts which had been drawn in *Bugg v Director of Public Prosecutions* (1993). In the case of the Town and Country Planning Act 1971, such construction showed that the reference to an enforcement notice in s 179(1) of the Act was to be understood as denoting an enforcement notice which, on its face, complied with the requirements of the Act and had not been quashed on appeal or by judicial review. Since the appellant had failed to comply with such a notice, he was guilty of the offence. The matters which he had sought to raise were irrelevant.

Boddington v British Transport Police (1998) HL: Principle set aside in criminal matters

Facts

The appellant was convicted of an offence under the Railways Bylaws 1965 (made under the Transport Act 1962), having smoked a cigarette in a railway carriage in which smoking was prohibited. His challenge to the validity of the bylaw was rejected by the stipendiary magistrate, who concluded on the basis of *Bugg* that subordinate legislation could only be challenged in a court with jurisdiction to rule on its validity. The appellant's appeal to the Divisional Court by way of case stated was also rejected.

Decision

The House of Lords held, dismissing the appeal, that the bylaw was valid, but that a question as to the validity of a bylaw could be determined in any court in which it arose. *Bugg* had held that subordinate legislation, such as a bylaw, remained effective until it was quashed, but had proceeded to draw a distinction between cases in which its validity was therefore beyond the jurisdiction of all but a court of supervisory jurisdiction, and cases in which subordinate legislation of patent (or 'substantive') invalidity could be called into question by way of defence in a criminal court. This distinction, in their Lordships' opinions, was based on the discredited distinction between 'voidness' and 'voidability', which had not survived the decision in *Anisminic* (see below). Only the clear language of a statute could take away the right of a defendant in criminal proceedings to challenge the validity of a bylaw or administrative decision where his prosecution was premised on its validity. *Bugg* was overruled.

9.5   Ouster clauses

9.5.1   *Total ouster clauses*

Anisminic v Foreign Compensation Commission (1969) HL: Total ouster clause cannot exclude judicial review without express words

Facts

Anisminic's property in Egypt was seized by the Egyptian Government at the time of the Suez crisis of 1956. Anisminic later sold its Egyptian business to an Egyptian company, but retained its right to claim compensation in respect of its earlier losses. In 1959, a treaty was concluded between the UK and Egyptian Governments, under which compensation was to be paid by the Egyptian Government to the UK in respect of certain properties, including Anisminic's. The UK Government set up the Foreign Compensation Commission in order to distribute the compensation.

Anisminic applied to the Commission for compensation. The Commission considered that it was obliged to be satisfied that Anisminic's successor in title to the property was or had been a British subject. It was not so satisfied and accordingly rejected Anisminic's claim. Anisminic argued that the nationality of a successor in title was irrelevant where the claimant was the original owner of the property. The main question for the House of Lords was whether, on the assumption that the Commission was mistaken in its interpretation of the legislative provisions, it had thereby exceeded its jurisdiction.

As a preliminary issue, the House of Lords had to consider the effect of s 4(4) of the Foreign Compensation Act 1950, which established the statutory regime pursuant to which the Commission was set up, and provided, 'The determination by the Commission of any application made to them under this Act shall not be called into question in any court of law'.

The Commission argued that the question whether its determination was *ultra vires* as a result of being based on an error of law was one which could be established only through legal proceedings, which were in terms prohibited by the Act.

Decision

The House of Lords held that s 4(4) of the Act did not preclude the court from quashing the Commission's determination. It was not necessary or even reasonable to construe the word 'determination' to include everything which purported to be a determination but in fact was no determination at all. It should be taken that Parliament, if it had intended that result, would have used clear words to achieve it.

South East Asia Fire Bricks v Non-Metallic Mineral Products Manufacturing Employees Union (1980) PC: Ouster effective on facts of case

Facts

A strike by employees of the appellants gave rise to a dispute concerning the legality of a lock-out (where employers prevent their employees from going to work until they accept terms imposed on them). The Industrial Court of Malaysia adjudicated upon the matter, finding against the appellants. The High Court granted the appellants' application for an order of certiorari to quash the decision of the Industrial Court on the ground that it was vitiated by an error of law on the face of the record. The Federal Court of Malaysia reversed the decision and on appeal to the Privy Council the question was whether the High Court had exceeded its powers by granting certiorari against the Industrial Court.

Section 29(3)(a) of the Malaysian Industrial Relations Act 1967 provided that 'an award of the court shall be final and conclusive, and no award shall be challenged, appealed against, reviewed, quashed or called into question in any court of law'.

Decision

The Privy Council held, dismissing the appeal, that the ouster was effective to exclude the grant of certiorari against a decision of the Industrial Court made within its jurisdiction.

9.5.2 Partial ouster clauses

R v Cornwall County Council ex p Huntington (1994): Imposition of strict time limits may be effective in excluding judicial review

Facts

The Wildlife and Countryside Act 1981 provided that any person aggrieved by a public right of way order made under the Act could apply to the High Court to question the order's validity, provided such application was made within 42 days of the publication of the order. The Act further stated that, 'Except as provided ... the validity of an order shall not be questioned in any legal proceedings whatsoever'. The respondent sought to have the grant of leave to apply for judicial review set aside on the ground that a public local inquiry into the order was still pending. The time period specified by the Act had therefore not begun to run and review outside the specified period was precluded by the terms of the Act.

Decision

The court held, setting aside leave, that where legislation prescribed a conditional opportunity for legal challenge, that prescription was effective to preclude challenge which did not comply with the conditions stipulated. This was so, irrespective of whether the decision sought to be challenged was fundamentally invalid and irrespective of the quasi-judicial or administrative character of the decision.

9.6 Nature of the matter

Case law shows in addition that the courts consider that certain matters should not be raised in the courts via judicial review, most notably the exercise by local authorities of their powers and responsibilities in relation to children.

In the Matter of Unborn Baby M sub nom R (on the Application of X and Y) v Gloucestershire County Council (2003) QBD Administrative Court: Principle that judicial review is inapplicable to child care proceedings

Facts

X and Y were the parents of an unborn baby ('M') due on 16 April 2003. X had five other children and Y had three, none of whom resided with them. X had been convicted several times of sexual intercourse with underage teenage girls and Y's abilities as a parent had been severely questioned in earlier care proceedings. It was X and Y's intention that M would live with them when born, together with one of X's children. The local authority considered that M was in need of protection from birth and registered it on the Child Protection Register and notified X and Y that care proceedings were to be instigated. In anticipation of this decision, X and Y commenced judicial review and injunction proceedings in order to challenge and prevent the decision to take M into care on an emergency basis. Contraventions of the European Convention on Human Rights were cited in support of the application, and it fell to be determined:

(1)   whether it was appropriate to bring judicial review proceedings in the circumstances;

(2)   if not, what the correct procedure was; and

(3)   in any event, whether care proceedings under the Children Act 1989 were compatible with the Convention.

Decision

The Court held as follows:

(1)   There were only fairly limited grounds on which the Administrative Court could intervene in the authority's decision making process and none of those grounds existed in the instant case. It was quite impossible to argue that it would be acting unlawfully, unreasonably, unfairly or in breach of anyone's human rights in making its application for a care order. The Family Proceedings Court (or the Family Division of the High Court following transfer of the proceedings) were the appropriate forums for an investigation and evaluation of the authority's case.

(2)   X and Y's application was wholly misconceived for the fundamental reason that a local authority had ongoing duties in respect of child protection and should not be barred from making the relevant application under the Children Act 1989, where it considered it necessary in order to safeguard a child's welfare. The need for highly intrusive emergency intervention to protect the interest of a baby was well recognised, albeit that such intervention was only to be allowed for extraordinary, compelling reasons (see *P, C and S v UK* (2002)) if it were to comply with Art 8 of the Convention. No arguable case had been made out by X and Y that the Children Act 1989 was incompatible with the Convention.

(3)   Save in wholly exceptional circumstances, it would not be appropriate to bring judicial review proceedings where the intention was to prevent a local authority from commencing emergency protection or care proceedings.

CHAPTER 10

WHO MAY SEEK JUDICIAL REVIEW – THE REQUIREMENT OF *LOCUS STANDI*

Introduction

In order to obtain judicial review of the action or decision of a public body, the applicant must demonstrate that he has 'sufficient interest' in the subject matter. This does not mean that the decision must concern him directly, but he must show that he is not simply a busybody.

10.1   The tests applied at the leave and at the substantive stages are not the same

R v Inland Revenue Commissioners ex p National Federation of Self-Employed and Small Businesses Ltd (1982) HL: More stringent test applied at substantive stage

Facts
See 8.4.1.3 above.

Per Lord Diplock:
The whole purpose of requiring that leave should first be obtained to make the application for judicial review would be defeated if the court were to go into the matter in any depth at that stage. If, on a quick perusal of the material then available, the court thinks that it discloses what might on further consideration turn out to be an arguable case in favour of granting to the applicant the relief claimed, it ought, in the exercise of a judicial discretion, to give him leave to apply for that relief. The discretion which the court is exercising at this stage is not the same as that which it is called on to exercise when all the evidence is in and the matter has been fully argued at the hearing of the application.

The Federation had no sufficient interest in the confidential affairs of another taxpayer (*per* Lord Wilberforce) and had failed to show any conduct that was *ultra vires* or unlawful (*per* Lord Diplock). Had it made out a case to the effect that the Inland Revenue had abused its managerial discretion, Lord Scarman would have held that it had shown a sufficient interest for the grant of leave to proceed further with its application.

10.2   The test for *locus standi* may vary according to the remedy sought

R v Felixstowe Justices ex p Leigh **(1987):** Test may be less stringent when declaration is sought

Facts

The applicant was a journalist who wanted to know the names of the individuals who had sat on the bench of a magistrates' court. He had not been involved in any capacity in the trial which he was seeking to report, nor had he been present at the proceedings. He sought a declaration that the justices had improperly decided that they should not disclose their names, and mandamus to compel them to disclose their names.

Decision

The court held that magistrates should not seek to carry out their functions anonymously. In view of the seriousness of this matter, the applicant did have sufficient standing to obtain the declaration. However, he did not have sufficient standing to obtain mandamus to compel the magistrates on this bench to disclose their names.

10.3   The test of *locus standi*

Decisions taken over the last decade or so have shown a considerable variation in the stringency of the test, a narrow view being first adopted. More recently, it would seem that the courts have begun to recognise that there may be a general public interest in the judicial review of a particular decision, and that too narrow an approach may make it impossible in practical terms for any person or body to bring an application.

R v Secretary of State for the Environment ex p Rose Theatre Trust Co **(1990):** The stringent approach

Facts

The remains of the Rose Theatre, which had seen the first performances of works by Shakespeare and Marlowe, were discovered during redevelopment works in the London Borough of Southwark. The applicant company, whose members included distinguished archaeologists and actors, was formed in order to campaign for the protection of the remains. The applicant applied to the Secretary of State to protect the remains by scheduling them pursuant to powers granted to him by the Ancient Monuments and Archaeological Areas Act 1979. He refused. The applicant sought judicial review.

Decision

The court held that the applicant did not have a sufficient interest to apply for judicial review. Where individuals did not have sufficient interest, they did not obtain it by incorporating themselves into an association. Although the Secretary of State had corresponded with the applicant, that could not and should not afford the applicant sufficient interest to challenge the decision.

R v Secretary of State for Social Services ex p Child Poverty Action Group (1990) CA: *Locus standi* is an issue for the court

Facts

The applicant contended that the provisions of ss 98 and 99 of the Social Security Act 1975 had been wrongly interpreted by the respondent, and therefore that claims for supplementary benefit had not been handled in accordance with the intentions of the legislature. In view of the importance of the issue, the respondent did not dispute the applicant's *locus standi* in the Divisional Court, although it reserved its right to argue the point in analogous cases in the future. Counsel for the respondent wished to adopt the same approach before the Court of Appeal.

Decision

The Court of Appeal held that the applicant would not be granted declaratory relief, and that the question of *locus standi* therefore did not arise. However, the respondent's reservation of its position on *locus standi* was inappropriate. *Locus standi* went to the jurisdiction of the court. The parties might not by agreement confer on the court a jurisdiction which it did not otherwise have.

Comment

These cases set a very narrow view of *locus standi*: that an applicant for judicial review must have been directly affected by the decision at issue, which has not been followed in case law since. More recently, the courts have tended to adopt a more liberal approach: that it is appropriate that a body in some way representative of persons with an interest in the decision should be permitted to make application, since individual interested persons may lack the necessary means or expertise.

R v Secretary of State for Foreign and Commonwealth Affairs ex p Rees-Mogg (1994): A more liberal approach

Facts

The applicant sought a declaration that the UK could not lawfully ratify the Treaty of European Union signed at Maastricht on 7 February 1992.

Decision

The court held that the application for judicial review, assuming it to relate to a justiciable issue, would be dismissed on the merits. There was no dispute between the parties as to the applicant's *locus standi*, and therefore it was not appropriate to say anything more about it. The court did, however, accept 'without question that Lord Rees-Mogg brings the proceedings because of his sincere concern for constitutional issues'.

Comment

This is an extremely broad approach to the issue of *locus standi*.

R v HM Inspectorate of Pollution ex p Greenpeace (1994) QBD: 'Public interest' in an application being brought is a factor in issues of *locus standi*

Facts

British Nuclear Fuels plc proposed to test its new thermal oxide reprocessing plant (THORP) in Cumbria before it became fully operational. To this end, a variation of existing authorisations was obtained from the respondent. The applicant, an environmental protection organisation of international standing, was concerned about levels of radioactive emission from the THORP. It sought an order of certiorari to quash the respondent's decision to vary the authorisations, and an injunction to stay the implementation of the authorisations and to prevent the testing. The respondent denied that the applicant had a sufficient interest in the matter.

Decision

The court held, dismissing the substantive application, that the decision to vary the authorisations had been properly made. The applicant did have a sufficient interest. In deciding on *locus standi*, a court was to take into account the nature of the applicant, the extent of its interest in the issues raised, the remedy sought to be obtained, and the nature of the relief sought to be achieved. Here, the applicant was an entirely responsible and respected body with a genuine concern for the environment. It had 2,500 members in the Cumbria region. If the applicant were denied *locus standi*, those it represented might not have an effective way to bring issues of concern to them before the court.

Per Otton J:

Consequently, a less well informed challenge might be mounted which would stretch unnecessarily the court's resources and which would not afford the court the assistance it requires to do justice between the parties. Further, if the unsuccessful applicant had the benefit of legal aid, it might leave the respondent and BNFL without an effective remedy in costs.

The applicant was enabled by its expertise to mount a carefully selected, focused, relevant and well argued challenge. The applicant was seeking certiorari, not mandamus: less stringent *locus standi* principles applied to the former remedy. The applicant had been treated as one of the consultees during the consultation process. However:

... it must not be assumed that Greenpeace (or any other interest group) will automatically be afforded standing in any subsequent application for judicial review ... This will have to be considered on a case by case basis at the leave stage and if the threshold is crossed again at the substantive hearing as a matter of discretion.

R v Secretary of State for Foreign Affairs ex p World Development Movement Ltd (1995) QBD: Refining of broad approach

Facts

The applicant sought judicial review of the Secretary of State's decision to make a grant to Malaysia under s 1(1) of the Overseas Development and Co-operation Act 1980. The grant was to be used for the funding of the Pergau Dam project. Section

1(1) confined the use of the power to the promoting of development. The applicant submitted that only sound development projects could lawfully be funded. The Secretary of State had received advice that the Pergau Dam project was not economically sound, had been motivated for purposes not permitted by the Act and had taken into account irrelevant considerations in making his decision.

Decision

The court held that the funding was not directed towards the promotion of development and that it was therefore *ultra vires* the Act. On the issue of the applicant's *locus standi*, the court considered that there was nothing in *ex p National Federation* (see 10.1 above) to deny standing. Further, an increasingly liberal approach to standing had been taken during the 12 years since that decision. The merits of the application were an important, if not a dominant factor when considering standing. Here, the issue raised was of importance, the rule of law required to be vindicated, there was unlikely to be any other responsible challenger, and the court further took into account the nature of the breach of duty alleged against the Secretary of State, and the prominence of the applicants in their field. If the court had been able to accept in *ex p Rees-Mogg* that the applicant there had standing in the light of his 'sincere concerns for constitutional issues', then *a fortiori* the present applicant had the expertise and interest to be granted standing.

R v Somerset County Council ex p Dixon (1997) QBD: *Rose Theatre Trust* disapproved

Facts

The applicant sought leave to challenge the county council's decision to permit the expansion of limestone quarrying. He was resident in the area affected, a parish councillor and a member of more than one body concerned with the environment. It was argued against him that he had no personal right or interest which was threatened by the proposed quarrying activities.

Decision

The court held that he had sufficient *locus standi* for leave to be granted, though it was in fact refused on other grounds. Sedley J rejected the argument that the applicant's interest needed to be superior to that of the general public, expressly disapproving *Rose Theatre Trust Co* on this point. At the leave stage, the test for *locus standi* was designed only to prevent abuse of the court by busybodies and troublemakers. To attempt to raise the threshold above that level was misconceived. At the substantive stage, the question of the applicant's standing was one factor to be weighed with others in the decision whether or not to grant a remedy. The real question was whether the applicant could argue that some substantial default or abuse had been committed by the respondent, and not whether his personal rights or interests were involved. Sedley J added that doctrinal distinctions between standing for the different remedies had been supplanted by the practical question of the application's substantive merit.

CHAPTER 11

GROUNDS FOR JUDICIAL REVIEW – INTRODUCTION

11.1 Background

Judicial review deals with the *operation* of government: the actions and decisions of the executive – known as the administrative process – at both central and local level. This includes day-to-day administration by central and local government, and the carrying into effect of government policy. Judicial review is therefore pre-eminently concerned with the powers and responsibilities of government in relation to the individual.

It must be borne in mind that the individual's rights in this sphere are seldom absolute. For example, parents have no absolute right to send their children to a particular school, simply to express a preference for that school, and a right of appeal to an independent tribunal if their preference is not given effect. Very often, therefore, the law is in the position of performing a balancing act between upholding the rights of individuals and ensuring efficient public administration.

Unlike some other European countries, such as France, Britain has no separate system of administrative courts. Cases concerning public bodies are brought in the normal courts, whether under the ordinary law applicable to all, or the more specialised administrative jurisdiction applicable only to public bodies. Therefore, an individual may in the same court sue a public body in contract or tort, or seek one of the remedies available via an application for judicial review of that body's exercise of its *public* powers, whichever is more appropriate to his situation, although if he seeks both types of remedy, it will be necessary to pursue separate actions.

Questions concerning the legality of the administrative actions of the executive may arise in a number of ways other than judicial review.

11.1.1 Defence in ordinary action

R v Reading Crown Court ex p Hutchinson (1988) QBD: Public law issue may be used as defence to criminal charge

Facts

The applicant, a professional protester against nuclear weapons, was arrested during a demonstration against cruise missiles at Greenham Common and charged with breach of a bylaw. She wished to raise the alleged invalidity of the bylaw as a defence in the magistrates' court, but this was refused, and on appeal by way of case stated the Crown Court concluded that such a question could only be raised via application for judicial review. The applicant then sought judicial review of the Crown Court's decision.

Decision

The Divisional Court held that a question of the validity of the law which forms the basis of a prosecution could be raised as defence to criminal proceedings.

11.1.2 In an action for damages

Holgate-Mohammed v Duke (1984) HL: Public law issue may be raised in action for damages against public body

Facts

A police officer suspected the appellant of the theft of jewellery, but considered that he needed further evidence in order to secure her conviction. Rather than interviewing the appellant under caution, the officer decided to arrest her and take her to a police station for questioning. The county court judge found the officer's intention was to subject the appellant 'to the greater stress and pressure involved in arrest and deprivation of liberty in the belief that if she was going to confess she would be more likely to do so in a state of arrest' (though it was not suggested that any impropriety took place). The judge awarded the appellant £1,000 damages for false imprisonment. The Court of Appeal allowed an appeal by the Chief Constable. The appellant appealed to the House of Lords.

Decision

The House of Lords held, dismissing the appeal, that the powers under which the arrest had been made were not common law powers, but derived from s 2(4) of the Criminal Law Act 1967. Accordingly, the court was concerned with the exercise of a discretion conferred by statute. It could be challenged only by reference to the *Wednesbury* principles. Applying those principles, Lord Diplock noted that it had been found as fact by the county court judge that the officer had acted in good faith. The court therefore had only to determine whether the officer's exercise of his discretion had been reasonable. This depended on whether the officer's motivation constituted an irrelevant consideration. Lord Diplock was of the opinion that it did not. Accordingly, the arrest was lawful.

There is also a statutory appeal procedure from certain administrative decisions.

11.2 Concepts

11.2.1 Ultra vires

Ultra vires means 'beyond the powers'. In order to act lawfully, a public body must:
(1) act *within* its legal powers (which may be conferred by statute, or exist under common law or by virtue of the royal prerogative);
(2) use those powers for their proper purpose; and
(3) use those powers in a proper manner.
There is some scope for confusion in this area, as two overlapping systems of classification are in common use.

11.2.1.1   The Wednesbury classification

Associated Provincial Picture Houses v Wednesbury Corp (1948): *Wednesbury* principles enunciated

Facts
Under powers contained in the Cinematograph Act, the local authority granted a licence allowing a cinema to open on Sundays only on the condition that children under 15 would not be permitted to attend, since the restriction would assist in maintaining Sunday school attendance.

Decision
The court found, on the facts, that the restriction was not *ultra vires* and went on to set out the principles, based on previous case law, on which a public body could be found to have acted *ultra vires* in the exercise of its statutory powers.

Per Lord Greene MR:
When an executive discretion is entrusted by Parliament to a body such as the local authority in this case, what appears to be an exercise of that discretion can only be challenged in the courts in a strictly limited class of case. As I have said, it must always be remembered that the court is not a court of appeal. When discretion of this kind is granted the law recognises certain principles upon which that discretion must be exercised, but within the four corners of those principles the discretion is an absolute one and cannot be questioned in any court of law. What then are those principles? ... The exercise of such a discretion must be a real exercise of the discretion. If, in the statute conferring the discretion, there is to be found, expressly or by implication, matters which the authority exercising the discretion ought to have regard to, then in exercising the discretion it must have regard to those matters. Conversely, if the nature of the subject matter and the general interpretation of the Act make it clear that certain matters would not be germane to the matter in question, the authority must disregard those irrelevant collateral matters.

There have been in the cases expressions used relating to the sort of things that authorities must not do, not merely in cases under the Cinematograph Act ... Bad faith, dishonesty – those, of course, stand by themselves – unreasonableness, attention given to extraneous circumstances, disregard of public policy and things like that have all been referred to, according to the facts of individual cases, as being matters which are relevant to the question ...

It is true the discretion must be exercised reasonably. Now what does that mean? Lawyers familiar with the phraseology commonly used in relation to exercise of statutory discretions often use the word 'unreasonable' in a rather comprehensive sense. It has frequently been used and is frequently used as a general description of the things that must not be done. For instance, a person entrusted with a discretion must, so to speak, direct himself properly in law. He must call his own attention to the matters which he is bound to consider. He must exclude from his consideration matters which are irrelevant to what he has to consider. If he does not obey these rules, he may truly be said, and often is said, to be acting 'unreasonably'. Similarly, there may be something so absurd that no sensible person could even dream that it lay within the powers of the authority.

Comment
The *Wednesbury* principles can conveniently be summed up as the requirement that an administrative decision must be reasonable, made after consideration of all relevant factors and only relevant factors, and made in good faith.

11.2.1.2   Lord Diplock's classification

Council of Civil Service Unions v Minister for the Civil Service (1985)

Facts

See 7.5 above.

Per Lord Diplock:

... Judicial review has I think developed to a stage today when ... one can conveniently classify under three heads the grounds upon which administrative action is subject to control by judicial review. The first ground I would call 'illegality', the second 'irrationality' and the third 'procedural impropriety'. That is not to say that further development on a case by case basis may not in the course of time add further grounds ... but to dispose of the instant case the three already well established heads will suffice.

By 'illegality' as a ground for judicial review I mean that the decision maker must understand correctly the law that regulates his decision making power and must give effect to it ...

By 'irrationality' I mean what can by now be succinctly referred to as '*Wednesbury* unreasonableness' ... It applies to a decision which is so outrageous in its defiance of logic or of accepted moral standards that no sensible person who has applied his mind to the question to be decided could have arrived at it ... I have described the third head as 'procedural impropriety' rather than failure to observe basic rules of natural justice or failure to act with procedural fairness towards the person who will be affected by the decision ...

11.3   The principles of natural justice

Unlike *ultra vires*, natural justice is a concept applicable to private law as well as public law matters. A body making a decision which affects the existing rights of individuals must observe the following principles:

(1)   *Audi alteram partem* – 'Hear the other side';

(2)   *Nemo judex in sua causa potest* – 'No one may be judge in his own cause'.

CHAPTER 12

GROUNDS FOR JUDICIAL REVIEW: ILLEGALITY (1) THE *ULTRA VIRES* DOCTRINE

Introduction

'Illegality' essentially involves acting outside a power conferred by statute, prerogative or common law. Originally a narrow concept, it has broadened in recent years and acts as an umbrella for several concepts.

12.1 The limited nature of the powers of public bodies

A public body may only perform actions which are within its statutory, prerogative or common law powers, or are reasonably incidental to such powers.

R v Somerset County Council ex p Fewings (1995) CA: The general principle

Facts
See 8.1 above.

Per Laws J:
Public bodies and private persons are both subject to the rule of law; nothing could be more elementary. But the principles which govern their relationships with the law are wholly different. For private persons, the rule is that you may do anything you choose which the law does not prohibit ... But for public bodies the rule is opposite, and so of another character altogether. It is that any action to be taken must be justified by positive law. A public body has no heritage of legal rights which it enjoys for their own sake; at every turn, all of its dealings constitute the fulfilment of duties which it owes to others; indeed, it exists for no other purpose.

Attorney General v Fulham Corp (1921) KBD: Public body must act within statutory powers

Facts
Under the Baths and Wash-Houses Acts 1846–78, the Corporation had power to establish baths, wash-houses and open bathing places. For many years, it had operated a wash-house where residents could come and wash their clothes themselves. The Corporation resolved to replace this by a system in which a customer left a bag of washing to be washed by Corporation employees. The Attorney General, at the relation of certain Fulham ratepayers, alleged that the system operated by the Corporation was *ultra vires* the enabling legislation.

Decision
The court held, granting a declaration to that effect, that it was important that the doctrine of *ultra vires* should be maintained. It was for the Corporation to show that it had authority to do the acts specified, or that it was doing merely what was reasonably

incidental to or consequential upon what it was authorised to do. The Corporation was authorised by statute to provide washing facilities. To wash customers' clothes for them was not incidental to or consequential upon that power.

Bromley London Borough Council v Greater London Council (1982)
HL: Public body must not disregard caveats attached to its statutory powers

Facts
In order to finance the manifesto policy of the controlling Labour group of reducing fares on London Transport by 25%, the Greater London Council (GLC) levied a supplementary rate. Bromley Council applied for an order of certiorari to quash this decision on the grounds, *inter alia*, that it was *ultra vires* the Transport (London) Act 1969. Under s 1 of the Act, the GLC had a general duty to develop and encourage measures which would promote the provision of 'integrated, efficient and economic transport facilities and services for Greater London'.

Decision
The House of Lords held that the actions of the GLC were *ultra vires*. The statutory framework made it clear that the London Transport Executive was not to conduct its undertaking other than on economic lines. The Executive in making its proposals, and the GLC in accepting them, had no power to totally disregard any responsibility for seeking to ensure that outgoings were met from revenue.

Comment
A further factor in the decision was that the GLC was under a fiduciary duty towards its ratepayers, not all of whom were necessarily transport users, particularly as many users of London Transport commuted into London from elsewhere.

12.2   The exercise of powers reasonably incidental to those specifically granted

Attorney General v Crayford Urban District Council (1962) **CA:** Concept of power which is 'reasonably incidental' to powers expressly granted by statute

Facts
Section 111(1) of the Housing Act 1957 gave local authorities powers of 'general management' in connection with their stock of council houses. Claiming to use this power, Crayford UDC agreed to recommend to its tenants that they insure themselves on the favourable terms of a scheme negotiated by the council with the Municipal Mutual Insurance Ltd. The council acted as agent for the insurance company, using its rent collectors to receive insurance premiums and retaining a commission. A rival insurance company maintained that this scheme was *ultra vires* the powers granted by the 1957 Act. The question for the court was whether the operation of the scheme could be regarded as 'general management' within the terms of the 1957 Act.

Decision
The court held that the scheme was either within, or fairly incidental to, the general management remit of the council. If the tenants did not insure themselves, and then

suffered loss, they would be likely to default on their rent. It was the concern, if not the duty, of the council to ensure that its tenants paid their rents. Lord Evershed MR approved the following words of Lord Selborne LC in *Attorney General v Great Eastern Railway Co* (1880) HL:

I agree with James LJ that this doctrine ought to be reasonably, and not unreasonably, understood and applied, and that whatever may fairly be regarded as incidental to, or consequential upon, those things which the legislature has authorised, ought not (unless expressly prohibited) to be held, by judicial construction, to be *ultra vires*.

Comment

This case involves a council action which seems close to the boundary of what is reasonably incidental, though there would be no difficulty if the council had merely required the tenants to insure their property, and encouraged them to insure with Municipal Mutual Insurance under favourable terms which the council had negotiated.

McCarthy & Stone (Developments) Ltd v Richmond Upon Thames LBC (1991): Limits of what is 'reasonably incidental'

Facts

Section 111(1) of the Local Government Act 1972 gave local authorities power to do 'anything ... which is calculated to facilitate or is conducive, or incidental to, the discharge of any of their functions'.

The defendant council had adopted the practice of providing preliminary advice to applicants for planning permission and making a charge for this advice. The plaintiffs contended that this charge was unlawful.

Decision

The court found in favour of the plaintiffs on two grounds:

(a) The making of the charge came within the scope of Art 4 of the Bill of Rights, which prohibits the raising of revenue on behalf of the Crown without grant of Parliament. The court was not prepared to imply a power to raise revenue into s 111(1).

(b) Although the giving of preliminary advice was 'reasonably incidental' to the Council's powers and duties in relation to planning and came within the scope of s 111(1), neither s 111(1) nor the common law rule authorised the making of a charge. The Council could not argue that something was lawful on the basis that it was reasonably incidental to something which was itself reasonably incidental.

12.3   The effect of a decision maker's error of law

12.3.1   Errors of law not on the face of the record

Anisminic v Foreign Compensation Commission (1969) HL: Mere fact that a decision is 'wrong' on merits does not mean that it must have been reached unlawfully

Facts
See 9.5.1 above.

The main question for the House of Lords was whether, on the assumption that the Commission was mistaken in its interpretation of the legislative provisions, it had thereby exceeded its jurisdiction.

Decision
The House of Lords held, allowing Anisminic's appeal by a majority, that the Commission's mistake had resulted in its deciding a question which it had no jurisdiction to decide, and its decision was therefore a nullity.

Per Lord Reid:
… There are many cases where, although the tribunal had jurisdiction to enter on the inquiry, it has done or failed to do something in the course of the inquiry, which is of such a nature that its decision is a nullity. It may have given its decision in bad faith. It may have made a decision which it had no power to make. It may have failed in the course of the inquiry to comply with the requirements of natural justice. It may in perfect good faith have misconstrued the provisions giving it power to act so that it failed to deal with the question remitted to it and decided some question which was not remitted to it … I do not intend this list to be exhaustive. But, if it decides a question remitted to it for decision without committing any of these errors, it is as much entitled to decide that question wrongly as it is to decide it rightly.

Pearlman v Keepers and Governors of Harrow School (1979) CA: 'Wrong' decision may inevitably involve error of law on part of decision maker

Facts
Under Sched 8 to the Housing Act 1974, a county court judge had to determine whether the installation of central heating in a dwelling house amounted to 'structural alteration, extension or addition'. Without proffering a definition of the statutory words, the judge held that the work under consideration did not fall within them. The appellant sought an order of certiorari to quash the judge's decision, on the ground that it depended on an error of law and accordingly was beyond his jurisdiction.

Decision
The Court of Appeal held, by a majority, that the judge's decision on the issue was such that he must be taken to have made an error of law in the interpretation of the statutory words.

Per Lord Denning MR:
… The distinction between an error which entails absence of jurisdiction – and an error made within the jurisdiction – is very fine. So fine indeed that it is rapidly being eroded … I would suggest that this distinction should now be discarded … The way to get things right is to hold

thus: no court or tribunal has any jurisdiction to make an error of law on which the decision of the case depends. If it makes such an error, it goes outside its jurisdiction and certiorari will lie to correct it.

Per Geoffrey Lane LJ (dissenting):

The judge is considering the words ... which he ought to consider. He is not embarking on some unauthorised or extraneous or irrelevant exercise. All he has done is to come to what appears to this court to be a wrong conclusion on a difficult question. It seems to me that, if this judge is acting outside his jurisdiction, so then is every judge who comes to a wrong decision on a point of law.

Comment

Note the caution counselled by Geoffrey Lane LJ on leaping to conclusions on the basis of the decision alone.

Re Racal Communications Ltd (1981) HL: Limitation of principle in *Anisminic* to decisions of administrative tribunals

Facts

Racal was suspected of defrauding the Ministry of Defence. The Director of Public Prosecutions made an application to court to examine Racal's documents under s 441(1) of the Companies Act 1948. The High Court judge at first instance refused to grant the order, holding that he had jurisdiction to do so only in respect of the internal management of a company's affairs, and that the matters alleged fell outside that area.

Despite the provision in s 441(3) of the Act, that a decision of a judge of the High Court under the section should not be appealable, his decision was reversed by the Court of Appeal. The court considered that s 441(3) had no relevance to a case like the present in which an error of law had been made. Racal appealed to the House of Lords, arguing that the Court of Appeal had lacked jurisdiction to consider whether the judge's decision was right or wrong.

Decision

The House of Lords held, allowing the appeal, that the Court of Appeal had been wrong to create a distinction between mistakes of fact and mistakes of law. The jurisdiction of the Court of Appeal was exclusively statutory. It could be – and here it had been – excluded by statute whether in respect of alleged mistakes of fact or of law. Further, there was a distinction to be drawn between challenges to the decisions of administrative tribunals and challenges to the decisions of courts of law. In the former case, where Parliament conferred power to decide questions defined by the Act conferring the power, there was a presumption that Parliament intended the tribunal only to answer questions as so defined. In the case of courts of law, there was no presumption that Parliament did not intend to give those bodies authority to decide questions of law. *Anisminic* was concerned only with the determination of an administrative tribunal. The decision of the majority in *Pearlman* was wrong, since the judge in that case, as in this, had had exclusive jurisdiction to construe the meaning of statutory words.

Page v Hull University Visitor (1993) HL: Re-interpretation of principle in *Anisminic*

Facts

The appellant, a university lecturer, was dismissed from his post on the ground of redundancy. He petitioned the Visitor of the University, who had appellate jurisdiction over decisions by the University authorities, contending that under the University's statutes it had no power to dismiss him for that reason. The Visitor rejected the petition and the appellant successfully sought judicial review.

The Court of Appeal allowed the Visitor's appeal, holding that the Visitor had correctly understood the University's powers, but affirming the Divisional Court's determination that judicial review was available against a decision of the Visitor construing the University's statutes. The appellant appealed against the decision of the Court of Appeal, and the University and Visitor cross-appealed from the determination that the Visitor was amenable to judicial review for errors of construction.

Decision

The House of Lords held, dismissing the appeal and allowing the cross-appeal by a majority, that the question was whether the remedy of certiorari would lie against the Visitor to quash his decision as being erroneous in point of law, notwithstanding that the question of law arose under the domestic law of the University which the Visitor had exclusive power to decide. Provided the Visitor was within his jurisdiction, in the narrow sense that he had power under the regulating documents to enter into the adjudication of the dispute, the court could not intervene to quash his decision either for error of fact or of law. However, judicial review would lie where the Visitor had acted outside his jurisdiction understood in that narrow sense or where he had abused his powers or acted in breach of the rules of natural justice. In fact, the Visitor had made no error of law in any event.

Commenting on the effect of the decision in *Anisminic*, Lord Browne-Wilkinson said that it 'rendered obsolete the distinction between errors of law on the face of the record and other errors of law by extending the doctrine of *ultra vires*'. Thenceforward, it was to be taken that Parliament had only conferred the decision making power on the basis that it was to be exercised on the correct legal basis: a misdirection in law in making the decision therefore rendered the decision *ultra vires*.

12.3.2   Errors of law on the face of the record

R v Northumberland Compensation Appeal Tribunal ex p Shaw (1952) CA: Availability of remedy

Facts

The applicant sought compensation under the National Health Service (Transfer of Officers and Compensation) Regulations 1948 for loss of employment. He appealed to the Tribunal against the quantum of compensation awarded by the local authority. The Tribunal upheld the award, and the applicant successfully obtained an order of certiorari from the Divisional Court. Here, and on the Tribunal's appeal to the Court of Appeal, it was common ground that the compensation decision was flawed.

However, the Tribunal argued that the remedy of certiorari did not lie in respect of an error of law appearing on the face of the record where the decision maker had not exceeded its jurisdiction and, further, that although there had been error here, it did not appear on the record.

Decision

The Court of Appeal held, dismissing the appeal, that until some 100 years before the present case, the authorities showed that certiorari had regularly been used to challenge errors of law on the face of the record. In so far as it had fallen into disuse, that was because there had until recently been little occasion for its exercise, but with the advent of many new tribunals and the plain need for supervision over them, the remedy should be revived. It was unnecessary to discuss the types of error which respectively would or would not go to jurisdiction, because that question did not arise in the present case. Here, the error did not distinctly appear on the face of the record, but that was because the record was incomplete; if complete, it would have disclosed the error. Certiorari would lie not only to quash an error of law on the face of the record, but also an error admitted openly in the face of the court.

R v Supplementary Benefits Commission ex p Singer (1973) QBD: What is the record?

Facts

The applicant sought an order of certiorari to quash the Supplementary Benefits Commission's determination that he was ineligible for legal aid since his disposable income exceeded the statutory limit. As a basis for the assessment of income, the Commission had taken into account loans and gifts to the applicant. However, this fact appeared only from a letter of explanation sent on behalf of the Commission in response to an inquiry by the applicant following the making of the determination. The applicant contended that this basis was erroneous and that the letter formed part of the record of the Commission's decision.

Decision

The Court held, granting certiorari to quash the determination, that the applicant's arguments were both correct.

Per Bridge J:

Counsel for the Commission has taken the point that the letter of 29 June is not part of the record relating to the determination which is questioned; indeed that there is no such record available for the court to consider. We cannot accept this submission. It seems to us that whenever a statutory body, having made a decision of a kind which can be questioned in proceedings for an order of certiorari, has subsequently chosen to disclose the reasons for the decision ... however informal the document embodying the reasons, the decision with the added reasons becomes a 'speaking order' and, if an error of law appears in the reasons, certiorari will lie to quash the decision.

R v Crown Court at Knightsbridge ex p International Sporting Club (London) Ltd (1981) QBD: 'Record' includes informal records and oral statements

Facts

The applicant company, which had recently acquired three casinos, appealed to the Crown Court from the decision of magistrates to withdraw its gaming licences. The appeal was dismissed and the dismissal was embodied in a formal order. The Crown Court judge also gave an oral judgment in which it was made clear that his decision rested on the way in which the casinos had been managed in the past and took no account of the complete restructuring of the applicant company since the withdrawal of the licences. The applicant submitted that this was an error of law and that the record of the appeal hearing included the judge's oral judgment.

Decision

The court held, granting certiorari to quash the decision of the Crown Court, that the applicant's submissions were both correct. Although there were passages in the older authorities which suggested that the court would not look at the reasons given by an inferior tribunal unless they were embodied in a formal order, they reflected a time when shorthand had only recently been invented and there was no electronic recording apparatus in courts. Administrative law was in a phase of active development and the judges would adapt the rules applying to the issue of the prerogative orders to protect the rule of law in a changing society.

12.3.3 Errors of fact/evidential insufficiency

Ashbridge Investments Ltd v Minister of Housing and Local Government (1965) CA: Court could only act in respect of an error of law or absence of evidence

Facts

Upon the making of a compulsory purchase order in connection with a slum clearance scheme, a local authority was bound to compensate the owners of habitable houses or other buildings to the value both of the site and of the building on it, but compensation in respect of uninhabitable houses was limited to the value of the site. A local inspector determined that two adjoining buildings within a terrace were uninhabitable. On the basis of the inspector's report, the Minister further considered that one of the buildings, which had undergone some structural alteration, was not to be regarded as a house. The owners of the buildings sought to quash the Minister's confirmation of the compulsory purchase order on the ground that neither building was a house and invited the court to receive evidence afresh on this point. At first instance, Mocatta J held that the court should receive evidence of the facts and reach its own conclusion thereon.

Decision

The Court of Appeal held, allowing the Minister's appeal, that the court could interfere with his decision only if the Minister had acted on no evidence, or unreasonably, or through misinterpreting the statute, or in consequence of some other error of law. Here, the Minister had acted on the local inspector's report. It was not for the court to substitute its own opinion for that of the Minister to whom Parliament had entrusted the decision.

Coleen Properties Ltd v Minister of Housing and Local Government (1971) CA: Issues of fact are a matter for the decision maker

Facts
The appellants owned a modern building which had been included as added land within a slum clearance scheme. At a public local inquiry, an inspector had concluded that the compulsory purchase of the appellants' building was not (as the Housing Act 1957 required it to be) 'reasonably necessary' for the satisfactory development or use of the cleared area. The Minister reversed the inspector's decision. His decision was upheld at first instance.

Decision
The court held, allowing the appeal, that the fact of reasonable necessity had to be established as a condition precedent to the exercise of power to defeat the subject's proprietary rights by compulsory purchase. The question was not a matter of policy and therefore the Minister could determine it only on the evidence before the inspector. Since no such evidence supported the Minister's decision, it was *ultra vires*.

Puhlhofer v Hillingdon London Borough Council (1986) HL: Lords confirm principle that issues of fact are matters for decision maker

Facts
The local authority refused the appellants' application for accommodation under s 4(5) of the Housing (Homeless Persons) Act 1977 on the ground that they were not 'homeless' within the meaning of the Act. Section 1 of the Act provided that a person was homeless if he had no accommodation. The appellants contended that the Act's reference to 'accommodation', although unqualified, was to be understood to mean 'appropriate accommodation', and that, in the light of the conditions in which they were living, they were not appropriately accommodated. The appellants succeeded at first instance, but the Court of Appeal allowed the local authority's appeal. The appellants appealed to the House of Lords.

Decision
The House of Lords held, dismissing the appeal, that what was properly to be regarded as 'accommodation' was a question of fact for the local authority to determine. In determining that question, the circumstances of the occupants were relevant, but, in the present case, the council had been entitled to find that the applicants were not homeless for the purposes of the Act because they had accommodation within the ordinary meaning of that expression.

Per Lord Brightman:
Although the action or inaction of a local authority is clearly susceptible to review where they have misconstrued the Act, or abused their powers or otherwise acted perversely, I think that great restraint should be exercised in giving leave to proceed by judicial review ... Where the existence or non-existence of a fact is left to the judgment and discretion of a public body and

that fact involves a broad spectrum ranging from the obvious to the debatable to the just conceivable, it is the duty of the court to leave the decision of that fact to the public body to whom Parliament has entrusted the decision making power save in a case where it is obvious that the public body, consciously or unconsciously, are acting perversely.

Zamir v Secretary of State for the Home Department (1980) HL: Limits of court's role in relation to issues of fact

Facts

The appellant, whose parents had settled in the UK, applied for and received a certificate of entry to the UK. He was entitled to it under the Immigration Rules because at the time he was, among other qualifications, unmarried. He married in February 1976 and entered the UK alone the following month. He neither volunteered any information nor was asked any questions about his status and was granted leave to enter for an indefinite period.

It was later discovered that he had been married at the time of entry, whereupon he was detained as an illegal immigrant on the ground that the grant of leave to enter had been vitiated by his failure to disclose a change of circumstances which he knew or ought to have known would affect his qualification for entry. He applied unsuccessfully for a writ of habeas corpus to the Divisional Court and the Court of Appeal, and appealed to the House of Lords, arguing that the power to detain and remove him depended on the precedent establishment of the alleged deception as an objective fact.

Decision

The House of Lords held, rejecting the appeal, that the nature and process of decision making powers conferred on immigration officers by existing legislation was incompatible with any requirement for the establishment of precedent objective facts whose existence the court could verify. The court was not in a position to act, in effect, as a court of appeal as to the facts on which the immigration officer decided. The limit of the court's competence lay in ascertaining that there was evidence on which the immigration officer, acting reasonably, could decide as he had.

Khawaja v Secretary of State for the Home Department (1983) HL: Lords extend jurisdiction in relation to issues of fact

Facts

The case involved conjoined appeals. In the first, the applicant had obtained leave to enter the UK for one month. He was already bigamously married to a woman settled in England. He said nothing about this marriage. He later applied for an extension of leave, informing the Home Office of the marriage (which had now been regularised). His application was refused and his detention pending removal was ordered on the ground that leave to enter had been obtained by deception. The facts of the second case were similar to those of *Zamir* (above). In both cases, the notification of removal provided to the applicant contained the statement of an immigration officer that there were 'reasonable grounds to conclude' that the applicant was an illegal entrant. On appeal to the House of Lords, the question arose, *inter alia*, whether the court was limited to determining whether the immigration officer had had reasonable grounds for that conclusion, or whether the court was required itself to decide whether the applicants were illegal entrants.

Decision

The House of Lords held that the appeal in the first case would be dismissed, and the second appeal allowed. In so deciding, the House itself determined the status of the appellants, finding the first clearly to have been guilty of procuring entry by deception, and finding the second innocent of deception on the evidence before the immigration officer. The construction of the Immigration Rules favoured in *Zamir* had limited judicial review in such a case to the *Wednesbury* heads of challenge comprising error of law, unreasonableness and breach of natural justice. Thus limited, the court would not be competent to substitute its own view of the facts for that of the decision making authority. However, that limitation was contrary to the development of the safeguards which the law provided to an individual whose liberty was vulnerable to the exercise of executive power. In such cases, the courts would decide whether facts precedent to the availability of the power had been established. The standard of proof involved would be the civil standard applied with reference to the gravity of the issue at stake.

12.4   Delegation of powers

12.4.1   *Permissible delegation*

Carltona v Commissioners of Works (1943) CA: The 'alter ego' doctrine

Facts

The appellants owned a food factory. In 1942, the factory was requisitioned by the Commissioners of Works under the Defence (General) Regulations 1939. The appellants claimed, *inter alia*, that the notice to requisition was invalid because the persons constituting the requisitioning authority had never brought their minds to bear on the question. The body known as the Commissioners of Works in fact never met; its functions were exercised by the Minister of Works and Planning who also held the office of First Commissioner. The notice issued to the appellants had been signed by his assistant secretary.

Decision

The Court of Appeal held, dismissing the appeal, that the person acting for the First Commissioner in this matter was the assistant secretary, and that the question therefore was whether he had directed his mind to the decision in question.

Per Lord Greene MR:

In the administration of government in this country, the functions which are given to ministers (and constitutionally properly given to ministers because they are constitutionally responsible) are functions so multifarious that no minister could ever personally attend to them ... The duties imposed upon ministers and the powers given to ministers are normally exercised under the authority of the ministers by responsible officials of the department. Public business could not be carried on if that were not the case. Constitutionally, the decision of such an official is, of course, the decision of the Minister. The Minister is responsible. It is he who must answer before Parliament ...

12.4.2 Impermissible delegation

Barnard v National Dock Labour Board **(1953) CA:** Limits of permissible delegation

Facts

The National Dock Labour Board was set up by Parliament under the Dock Workers (Regulation of Employment) Order 1947. It was the duty of the National Board to administer a scheme under which only dockers registered under the scheme could work in British ports. A number of the Board's functions, including disciplinary powers over registered dockers, were to be delegated to local dock labour boards. The London Dock Labour Board further delegated its disciplinary powers to the London port manager. The port manager suspended a number of dockers in connection with an industrial dispute. The dockers applied for a declaration that their suspension was unlawful on the grounds that the local board had no power to delegate its disciplinary powers.

Decision

The Court of Appeal held, allowing the appeal, that the disciplinary powers in question were of a judicial character, rather than merely administrative. Only administrative powers might be delegated under the alter ego doctrine.

CHAPTER 13

GROUNDS FOR JUDICIAL REVIEW: ILLEGALITY (2)

13.1 The exercise of discretion

Though the courts are careful to emphasise that public bodies have discretion in the exercise of their powers, that discretion must be exercised in a lawful manner. In particular, the decision maker must consider all relevant factors, but only relevant factors. Though it is entitled to have regard to a policy of its own creation, that policy must be based only on relevant factors, and must not be followed blindly.

13.1.1 The fettering of discretion by the adoption of policy

13.1.1.1 The general principle

***R v Port of London Authority ex p Kynoch Ltd* (1919) CA:** The decision maker may adopt a policy but must not follow it to the exclusion of all other considerations

Facts
The appellant owned land and wished to use it for the construction of a deep water wharf. For this, a licence was required from the Port of London Authority. The Authority declined to issue a licence, stating that the facility proposed was one which the Authority itself had been charged by Parliament to provide. The appellant argued that the port authority had not properly heard and determined its licence application.

Decision
The court held, dismissing the appeal, that the Authority's affidavit made it clear that the merits of the application had been fully considered. However, even if they had not, the grounds specifically referred to by the Authority for its refusal were rightly taken into consideration, and it was not wrong to apply them by a policy.

Per Bankes LJ:
There are, on the one hand, cases where a tribunal in the honest exercise of its discretion has adopted a policy, and, without refusing to hear an applicant, intimates to him what its policy is, and that after hearing him it will in accordance with its policy decide against him, unless there is something exceptional in his case. I think counsel for the appellants would admit that, if the policy has been adopted for reasons which the tribunal may legitimately entertain, no objection could be taken to such a course. On the other hand, there are cases where a tribunal has passed a rule, or come to a determination, not to hear any application of a particular character by whomsoever made …

Stringer v Minister for Housing (1971) QBD
Facts
The applicant applied for and was refused planning permission for a residential development at Brereton Heath, four miles from the Jodrell Bank Telescope. An

agreement had been entered into by the local authorities with the operators of the telescope 'to discourage development within the limits of their powers at Brereton Heath until 1990'. Among the reasons given for the refusal of planning permission was the proximity of the proposed development to the radio telescope, and the likelihood of interference with the telescope's efficient running. The applicant appealed to the Minister. Following a local inquiry, the Minister upheld the refusal of planning permission on the ground, *inter alia*, that the proposed development would be contrary to the policy for the area around Jodrell Bank. The applicant argued, *inter alia*, that the Minister, in determining the appeal, had failed to discharge his duty to act fairly and judicially.

Decision

The court held, dismissing the application, that the Minister had fairly considered the applicant's appeal.

Per Cooke J:

It seems to me that the general effect of the many relevant authorities is that a minister charged with the duty of making individual administrative decisions in a fair and impartial manner may nevertheless have a general policy in regard to matters which are relevant to those decisions, provided that the existence of that general policy does not preclude him from fairly judging all the issues which are relevant to each individual case as it comes up for decision.

13.1.1.2   Fettering of discretion by rigid adherence to policy

H Lavender & Son Ltd v Minister of Housing and Local Government (1970) QBD: The decision maker adhered too rigidly to policy

Facts

The applicants were refused planning permission to extract sand, gravel and ballast from a site near Walton-on-Thames, designated as an area of high quality agricultural land. There was evidence that the applicants would be able to restore the land to a high level of agricultural quality. The only substantial objection to the application was submitted by the Ministry of Agriculture, which wished to see the land maintained as agricultural land. No other reason for the refusal of planning permission was found by the planning authority. Appeal from the refusal of the application lay to the Minister of Housing and Local Government, who dismissed it on the grounds that it was his policy not to release land for mineral working unless there was no objection from the Minister for Agriculture. The applicants argued that the Minister of Housing and Local Government had fettered his own discretion by treating as decisive not his own view, but that of the Minister for Agriculture, and that he had thereby effectively delegated his discretion without authority.

Decision

The court held, allowing the appeal, that the Minister of Housing and Local Government was entitled to have a policy, and to decide appeals in accordance with it. If, however, he had pre-empted himself from giving any genuine consideration to the matter before him, he would have failed to carry out his statutory duties properly. There was nothing in the language of the Minister's decision to suggest that he had considered whether this might be an exceptional case which might have justified his departing from his policy. In the circumstances, it was not the authority made responsible by Parliament for the decision who had made it, but a different authority.

Comment
As well as an unlawful fettering of discretion, there had been an effective delegation of decision making power to another body.

British Oxygen v Minister of Technology (1971) HL: Duty of the decision maker to listen to alternative views

Facts
British Oxygen had purchased a large quantity of gas cylinders, each costing £20. The total purchase came to more than £4 million. British Oxygen applied to the Board of Trade for an investment grant under the Industrial Development Act 1966 in respect of the purchase. The Board refused to make any grant, giving as its reason, *inter alia*, that there was a lower limit of £25 of cost for single items eligible for grants. In addition to other remedies, British Oxygen sought a declaration that the Board was not entitled to decline to make a grant on the grounds solely of its self-imposed lower price limit.

Decision
The court held, refusing the declaration, that there was nothing in the Industrial Development Act 1966 which would guide the Board as to the circumstances in which it should or should not pay grants. If the Board considered that policy or good administration required the operation of some limiting rule, there was nothing to prevent its adoption. The most that could be said was that the absolute discretion conferred on the Board should not be exercised in bad faith or exercised so unreasonably as to show that there had been no real or genuine exercise of the discretion. Further (*per* Lord Reid):

There may be cases where an officer or authority ought to listen to a substantial argument reasonably presented urging a change of policy. What the authority must not do is to refuse to listen at all. But a ministry or large authority may have had to deal already with a multitude of similar applications and then they will almost certainly have evolved a policy so precise that it could well be called a rule. There can be no objection to that provided the authority is always ready to listen to anyone with something new to say ... In the present case, the Minister's officers have carefully considered all that the appellants have had to say and I have no doubt that they will continue to do so.

Bromley London Borough Council v Greater London Council (1982) HL: Council cannot blindly follow election manifesto

Facts
See 12.1 above.

Per Lord Diplock:
I would also have held the decision and the precept to be void upon another ground ... the members of the majority party by whose votes the effective resolutions were passed acted upon an erroneous view ... that from first to last they regarded the GLC as irrevocably committed to carry out the reduction, whatever might be the additional cost to the ratepayers, because a

reduction of that amount had been pre-announced in the election manifesto issued by the political party whose candidates formed a majority of the members elected ...

R v Ministry of Agriculture, Fisheries and Food ex p *Hamble (Offshore) Fisheries Ltd* (1995) QBD: Effect of change of policy

Facts

The applicant acquired two fishing vessels with a view to transferring their beam trawl licences to a larger trawler (the *Nellie*) which it had earlier acquired for the purposes of the transfer. The Ministry's then policy permitted this transfer. In the meantime, the applicant transferred general trawling licences to the *Nellie*. Following a change in policy and the introduction of a moratorium on the transfer of licences onto beam trawlers, the Ministry wrote to the applicant informing it that the *Nellie* would not qualify for a beam trawl licence since she currently held a general licence and had no track record of beam trawling. The letter indicated that this changed policy was being applied in all similar cases and that any deviation from it would be discriminatory. The applicant contended that it had a legitimate expectation that an exception to the policy would be made for those who had already acted with a view to a licence transfer, and further maintained that the application of the new policy without regard to the appropriateness of exception amounted to a failure to exercise discretion.

Decision

The court held that the applicant's arguments could not succeed. There had been no failure to exercise discretion because the cases of those in the applicant's position had been taken into account in the framing of the policy.

Per Sedley J:

While the framer of a policy for the exercise of a governmental discretion must be prepared to consider making exceptions where these are merited, the inclusion of thought-out exceptions in the policy itself may well be exhaustive of the obligation. While any further candidates for exemption must be considered, it will always be a legitimate consideration that to make one such exception may well set up an unanswerable case of partiality or arbitrariness. The decision maker must therefore balance the case for making no such exception against the case for generalising it ...

13.1.2 The fettering of discretion by the giving of private undertakings

13.1.2.1 The general principle

Birkdale District Electric Supply Co Ltd v Southport Corp (1926) HL: The decision maker cannot fetter discretion by giving an undertaking to a specific body

Facts

Pursuant to an electric lighting order made under statutory powers, the appellants took over the supplying of electricity from Birkdale Council. At that time they covenanted not to charge private consumers more than was charged by Southport Corporation in the neighbouring borough. In 1911, Southport Corporation took over responsibility for the Birkdale area. From 1921, the appellants began to charge more for electricity than was charged by Southport Corporation. The Corporation sought an injunction to restrain the appellants from exceeding the Southport price.

The appellants argued that the initial agreement was *ultra vires* as a fetter on their power to fix their own prices (subject to certain statutory maximum charges). This was a power which they might in the future need to exercise in order to maintain the commercial conditions necessary to the performance of their statutory function. The Corporation replied that the initial agreement was a commercial arrangement which might have proved unwise for the appellants, but which was compatible with the performance of their statutory duty. The question of compatibility had to be judged at the date of the agreement.

Decision

The House of Lords held, dismissing the appeal, that the appellants' arguments depended on the proposition that it was one of the statutory objects of the electric lighting order that the appellants should make a profit. This was impossible to maintain; the order itself imposed a maximum price for the supply of electricity and so was logically capable of interfering with the appellants' freedom of charging in the same way as their initial agreement.

Per the Earl of Birkenhead:

... [It is] a well established principle of law that, if a person or public body is entrusted by the legislature with certain powers and duties expressly or impliedly for public purposes, those persons or bodies cannot divest themselves of these powers and duties. They cannot enter into a contract or take any action incompatible with the due exercise of their powers or the discharge of their duties.

13.1.2.2   Applications of the principle

Ayr Harbour Trustees v Oswald (1883)

Facts

The Harbour Trustees had statutory powers and duties to acquire land to be used as need might arise for coastal or harbour works. On the compulsory purchase of a piece of land, they sought to save money by offering its owner a perpetual covenant not to carry out any works on the land acquired so as to cut off the land left to him from access to the harbour.

Decision

The court held that the covenant was *ultra vires*. Where the legislature conferred powers to take land compulsorily for a particular purpose, it had to be assumed that it was on the ground that the using of the land for that purpose would be to the public good. A contract seeking to bind the authority not to use those powers in any circumstances would be void.

Stourcliffe Estates Co Ltd v Bournemouth Corp (1910) CA: Principle interpreted narrowly

Facts

The Corporation purchased land from the plaintiff for use as a public park. It covenanted with the plaintiff not to build on the land except to erect 'such structures as summer houses, a band stand or shelters'. Section 85 of the Bournemouth Improvement Act 1892 gave the Corporation power to build public conveniences in any of their public parks. The plaintiff sought and was granted an injunction to restrain the Corporation from erecting public conveniences on the land affected by the covenant. The Corporation argued that the covenant was *ultra vires*.

Decision
The court held that the plaintiff was entitled to the injunction. The Corporation's argument amounted to an assertion that it should be permitted to retain the land bought from the plaintiff while repudiating a part of the consideration. Further, the present case was distinguishable from *Ayr Harbour Trustees v Oswald* (above) because, there, the power granted by Parliament had been to purchase specific land; here, the Corporation might purchase where it pleased.

13.1.3   Conflicting or overlapping powers

R v Hammersmith and Fulham London Borough Council ex p Beddowes (1987) CA: Approach where two or more powers conflict or overlap

Facts
The council owned an estate of blocks of flats, Fulham Court, which was urgently in need of repairs. The Conservative majority on the council favoured dealing with the problem by selling the blocks of flats for development for owner-occupation. Labour councillors opposed the loss of council housing stock, which this would entail. In 1986, the council resolved that one of the blocks should be sold to a private developer. In order to avoid being left in control of a single renovated block in the middle of an otherwise blighted estate, the developer required and obtained the council's covenant to continue its policy of selling the blocks for private development. The applicant, a resident of the estate, challenged the council's decision to sell the first block, arguing that the covenant obtained from the council constituted an unlawful fetter on its powers as a housing authority.

Decision
The Court of Appeal held, by a majority, that the council's actions were not open to criticism. The council possessed overlapping or conflicting statutory powers; it had powers to create covenants restrictive of the use of the land it retained, and powers in relation to the use of the retained land for housing purposes. In these circumstances, it was necessary to ascertain the primary purpose for which the retained land was held. That purpose was the provision of housing accommodation in the area. The provision of good accommodation at reasonable prices for owner-occupiers was no less within the purposes of the Housing Acts than the provision of rented housing.

Per Sir Denys Buckley:
... If a statutory authority acting in good faith in the proper and reasonable exercise of its statutory powers undertakes some binding obligation, the fact that such obligation may thereafter preclude the authority from exercising some other statutory power, or from exercising its statutory powers in some other way, cannot constitute an impermissible fetter on its powers ...

Kerr LJ (dissenting) considered that the council's primary motivation was to ensure the continuance of its policy in the event of a political change in forthcoming elections. Accordingly, its actions were designed to fetter future policies and were not motivated by any current requirements.

13.1.4 Improper motives

R v Port Talbot Borough Council ex p Jones (1988): Power cannot be used for purely party-political purposes

Facts
In breach of its own policy on the allocation of council houses, which gave priority to families with dependent children, a Labour-controlled local authority granted a tenancy to a single woman with no dependants, on the basis that she was a Labour member of the council, and that living in the ward she represented would improve her chances of re-election. The applicant sought an order of certiorari to quash the council's decision.

Decision
The grant of the tenancy was *ultra vires* in that it was made solely for a party-political purpose.

Comment
This case is unusual in that the council's action was inspired solely by party-political motives. Other case law demonstrates that a party-political policy is not unlawful in itself and a party-political consideration is capable of being a relevant factor.

13.2 The availability of estoppel against a public authority

Old case law established that estoppel could not lie against a public authority. For a brief period, these precedents were set aside, but the courts have since returned to them except where one of two exceptions applies.

Lever (Finance) Ltd v Westminster Council (1971) CA: Estoppel available in principle

Facts
It was common practice for planning officers to accept minor modifications to plans sent with successful applications for planning permission. One of the defendant corporation's planning officers sanctioned a modification which (in the opinion of the Court of Appeal) was not minor but required independent planning permission. When this was discovered, the corporation suggested that the defendant apply for planning permission. Permission was refused. The plaintiff sought, and at first instance obtained, a declaration that there was valid planning permission in force which included the modification.

Decision
The Court of Appeal held that the declaration had been properly granted. Lord Denning MR referred to the authorities which set out the general rule that estoppel

could not be pleaded against a public authority so as to prevent it performing its public duty, and went on:

But those statements must now be taken with considerable reserve. There are many matters which public authorities can now delegate to their officers. If an officer, acting within the scope of his ostensible authority, makes a representation on which another acts, then a public authority may be bound by it, just as much as a private concern would be.

Brooks and Burton Ltd v Secretary of State for the Environment (1976): Courts should be slow to find estoppel

The facts are not material.

Per Lord Widgery CJ:

There has been some advance in recent years of this doctrine of estoppel as applied to local authorities through their officers, and the most advanced case is ... *Lever Finance Ltd v Westminster (City) London Borough Council.* I do not propose to read it. It is no doubt correct on its facts, but I would deprecate any attempt to expand this doctrine because it seems to me, as I said a few minutes ago, extremely important that local government officers should feel free to help applicants who come and ask them questions without all the time having the shadow of estoppel hanging over them and without the possibility of their immobilising their authorities by some careless remark which produces such an estoppel.

Comment

Lord Widgery's remarks precisely sum up the policy difficulty in this area.

Laker Airways v Department of Trade (1977) CA: Limitation of doctrine

Facts

See 7.4.1 above.

Decision

The Court of Appeal held that estoppel could not be pleaded against a public authority. Whatever representations had been made to Laker Airways by the Secretary of State between 1972 and 1974, his successor necessarily remained free to go back on them provided he was satisfied that the public interest required him to do so. Estoppel could not be allowed to hinder the formation of government policy, even though Laker sustained loss as a result.

Western Fish Products Ltd v Penwith District Council (1981) CA: Estoppel not generally available – litigant may only plead estoppel in strictly defined circumstances

Facts

The company bought a disused factory which had been used for the production of fertiliser from fish and fishmeal. The company intended to use the factory to manufacture fishmeal and fish oil, and to prepare and package fresh fish for human consumption. The chairman of the company informed a representative of the council's chief planning officer that there existed an 'established user right' by virtue of the previous use of the factory which entitled the company to carry on their intended processes without the need for a new grant of planning permission. The officer said that, if the company could satisfy him of the claimed right in writing, the council would do everything it could to facilitate the company's plans. In reply to information provided by the company, the officer confirmed that the claimed rights appeared to be established.

On the strength of this reply and with the knowledge of the council, the company expended money modifying the factory premises. The council requested that the company seek planning permission, but explained that this was a formality only. Permission was refused. The company sought, *inter alia*, a declaration of its claimed rights. It was refused at first instance and the company appealed to the Court of Appeal.

Decision

The Court of Appeal held, dismissing the appeal, that the case did not fall within any exception to the general rule that a statutory body could not be estopped from performing its statutory duty. There were two exceptions to the rule:

(1) If a planning authority delegated power to its officers to determine specific questions, their decisions could not be revoked. *Lever (Finance) Ltd v Westminster Corp* (above) was to be regarded as an example of this exception.

(2) If a planning authority waived any procedural requirement relating to an application made to it for the exercise of its statutory powers, it might be estopped from relying on lack of formality as a ground for rejecting the application. Neither exception covered the present case and the exceptions would not be broadened.

13.3   Relevant and irrelevant considerations

This is perhaps the most important single reason by which the courts find executive decisions *ultra vires*. An obvious area of difficulty is the way in which the courts decide which considerations are relevant or irrelevant for this purpose.

CREEDNZ v Governor General (1981) New Zealand: Not all factors which might properly be considered necessarily come within the scope of the doctrine

The facts are not material.

Per Cooke J:

What has to be emphasised is that it is only where the statute expressly or impliedly identifies considerations required to be taken into account by the authority as a matter of legal obligation that the court holds a decision invalid on the ground now invoked. It is not enough that a consideration is one which may properly be taken into account, nor even that it is one which many people, including the court itself, would have taken into account if they had to make the decision ... [However] there will be some matters so obviously material to a decision on a particular project that anything short of direct consideration of them ... would not be in accordance with the intention of the Act.

Bolton Metropolitan District Council v Secretary of State for the Environment (1995) HL: Decision maker must have regard to all relevant considerations, but need not refer to them all in his statement of reasons

Facts
The respondents to the appeal, a consortium of local authorities, property companies and other commercial organisations, objected to the Secretary of State's adoption of a planning inspector's recommendations regarding the grant of planning permission for a shopping centre development in the Greater Manchester area. They alleged, *inter alia*, that the Secretary of State had failed to take certain material considerations into account, relying on the fact that his decision letter did not refer to all the material considerations. The Court of Appeal accepted that a planning decision letter had to refer to each material consideration bearing on the decision. The Secretary of State appealed to the House of Lords.

Decision
The House of Lords held, allowing the Secretary of State's appeal, that, while he had to have regard to all material considerations before reaching his decision, he did not have to mention all of them in giving his reasons for it.

Per Lord Lloyd of Berwick:
What the Secretary of State had to do was to state his reasons in sufficient detail to enable the reader to know what conclusion he had reached in the 'principal important controversial issues'. To require him to refer to every material consideration, however insignificant, and to deal with every argument, however peripheral, would be to impose an unjustifiable burden.

Roberts v Hopwood (1925) HL: A decision may be so divorced from reality as to be made without consideration of relevant factors

Facts
Under s 62 of the Metropolis Management Act 1855, Poplar Borough Council had power to pay to its employees 'such salaries and wages ... as [the council] may think fit'. At a time when the cost of living was rising, the council increased its minimum wage for men and women alike to 80 shillings a week, well above the typical level of the day and at a time when there was no requirement for equal pay between men and women doing the same job. It maintained its minimum wage at that level, despite later reductions in the cost of living.

The district auditor, who had made no objection when he first noticed the increase, found that the council's total wage bill substantially exceeded the amount which would have been paid if trade union rates had been applied. He heard representations from the Socialist majority on the council that they regarded themselves as bound to maintain these wage levels by a mandate of the electors. Claiming to act pursuant to his duty under s 247(7) of the Public Health Act 1875 to disallow unlawful items of expenditure and to impose a surcharge on those making or authorising the payment, he disallowed £5,000 of expenditure on wages and surcharged it on the councillors concerned, so making them personally liable for the loss to the council. The councillors sought an order of certiorari to quash the auditor's decision. The Court of Appeal allowed their appeal, and the auditor appealed to the House of Lords.

Decision

The House of Lords held, allowing the auditor's appeal, that the council had ceased to regard the payments as wages due in proportion to work done or to consider the purchasing power of the sums paid at a time of falling cost of living. The council stated that it had taken these matters into account, but it appeared to the court impossible to reconcile that assertion with setting of a flat rate of payment which (*per* Lord Buckmaster) 'standardised men and women not according to the duties which they performed, but according to the fact that they were adults'. The council had failed to have proper regard to the fiduciary duty it owed to ratepayers to conduct administration in a fair and businesslike manner with reasonable care, skill and caution. Since they had taken an arbitrary principle and fixed an arbitrary sum, they had not genuinely exercised the discretion imposed upon them by the Metropolis Management Act 1855.

Prescott v Birmingham Corp (1955) CA: Matters other than strict financial considerations may be relevant factors

Facts

A ratepayer brought an action for a declaration that the Corporation had acted unlawfully in implementing a scheme for free bus travel for the elderly. The Corporation had statutory power to charge 'such fares as they may think fit' on their public transport system.

Decision

The Court of Appeal held, granting the declaration, that it was clearly implicit in the legislation that the transport undertaking was to be run as a business venture. Further, local authorities owed a fiduciary duty to their ratepayers in relation to the application of funds contributed by the latter. Concessions such as half-price travel for children were justifiable on business principles, and free travel for the disabled, if not strictly justifiable, was a minor act of elementary charity to which no reasonable ratepayer would be likely to object. The Corporation had misapprehended the nature and scope of the discretion conferred on it.

Comment

It is interesting that free travel for the disabled was viewed as legitimate as an act of charity, but free travel for the elderly was not. The case also demonstrates, as does *Roberts v Hopwood*, that ideas as to what constitute relevant considerations may change over time.

Bromley London Borough Council v Greater London Council (1982) HL: Local authorities must have regard to their fiduciary duty to act fairly between different groups to whom they are responsible

Facts

See 12.1 above.

Decision

In addition to finding that the statutory framework imposed a duty on the London Transport Executive to run the transport system on economic lines, the House of Lords held that the GLC owed a fiduciary duty to ratepayers. That duty had to be balanced against its duty to provide for transport users, by no means all of whom were also ratepayers. The GLC had power to make a grant to the London Transport Executive, but might only do so with proper regard to its fiduciary duty.

R v Somerset County Council ex p Fewings (1995) CA: Decision maker must have regard to relevant considerations, but need not give them all equal weight

Facts

See 8.1 above.

At first instance, Laws J quashed the hunting ban on the ground that the council had taken into account an irrelevant consideration by basing its decision chiefly on a freestanding distaste for the alleged cruelty of hunting. The council appealed to the Court of Appeal.

Decision

The Court of Appeal held (Simon Brown LJ dissenting) that the judgment of Laws J would be upheld. There was a fundamental difference between the rights of private and public landowners: the former might do as they wished within the law, whereas the latter could act only with positive legal justification. The 'cruelty argument' was not necessarily an irrelevant consideration (Swinton Thomas LJ dissenting on this point), but the evidence showed that the limited scope of the council's powers of management had never been drawn to its attention. A relevant consideration had therefore been overlooked and the council could not be said to have exercised its power to further the object prescribed by the statute.

Simon Brown LJ was of the opinion that s 120(1)(b) merely mirrored common law restraints on the council's powers and he found no reason to conclude that the common law limits had not been present to the minds of the councillors. A relevant consideration had therefore not been overlooked. It was for the councillors to decide what weight to give to the cruelty argument; it was a relevant consideration and might properly be treated as decisive. Had it not been considered, the council would have been open to criticism.

Tesco Stores Ltd v Secretary of State for the Environment (1995) HL: Confirmation of dissenting approach in *Fewings*

Facts

The case concerned an application for review of the refusal of planning permission for a superstore. The intending developer had offered to fund a local relief road and argued that this relevant consideration had been ignored by the Secretary of State.

Decision

The House of Lords held that it had in fact been taken into account, so that the decision was not flawed, but observed (in terms related to planning law but seemingly of general application) that, while its relevance was a matter of law, the influence which the consideration exerted upon the decision making process was a matter for the discretion of the decision maker.

13.4 The exercise of discretion for an improper purpose

13.4.1 Applications of the principle

Padfield v Minister of Agriculture, Fisheries and Food (1968) HL: Discretion must be applied with regard to the reasons for which the power was granted

Facts

The Agricultural Marketing Act 1958 provided that, where complaints relating to the operation of a milk marketing scheme were made to the Minister, a committee of investigation should consider them and report on them to the Minister 'if the Minister in any case so directs'. The Minister received a complaint from milk producers in the south-east of unfair price differentials, but declined to appoint a committee of investigation. The south-eastern producers sought an order of mandamus to compel the Minister either to refer the complaint to a committee, or to deal effectively with the complaints on relevant considerations only.

The Court of Appeal, by a majority, allowed the Minister's appeal and the milk producers appealed to the House of Lords.

Decision

The House of Lords held, allowing the appeal by a majority, that the Minister was wrong to contend that the Agricultural Marketing Act 1958 gave him an unfettered discretion to choose whether or not to refer complaints.

Per Lord Reid:

Parliament must have conferred the discretion with the intention that it should be used to promote the policy and objects of the Act; the policy and objects of the Act must be determined by construing the Act as a whole and construction is always a matter of law for the court ... If the Minister, by reason of his having misconstrued the Act or for any other reason, so uses his discretion as to thwart or run counter to the policy and objects of the Act, then our law would be very defective if persons aggrieved were not entitled to the protection of the court ...

Lord Reid found that by the complaints procedure, the Act provided mechanisms calculated to safeguard those who were subject to its pricing machinery. By failing to refer it, the Minister was rendering nugatory a safeguard provided by the Act.

Oliver Ashworth (Holdings) Ltd v Ballard (Kent) (1999) CA: Deciding the purpose for which the power was granted

The facts are not material.

Per Laws LJ:

Sometimes, the statute's policy and objects are expressed in terms; sometimes, the Minister's power is made subject to the existence of a precedent fact or facts, whose nature plainly shows the purpose for which the power is to be exercised. But it may be that neither of these features is present. In that case, the court will gather the statute's policy and objects from a consideration of the Act's whole subject matter, and will by judicial review hold the Minister to account if he exceeds them.

Congreve v Home Office (1976) CA: Example of use of power for improper purpose

Facts

The Home Secretary decided to increase the cost of a television licence from £12 to £18 from 1 April 1975. Several licence holders renewed their existing licences prematurely in order to avoid paying the increased charge. Section 1 of the Wireless Telegraphy Act 1949 gave the Home Secretary power to issue licences 'subject to such terms, provisions and limitations as he may think fit'. It gave him an unfettered power to revoke licences. He threatened to revoke the licences prematurely renewed unless their holders paid the difference between the old and the new fees. Congreve, the holder of a prematurely renewed licence, sought a declaration that the threatened revocation would be unlawful.

Decision

The Court of Appeal held, granting the declaration, that the Minister did indeed have a discretion as to the issue and revocation of licences. However, the revocation in this case was tainted by an illegal threat, and it was an improper use of a discretionary power to use a threat to exercise that power as a means of raising money which Parliament had given the executive no mandate to raise.

Per Lord Denning MR:

… It is a discretion which must be exercised in accordance with the law, taking all relevant considerations into account, omitting irrelevant ones, and not being influenced by any ulterior motives … The licence is granted for 12 months and cannot be revoked simply in order to enable the Minister to make more money. Want of money is no reason for revoking a licence. The real reason, of course, in this case was that the Department did not like people taking out overlapping licences so as to save money. But there was nothing in the regulations to stop it. It was perfectly lawful; and the Department's dislike of it cannot afford a good reason for revoking them.

Comment

A further element in Lord Denning's judgment was that there was a breach of Art 4 of the Bill of Rights 1688, which forbids the raising of revenue by the Crown without the authority of Parliament, a provision always construed narrowly by the courts.

Wheeler v Leicester City Council (1985) HL: Decision maker cannot use powers to punish individuals or groups for actions which are not unlawful

Facts

The council administered a recreation ground to allow and promote its enjoyment by the public as an open space. It had the power to set aside pitches for the purpose of playing football. By s 56 of the Public Health Act 1925, the council had the power to permit the use by any club of such a pitch, subject to such charges and conditions as the council thought fit. The council passed a resolution banning Leicester (Rugby) Football Club from using the recreation ground, because it considered that the Club had not done sufficient to discourage three of its members from participating in a

British Lions tour of South Africa during the apartheid era. The council maintained that it was entitled to take into account its duty under s 71 of the Race Relations Act 1976, which read:

... It shall be the duty of every local authority to make appropriate arrangements with a view to securing that their various functions are carried out with due regard to the need ... to promote ... good relations, between different persons of different racial groups.

The Club sought an order of certiorari to quash the council's decision. The Court of Appeal (by a majority) dismissed the Club's appeal. The Club appealed to the House of Lords.

Decision

The House of Lords held, allowing the appeal, that the council had misused its statutory powers of management in order to punish the Club. That this was the intention of the council was clear from the evidence. The Club had done no wrong – they had merely left the issue to the consciences of the players involved. Lord Templeman quoted from the judgment of Lord Denning MR in *Congreve v Home Office* (above) and continued:

Similar considerations apply, in my opinion, to the present case. Of course, this does not mean that the Council is bound to allow its property to be used by a racist organisation or by any organisation which, by its actions or its words, infringes the letter or the spirit of the Race Relations Act 1976. But the attitude of the Club and of the committee of the Club was a perfectly proper attitude, caught as they were in a political controversy which was not of their making.

For Ackner LJ's and Lord Roskill's difference on the applicability of irrationality principles to the case, see 14.2 below.

R v Derbyshire County Council ex p The Times Supplements Ltd (1990) QBD: 'Revenge' is improper purpose

Facts

The Sunday Times published articles about Derbyshire County Council which led to the institution of libel proceedings by the council's leader, David Bookbinder. The council resolved to remove all its advertising from newspapers owned by Rupert Murdoch, including *The Times Educational Supplement* (TES), and, in consequence, it appeared that its advertisements for teaching posts in particular (traditionally advertised in the TES) would cost more and be seen by fewer of those at whom they were targeted. The applicant sought an order of certiorari to quash the decision.

Decision

The court held, granting the order, that the majority Labour group on the council had been motivated by bad faith or vindictiveness, despite claims in the affidavits before the court that educational considerations had prompted the transfer of the teaching post advertisements. The court would have been equally prepared to hold that the council's decision was unreasonable in the *Wednesbury* sense (*Associated Provincial Picture Houses Ltd v Wednesbury Corp*, see 14.1 below) as having no sensible or justifiable basis.

13.4.2   The co-existence of improper and legitimate purposes

Westminster Corp v London and North-Western Railway Co (1905)
HL: Importance of main purpose rather than subsidiary consequences

Facts
Under the Public Health (London) Act 1891, the Corporation had power to construct public lavatories. The railway company owned a building on the east side of Parliament Street, Westminster. The Corporation built underground public lavatories below the middle of Parliament Street, with entrances on either side of the street. On various occasions, the Corporation and its predecessor, the Vestry of St Margaret's, Westminster, had referred to the intended works as a subway. The railway company sought an injunction to prevent the Corporation's continued trespass on its premises and to obstruct the pavement opposite their premises, and damages. They argued that the Corporation's true purpose was to build a subway, and that it had therefore exceeded the powers given to it by the Act of 1891. The Court of Appeal considered that the Corporation had acted in bad faith.

Decision
The House of Lords held, by a majority, that the Corporation had not acted in bad faith. After emphasising that the charge of want of good faith was a serious one, Lord MacNaghten continued:

It is not enough to show that the Corporation contemplated that the public might use the subway as a means of crossing the street. That was an obvious possibility … In order to make out a case of bad faith, it must be shown that the Corporation constructed this subway as a means of crossing the street under colour and pretence of providing public conveniences which were not really wanted at that particular place.

Since the chairman of the works committee had declared on oath before the judge at first instance that the primary object of the committee was to provide the conveniences, and had been believed by the judge, his account should continue to prevail.

Comment
Here the improper purpose – the building of the subway – was secondary to the lawful purpose. This case can also be analysed as one in which the building of the subway was lawful as reasonably incidental to the statutory power.

R v Inner London Education Authority ex p Westminster City Council (1986) **QBD:** Approach to be taken by courts

Facts
Under the Local Government Act 1972, the authority had power to incur expenditure on publishing 'information on matters relating to local government' within its area. In 1984, a sub-committee resolved to mount an advertising campaign costing £651,000 in order to inform the public about government education proposals and to seek to persuade the public to share the authority's view of the proposals. The authority accepted that while the first of these objectives was lawful, the second was not. Westminster Council argued that the sub-committee's resolution was *ultra vires* the

Local Government Act 1972 because the authority had an improper purpose and, because, in allowing itself to be motivated by its desire to increase public opposition to government policy, it had taken into account an irrelevant consideration.

Decision

It was held that the declaration sought by Westminster Council would be granted on both grounds. Glidewell J stated that the question for the court was whether a decision taken to achieve two purposes, one authorised by statute and the other unauthorised, was invalid. He cited the following passage from *de Smith's Judicial Review of Administrative Action*, 4th edn, 1980, pp 329–32:

(1)   What was the true purpose for which the power was exercised? If the actor has in truth used his power for the purposes for which it was conferred, it is immaterial that he was thus enabled to achieve a subsidiary object …

(5)   Was any of the purposes pursued an unauthorised purpose? If so, and if the unauthorised purpose has materially influenced the actor's conduct, the power has been invalidly exercised because irrelevant considerations have been taken into account.

Glidewell J found as fact that the wish to persuade the public to adopt its own point of view was a (if not the) major purpose of the authority in making its decision. He further found that the authority had taken into account an irrelevant consideration, but declined to accept submissions that the authority had acted in disregard of its fiduciary duty to ratepayers, or that its decision was so unreasonable as to be perverse.

R v Broadcasting Complaints Commission ex p Owen (1985) QBD: Improper purpose does not invariably invalidate decision

Facts

The applicant, Dr David Owen, was the leader of the Social Democratic Party, which had entered into an alliance with the Liberal Party. At the 1983 general election, these two parties obtained only slightly fewer votes than the Labour Party, but won far fewer seats in the Commons. The applicant wrote to the BBC complaining of unfair treatment in that the Corporation had given more coverage to the views of the Labour Party than it had to those of the Alliance. The BBC replied that it had no jurisdiction to consider such a complaint, and that, even if it had, it would have exercised its discretion under ss 54 and 55 of the Broadcasting Act 1981 not to consider it. The BBC gave a number of reasons for this stance. The applicant sought to persuade the court that the invalidity of one of any of the stated reasons would invalidate the BBC's decision.

Decision

The court held, dismissing the application, that the BBC had been wrong to conclude that it did not have jurisdiction to consider the applicant's complaint, but that its exercise of its discretion would not be overturned. The third of the reasons given (that it would be burdensome to give fuller coverage to the Alliance's policies) was not a proper reason. In *R v Rochdale Metropolitan Borough Council ex p Cromer Ring Mill Ltd* (1982), Forbes J had held that academic and judicial authority established that the presence of an irrelevant consideration was sufficient to invalidate a decision even if its influence was not dominant; it was enough that it was substantial. However, that was a case in which the reasons given were impossible to disentangle; in a case like the present, where the reasons given were separate and alternative, and the decision was one which the authority would have reached even if it had not taken into account the improper consideration, the court would not intervene.

CHAPTER 14

THE GROUNDS FOR JUDICIAL REVIEW: IRRATIONALITY

Introduction

'Irrationality' is the most difficult of the grounds to satisfy, as the traditional test is extremely stringent. This is so in order to prevent the courts from becoming embroiled in arguments over the merits of a decision.

14.1   General definitions of irrationality

Associated Provincial Picture Houses Ltd v Wednesbury Corp (1948) CA: Traditional definition

Facts
See 11.2.1.1 above.

Per Lord Greene MR:
It is true to say that if a decision on a competent matter is so unreasonable that no reasonable authority could ever have come to it, then the courts can interfere. That, I think, is quite right; but to prove a case of that kind would require something overwhelming, and, in this case, the facts do not come anywhere near anything of that kind.

Council of Civil Service Unions v Minister for the Civil Service (1985) HL: Lord Diplock's definition

Facts
See 7.5 above.

Per Lord Diplock:
By 'irrationality', I mean ... a decision which is so outrageous in its defiance of logic or of accepted moral standards that no sensible person who had applied his mind to the question to be decided could have arrived at it ... To justify the court's exercise of this role, resort I think is today no longer needed to Viscount Radcliffe's ingenious explanation in *Edwards v Bairstow* (1956) of irrationality as a ground for a court's reversal of a decision by ascribing it to an inferred though unidentifiable mistake of law by the decision maker. 'Irrationality' by now can stand upon its own feet as an accepted ground on which a decision may be attacked by judicial review.

14.2   Application of the principle

Wheeler v Leicester City Council (1985) CA and HL: Rare instance of a decision being found *Wednesbury* unreasonable

Facts
See 13.4.1 above.

Decision

In the Court of Appeal, Ackner LJ considered whether the council's behaviour was irrational in the *Wednesbury* sense (see 14.1 above) in the following terms:

Can it be said in the circumstances of this case that no reasonable local authority could properly conclude that temporarily banning from the use of their recreation ground an important local rugger club, which declined to condemn a South African tour and declined actively to discourage its members from participating therein, could promote good relations between persons of different racial groups? ... In my judgment, it would be quite wrong to categorise as perverse the Council's decision ...

In the House of Lords, Lord Roskill was of the opinion that the council's decision was unreasonable in the *Wednesbury* sense. It had gone beyond persuasion and applied illegitimate pressure coupled with a threat of sanctions. Lord Roskill would equally have been prepared to hold that the council's decision was unfair, within the meaning of the third of the principles stated by Lord Diplock in the *GCHQ* case (see 15.1 below).

14.3   Stringent test of irrationality

***Champion v Chief Constable of Gwent* (1990) HL:** Criticism of way in which test is expressed

Facts

The appellant, a police officer, was elected a school governor. He was refused permission by his Chief Constable to attend meetings of the appointments sub-committee in duty time, or to serve on the committee. The refusal of permission purported to be pursuant to para 1 of Sched 2 to the Police Regulations 1979, which required a member of a police force 'at all times [to] abstain from any activity which is likely to interfere with the impartial discharge of his duties or which is likely to give rise to the impression amongst members of the public that it may so interfere; and, in particular, a member of a police force shall not take any active part in politics'.

The Chief Constable took the view that the appellant might have information about a candidate for appointment which he had obtained only because of his position as a police constable. He concluded:

(1)   That were this known to the candidate, he might suppose that the appellant had unfairly used this knowledge to prevent his appointment, and this would in turn give rise to an impression amongst members of the public that the appellant's activities as a member of the appointments sub-committee would interfere with the impartial discharge of his duties as a police officer.

(2)   That the appellant might be embarrassed by his inability to pass such information to other members of the committee without the Chief Constable's permission. The Chief Constable indicated that permission would never be given. Further, he feared for the reputation of the police force were the appellant to become involved in controversial decision making. The judge at first instance and the Court of Appeal refused the application for judicial review. The appellant appealed to the House of Lords.

Decision

The House of Lords held, by a majority, that the appeal would be allowed. Lord Griffiths was of the opinion that the Chief Constable had failed to give any weight to the use of the word 'likely' in the Regulations, and so had relied on that prohibition for a purpose for which it had never been intended. Lord Ackner stated that he could find nothing irrational or perverse in the Chief Constable's decision. Lord Lowry concluded that the decision was so unreasonable that no reasonable Chief Constable could ever have come to it, but continued:

> The use of this stark language may be a salutary reminder of the heavy burden assumed by those who would attack administrative decisions, but I regret the identification which it implies of unreasonableness with the decision maker as well as with the decision ... When the decision is made by a statutory authority or a public officer, I feel that it would be more becoming and more accurate to condemn (where that step must be taken) a decision 'so unreasonable that no statutory authority/public officer [to be specified] acting reasonably could ever have come to it', because it by no means follows that the authority or officer concerned has not in the past behaved or will not in future behave in the most reasonable way imaginable. The present case may be a case in point.

R v Ministry of Defence ex p Smith and Others (1996) CA: Decision cannot be irrational on the basis of defiance of accepted moral standards when there is no accepted moral standard

Facts

The appellants were three servicemen and one servicewoman who had been discharged towards the end of 1994 from the Armed Forces on the ground that they were homosexuals. Their discharge took place pursuant to a Ministry of Defence policy which stated, 'Service personnel who are known to be homosexual or who engage in homosexual activity are administratively discharged from the Armed Forces'. The operation of the policy was non-discretionary. Together with all legislation affecting the Armed Forces, it was reviewed every five years by a Select Committee of the House of Commons. The last review had taken place in 1991, when the Committee declined to recommend the policy's alteration. The appellants challenged the lawfulness of their discharges on the grounds that the policy was irrational, contrary to the European Convention on Human Rights, and contrary to the EC Directive on Equal Treatment of Men and Women (76/207).

The Divisional Court refused their application, noting that, when exercising its 'secondary' judgment on an irrationality challenge, it was bound, even within a human rights context, to act with some reticence. There was 'still room for two views' on the merits of the policy, and it could not therefore be stigmatised as irrational – completely at odds with accepted moral standards. In the opinion of Simon Brown LJ, the days of the policy were numbered; Curtis J disagreed, holding that the applications failed on their merits as well as in law. The appellants appealed to the Court of Appeal.

Decision

The Court of Appeal held, dismissing the appeals, that the policy could not be stigmatised as irrational at the time when the appellants were discharged. At the time of the discharges, the policy had support both from Parliament and from those to whom the Ministry of Defence looked for advice. The argument based on the European Convention was regarded, in the context of domestic law, as supporting the irrationality challenge, rather than as an independent ground for impugning an exercise of administrative discretion. The Equal Treatment Directive was not relevant, since it dealt with discrimination on the ground of gender, not sexual orientation. Sir Thomas Bingham MR approved the following test for irrationality, proposed by counsel for three of the applicants:

The court may not interfere with the exercise of an administrative discretion on substantive grounds save where the court is satisfied that the decision is unreasonable in the sense that it is beyond the range of responses open to a reasonable decision maker.

14.4   Irrationality and the European Convention on Human Rights

***Lustig-Prean and Becket v UK; Smith and Grady v UK* (1999) ECtHR:** Stringent test of irrationality creates a breach of Convention rights

Decision
On consideration of the facts of *ex p Smith* (above), the European Court of Human Rights held that the policy of administrative dismissal of known homosexuals from the Armed Forces contravened the applicants' rights to respect for their private lives under Art 8 of the European Convention on Human Rights, and that the applicants had been denied an effective remedy in domestic law contrary to Art 13. The Court cited the test for irrationality stated by Sir Thomas Bingham MR in *ex p Smith*, and noted the favourable attitude to the applicants' submissions which had been taken by both the High Court and the Court of Appeal. However, the threshold of irrationality was set so high by that test that it effectively precluded consideration of whether the interference with the applicants' private lives had answered a pressing social need, or whether it had been proportionate to national security or public order aims. It followed that the applicants had not had access to an effective remedy for violation of the rights guaranteed by Art 8.

***R v Lord Saville of Newdigate and Others ex p A and Others* (1999):** Less stringent test to be applied when fundamental human rights are at stake

Facts
The applicants, who had formerly served as soldiers in Northern Ireland, were the subject of proceedings before a tribunal appointed under the Tribunals of Inquiry (Evidence) Act 1921 to inquire into the deaths of marchers in Londonderry on 'Bloody Sunday' (30 January 1972). The tribunal resolved to withdraw anonymity from the applicants despite accepting that there would be a significant threat to their lives if their identities were known.

Decision

The court held, by a majority, quashing the tribunal's decision and remitting the matter to it, that the tribunal had not given due weight to the applicants' fundamental rights (here, the right to life). In cases where fundamental rights were involved, decisions would be subjected by the court to a more stringent and intensive review than was normal. In the light of this heightened intensity, the test for the reasonableness of a decision was not the same as the test for 'perversity' or 'absurdity'. Rather, the question to be asked was whether a reasonable body, on the material before it, could reasonably have concluded that the interference with human rights was justifiable.

14.5   The test as applied to decisions approved by the House of Commons

***Nottinghamshire County Council v Secretary of State for the Environment* (1986) HL:** Court's role is reduced where Parliament has a role

Facts

The council sought judicial review of guidance on expenditure issued by the Secretary of State. The guidance was framed with reference to a notional standard expenditure for local authorities known as 'grant-related expenditure' (GRE). The guidance differentiated between authorities which had budgeted at or below GRE in the preceding year, and those which had budgeted above the previous year's GRE. The council claimed that the guidance did not comply with a requirement in the Local Government Planning and Land Act 1980, in that it was not framed by reference to principles applicable to all local authorities. The council further claimed that the guidance was unreasonable because it was disproportionately disadvantageous to certain authorities. Pursuant to s 60 of the Local Government Planning and Land Act 1980, the guidance had been laid before the House of Commons and approved by a resolution of the House.

Decision

The court held, holding for the Secretary of State on both arguments, that guidance might validly differentiate between different authorities on the basis of their past expenditure records. Giving his opinion on the council's second submission, Lord Scarman refused to examine the detail of the guidance or its consequences. By the Commons' approval procedure enacted in s 60 of the Local Government Planning and Land Act 1980, Parliament had effectively made one of its Houses responsible for judging the guidance. The court's power of review was therefore diminished in so far as it overlapped with that function.

Per Lord Scarman:

Such an examination by the court would be justified only if a *prima facie* case were to be shown for holding that the Secretary of State has acted in bad faith, or for an improper motive, or that the consequences of his guidance were so absurd that he must have taken leave of his senses. The evidence comes nowhere near establishing any of these propositions.

R v Secretary of State for the Environment ex p Hammersmith and Fulham London Borough Council (1991) HL: Limitation of court's power where decisions are essentially political in nature

Facts

As a consequence of decisions by the Secretary of State under the Local Government Finance Act 1988 to impose budgetary restrictions on certain local authorities, each would be required to make proportionate reductions in the level of its community charge (poll tax). The local authorities sought judicial review of the Secretary of State's decision on the grounds of illegality, irrationality, and procedural impropriety.

Decision

The House of Lords held, rejecting the council's application on all grounds, that the restrictions placed on the scope of judicial review in the *Nottinghamshire* case (above) were equally appropriate here.

Per Lord Bridge:

The restriction which the *Nottinghamshire Case* ... imposes on the scope of judicial review operates only when the court has first determined that the ministerial action in question does not contravene the requirements of the statute, whether express or implied, and only then declares that, since the statute has conferred a power on the Secretary of State which involves the formulation and the implementation of national economic policy and which can only take effect with the approval of the House of Commons, it is not open to challenge on the grounds of irrationality short of the extremes of bad faith, improper motive or manifest absurdity. Both the constitutional propriety and the good sense of this restriction seem to me to be clear enough. The formulation and the implementation of national economic policy are matters depending essentially on political judgment ... If the decisions have been taken in good faith within the four corners of the Act, the merits of the policy underlying the decisions are not susceptible to review by the courts and the courts would be exceeding their proper function if they presumed to condemn the policy as unreasonable.

CHAPTER 15

THE GROUNDS FOR JUDICIAL REVIEW: PROCEDURAL IMPROPRIETY

15.1   General definition of the principle

Procedural impropriety essentially involves failure to follow procedures specified in the instrument granting the power at issue, rather than the broader concept of breach of the principles of natural justice (see Chapter 16).

Council of Civil Service Unions v Minister for the Civil Service (1985) **HL:** Lord Diplock's definition

Facts
See 7.5 above.

Per Lord Diplock:
I have described the third head [of judicial review] as 'procedural impropriety' rather than failure to observe basic rules of natural justice or failure to act with procedural fairness towards the person who will be affected by the decision. This is because susceptibility to judicial review under this head covers also failure by an administrative tribunal to observe procedural rules that are expressly laid down in the legislative instrument by which its jurisdiction is conferred, even where such failure does not involve any denial of natural justice.

15.2   Effect of failure to observe express procedural requirements

Howard v Bodington (1877): Failure to observe mandatory procedural requirement renders decision void

Facts
Section 9 of the Public Worship Regulation Act 1874 provided that, where a bishop received a complaint about any clergyman in his diocese, he should transmit a copy to the person complained of within 21 days of receiving it, unless satisfied that proceedings should be taken no further. The archbishop, acting on behalf of a bishop, received a complaint, but failed to forward it as required by s 9.

Decision
The House of Lords held that the requirement was imperative (mandatory) and that the subsequent proceedings were therefore void.

Per Lord Penzance:
I believe that, as far as any rule is concerned, you cannot safely go further than that in each case you must look to the subject matter; consider the importance of the provision that has been disregarded, and the relation of that provision to the general object intended to be secured by

the Act; and upon a review of the case in that aspect decide whether the matter is what is called imperative or only directory.

Comment

Here we see the distinction made by the courts between mandatory (compulsory) and directory (advisory) requirements, which is the main source of difficulty in this area.

15.2.1   Rigid and flexible approaches to mandatory and directory requirements

Bradbury v Enfield London Borough Council (1967) CA: Procedural requirements exist as safeguards, and so should be observed

Facts

By s 13 of the Education Act 1944, an education authority which planned to reorganise its schools had to give notice of its plans by posting details of them at or near the main gates of schools and by publishing them in the local press, 'and in such other manner as appears to be desirable for giving publicity to the notice'. The council, which planned to reorganise its schools along comprehensive lines, failed to give notice of its intentions to the public. Local ratepayers obtained an injunction to prevent the council implementing its plans until the statutory procedure had been followed.

Decision

The court held, dismissing the council's appeal, that the injunction had been properly granted despite the chaos which it would cause. The notice requirements were mandatory.

Per Danckwerts J:

... In cases of this kind, it is imperative that the procedure laid down in the relevant statute should be properly observed. The provisions of statutes in this respect are supposed to provide safeguards for Her Majesty's subjects. Public bodies and ministers must be compelled to observe the law; and it is essential that the bureaucracy be kept in its place.

Coney v Choice (1975): Strict compliance with procedures is not always necessary, provided objective of requirement has been achieved

Facts

The facts were similar to those of *Bradbury v Enfield LBC* above. The reorganisation plans were not posted in the statutory manner at two schools in the area.

Decision

The court held that the specific requirements were only directory. Templeman J construed the object of the legislative provisions to be that 'notice should be published in a manner designed to show a representative number of people what their rights are'. This object was mandatory. The notice provided had achieved substantial compliance with this object, so that no substantial prejudice would have been suffered by those for whose benefit the provisions had been made.

Comment

These two apparently conflicting decisions may be reconciled on the basis that in the first case there had been a large-scale failure to notify the public, whereas in the second the requirements of s 13 had been substantially satisfied and the failure was relatively technical.

15.2.2   The gravity and relevance of the breach alleged

London & Clydeside Estates Ltd v Aberdeen District Council (1980) HL: Approach to be taken by courts in deciding whether requirement is mandatory or directory

Facts

By s 25 of the Land Compensation (Scotland) Act 1963, an authority which compulsorily purchased land was to provide a certificate at the request of its owner stating the uses for which planning permission might have been granted in respect of the land had it not been compulsorily acquired for a different purpose. The certificate was required to state that the owner had a right of appeal within one month to the Secretary of State. The council issued a certificate to the company in which it stated that the grant of planning permission would have been limited to the purpose for which the land was in fact being compulsorily acquired. The certificate did not mention the right of appeal. The company's eventual appeal was rejected on the ground that it was out of time. It renewed its appeal to the House of Lords and sought to impugn the validity of the certificate, arguing that the notice of appeal requirement was mandatory. The council claimed that the requirement was merely directory and fell either into the category of directory requirements with which substantial compliance was necessary, or into a secondary category of merely regulatory requirements.

Decision

The House of Lords held that the requirement was mandatory.

Per Lord Hailsham:

When Parliament lays down a statutory requirement for the exercise of legal authority, it expects its authority to be obeyed down to the minutest of details. But what the courts have to decide in a particular case is the legal consequence of non-compliance on the rights of the subject viewed in the light of a concrete state of facts and a continuing chain of events. It may be that what the courts are faced with is not so much a stark choice of alternatives but a spectrum of possibilities ... At one end of this spectrum, there may be cases in which a fundamental obligation may have been so outrageously and flagrantly ignored or defied that the subject may safely ignore what has been done and treat it as having no legal consequences upon himself ... At the other end ... the defect in procedure may be so nugatory or trivial that the authority can safely proceed without remedial action, confident that, if the subject is so misguided as to rely on the fault, the courts will decline to listen to his complaint. But in a very great number of cases ... it may be necessary for a subject, in order to safeguard himself, to go to the court for declaration of his rights ... In such cases, though language like 'mandatory', 'directory', 'void', 'voidable', 'nullity' and so forth may be helpful in argument, it may be misleading in effect if relied on to show that the courts, in deciding the consequences of a defect in the exercise of power, are necessarily bound to fit the facts of a particular case and a developing chain of events into rigid legal categories or to stretch or cramp them onto a bed of Procrustes invented by lawyers for the purposes of convenient exposition.

CHAPTER 16

THE GROUNDS FOR JUDICIAL REVIEW: NATURAL JUSTICE

Introduction

The principles of natural justice – they are principles rather than rules, since their application varies according to circumstances – are traditionally expressed in the form of two Latin maxims. *Audi alteram partem* translates as 'Hear the other side', but essentially requires that a person affected by a decision must have a proper opportunity to put his case. *Nemo judex in sua causa potest* means literally, 'No man shall be judge in his own cause', but acts as a requirement that not only must there be an absence of actual bias in decision making, but there must be an absence of an appearance of bias.

16.1 The application of the principles

Initially, the principles of natural justice were only applicable to 'judicial' decisions, but case law over the past 150 years has gradually extended their relevance.

16.1.1 The demise of a rigid distinction between judicial and administrative decisions

Early decisions assumed that the principles of natural justice were only applicable to judicial or quasi-judicial decisions, not to decisions which were purely administrative, but this dichotomy was held inappropriate in the following case.

Ridge v Baldwin (1964) HL: Principles must be applied where a person's existing rights are at stake

Facts

Ridge, the Chief Constable of Brighton, was charged with conspiracy to obstruct the course of justice. The trial judge, directing his acquittal, nevertheless criticised Ridge and suggested that the Brighton police force required new and better leadership. The local watch committee (forerunner of the modern police authority) met and decided that Ridge should be dismissed. Ridge was not given notice of the meeting. His solicitor was granted permission to address a later meeting of the committee, which nevertheless resolved to adhere to the earlier decision. Ridge appealed on the grounds, *inter alia*, that the committee's decision was void for breach of the principles of natural justice. The Court of Appeal rejected his appeal, on the grounds that the decision to dismiss was an executive act and that the committee was therefore not bound to hold an inquiry of a judicial or quasi-judicial nature.

Decision

The House of Lords held, allowing the appeal, that a consistent line of authority would apply the requirement to observe the rules of natural justice to the present case. A tendency had more recently developed for the effect of those authorities to be limited. That was due in part to wartime circumstances in which the principles of natural justice had been neglected, and in part to a misunderstanding of a passage from the judgment of Atkin LJ in *R v Electricity Commissioners ex p London Electricity Joint Committee Co* (see 8.2.1 above). The duty to act judicially referred to in that case was, in fact, to be inferred from the nature of the decision maker's power.

Comment

On the basis of *Ridge v Baldwin*, the principles of natural justice were applicable in the case of office-holders, 'where there must be something against a man to warrant his dismissal' (at this time the statutory concept of unfair dismissal applicable to employees had yet to be created), and, more generally, where a person's existing rights were at stake. If dismissed, Ridge stood to lose the police pension he had already accumulated, thus his existing rights were at stake. It was argued for the watch committee that allowing him to address the committee would serve no purpose, as in the circumstances he could not remain Chief Constable. However, the Lords concluded that he could have been required to retire as an alternative to dismissal, which would not have cost him his pension.

Since *Ridge v Baldwin*, case law has established that the principles of natural justice must be observed where a person has a 'legitimate expectation' that he will be granted a right (see Chapter 17), commonly in circumstances where a grant has been granted for a time-limited period, renewable on application.

Chief Constable of the North Wales Police v Evans (1982) HL: Issue of whether the principles of natural justice are separate from those of fairness of decision reached

Facts

See 8.4.1.3 above.

Decision

The House of Lords held, dismissing the Chief Constable's appeal, that the treatment meted out to the respondent had been little short of outrageous. However, the grant of an order of mandamus would border on a usurpation of the Chief Constable's powers, and a declaration stating the rights of the respondent was granted. The statement of Lord Denning MR in the Court of Appeal, to the effect that the respondent was entitled not only to a fair hearing, but also to a fair and reasonable decision by the Chief Constable, was disapproved.

Per Lord Hailsham LC:

The function of the court is to see that lawful authority is not abused by unfair treatment and not to attempt itself the task entrusted to that authority by law ... I am not sure whether Lord Denning MR really intended his remarks to be construed in such a way as to permit the court to examine ... the reasoning of the subordinate authority with a view to substituting its own opinion ... The purpose of judicial review is to ensure that the individual receives fair treatment, and not to ensure that the authority, after according fair treatment, reaches on a matter which it is authorised or enjoined by law to decide for itself a conclusion which is correct in the eyes of the court.

16.1.2   The standard of the duty varies according to the rights at stake

***McInnes v Onslow-Fane* (1978):** More stringent standard applies where an existing right is at stake

Facts
The plaintiff had held various licences in connection with boxing in the past, but all had been withdrawn and he had since made no fewer than six unsuccessful applications for a trainer's licence. The plaintiff applied again to the British Boxing Board of Control for a trainer's licence, and requested an oral hearing and advance notice of anything which might militate against a favourable outcome. The Board refused his application without giving him a hearing and gave him no reasons for the refusal of the licence. He sought, *inter alia*, a declaration that the Board had acted in breach of natural justice and unfairly.

Decision
The court held, dismissing the plaintiff's summons, that the requirements of natural justice or the duty to act fairly would vary according to the type of decision to be made. The present case did not involve the forfeiture of an existing right: in such cases, there would be a right to an unbiased tribunal, to notice of the charges and to be heard in answer to them. The plaintiff had no legitimate expectation that his application would be granted. He had simply been refused a right (see Chapter 17 for the doctrine of legitimate expectation). In fulfilment of its duty to act fairly in these circumstances, the Board was under a duty only to reach an honest conclusion without bias, and not in pursuit of any capricious policy. In the absence of anything to suggest that the Board's decision had been affected by any impropriety, there was no obligation on the Board to give the plaintiff even the gist of its reasons for refusing his application.

16.1.3   Loss of common law procedural rights

***Cinnamond v British Airports Authority* (1980) CA:** The applicant's past conduct may disentitle him to be heard

Facts
The authority had statutory power to make bylaws regulating the use of Heathrow Airport and the conduct of persons within the airport. The appellants, who were minicab drivers, had regularly overcharged their customers, had convictions under the bylaws for offences of loitering, and had not paid fines imposed by the Authority. The Authority wrote to them informing them that they were banned until further notice from entering the airport, save as *bona fide* passengers. The appellants sought to overturn the ban. They argued, *inter alia*, that they should have been given the opportunity to be heard before the ban was imposed.

Decision

The Court of Appeal held, dismissing the appeal, that if the appellants had been of good character, fairness would have demanded that they be heard. However, it must have been apparent to them why the ban was ordered, and their record of persistent bad behaviour had disentitled them to a legitimate expectation of a hearing.

16.1.4   The merits of the subject's substantive case go to the discretion of the court

Glynn v Keele University (1971): No requirement to observe the principles of natural justice when the decision was a foregone conclusion

Facts

A student was discovered sunbathing naked on university premises. Without being given any notice of the charges against him or any hearing, he was fined £10 by the Vice Chancellor and excluded from the University for a year. The student learnt about the action taken against him only when he received a letter detailing the penalties imposed.

Decision

The court held that the Vice Chancellor had been acting in a quasi-judicial capacity and there had been a clear breach of the principles of natural justice. However, in the opinion of Pennycuick VC, the offence was a grave one, the penalties imposed were appropriate, and the student had put forward no specific justification for what he did. Had he been granted a hearing, he could only have put forward a plea in mitigation. The fact that he had been deprived of the opportunity to throw himself on the mercy of the Vice Chancellor was not sufficient to justify setting aside a perfectly proper decision. A remedy would be refused in the exercise of the court's discretion.

16.1.5   Loss of procedural rights attributable to the failure of the subject's legal advisers

Al-Mehdawi v Secretary of State for the Home Department (1990) HL: Court would not intervene when failure to observe principles of natural justice was due to matters outside the decision maker's control

Facts

The respondent, an Iraqi citizen, was notified in March 1985 that the Secretary of State had resolved to make a deportation order against him, following the expiry of his leave to remain in the UK and the refusal of his application for an extension of time. He instructed solicitors to appeal against the decision to an immigration adjudicator. Neither he nor his solicitors attended the hearing, and the adjudicator decided the appeal against him on the papers. He failed to lodge an appeal against the adjudicator's decision within time. Subsequently, it emerged that the solicitors had sent notice of the hearing date and of the adjudicator's decision to the wrong address. The respondent sought judicial review of the adjudicator's decision on the basis that he had been denied a hearing. The High Court and the Court of Appeal held for the respondent; the Secretary of State appealed to the House of Lords, arguing that the rules of natural justice concerned only the propriety of the procedure adopted by the decision maker.

Decision

The House of Lords held, allowing the appeal, that, in private law, the litigant who had lost the opportunity to have his case heard through the default of his own advisers could not complain that he had been the victim of a procedural impropriety. No principle had been suggested which would lead to a different conclusion in the field of public law. The decision of the Court of Appeal could only be supported at the cost of seriously undermining the principle of finality in decision making.

16.1.6 Reduction in procedural rights in an emergency

R v Secretary of State for Transport ex p Pegasus Holdings (1988): Urgency of matter may justify less stringent observance of principles of natural justice

Facts

The applicants chartered aircraft and flying crews from the Romanian airline Tarom. Tarom held a permit from the Secretary of State for this purpose. Five of its pilots voluntarily took flying tests conducted by the British Civil Aviation Authority. Four of them failed on grounds that they displayed an inability to manoeuvre the aircraft. The Secretary of State provisionally withdrew Tarom's licence within a matter of hours of the results of the tests becoming known. This caused the applicant package holiday company great difficulties in transporting its customers. The applicant claimed that the Secretary of State had failed to grant it a fair hearing before withdrawing the licence.

Decision

Schiemann J declared that he was content to proceed on the basis that the rules of natural justice did apply, but that, in the words of counsel for the respondent, in such an emergency as the present, with a provisional suspension being all that the court was concerned with, one was at the low end of the scale of duties of fairness. The Civil Aviation Authority had admittedly taken some time to refer the matter to the Secretary of State, but that delay would not lessen the appropriateness of the speedy action taken by the Secretary of State.

16.1.7 The inherent flexibility of procedural rights and the duty to act fairly in the circumstances

Re HK (An Infant) (1967): Duty was limited to what was appropriate in the circumstances

Facts

Under the Commonwealth Immigrants Act 1962, the applicant's right to enter the country was dependent on his showing that he was less than 16 years old. It was argued on behalf of the applicant that the immigration officer was under a duty to conform to the principles of natural justice. Thus, the applicant should have had the opportunity to persuade the immigration officer that he was under 16.

Decision

The court held, dismissing the application, that an immigration officer was indeed under such a duty, but that it amounted to a duty to act fairly in the circumstances. It was not a duty to hold a full-scale inquiry, or to adopt judicial process and procedure. The applicant had known of what he had to do to satisfy the authorities and had been given ample opportunity to do so.

16.2   *Audi alteram partem*

The *audi alteram partem* principle encompasses a number of areas of procedure, under the umbrella of giving the person affected by the decision a proper opportunity to put his case to the decision maker. It includes ensuring that he knows the basis on which a decision will be made, the case against him (if any), as well as giving him an opportunity to challenge evidence brought against him. Case law shows that the stringency of the requirements depends very much on the decision to be made.

16.2.1   *The right to cross-examine witnesses*

Bushell v Secretary of State for the Environment (1981) HL: No automatic right to cross-examine witnesses

Facts

Numerous parties objected to proposals to build stretches of motorway. The Secretary of State was statutorily obliged to hold an inquiry into the objections. The objectors sought to challenge statistical methods used by the Minister's department to predict future levels of traffic. The inspector who conducted the inquiry permitted the objectors to call expert witnesses to give evidence criticising the Department's methodology, but he did not permit cross-examination of the departmental officials. The Secretary of State, acting on the basis of the inspector's report, approved the construction of the roads. The objectors exercised a statutory right of challenge to the decision on the grounds that the inspector had been wrong in law to disallow cross-examination. The Court of Appeal (by a majority) allowed their appeal. The Secretary of State appealed to the House of Lords.

Decision

The House of Lords held, allowing the appeal by a majority, that the question whether it was unfair to disallow cross-examination depended on all the circumstances of the inquiry. It could not be said to be unfair *per se*, since it was not accorded in many legal systems, but was peculiar to the common law conception of procedure. A distinction was to be drawn between areas of government policy, with regard to which there was no discretion to allow cross-examination, and other matters, in regard to which there was a discretion. The choice of method used by the Department to assess future traffic needs fell within a 'grey area' between the two categories, but was best regarded as a matter of policy which it was not appropriate to investigate on the limited facts of a single inquiry. Further, in the present case, the matters on which the right to cross-examine was sought were very complicated. No one who was not an expert in the subject could form a useful judgment on it. The evidence of the expert witnesses called by the objectors was fully recorded for the consideration of the Secretary of State.

Per Lord Edmund-Davies (dissenting):

The general law may, I think, be summarised in this way:

(a)   In holding an administrative inquiry (such as that presently being considered), the inspector was performing quasi-judicial duties;

(b)   He must therefore discharge them in accordance with the rules of natural justice;

(c)   Natural justice requires that objectors (no less than departmental representatives) be allowed to cross-examine witnesses called for the other side on all relevant matters, be they matters of fact or matters of expert opinion;

(d)   In the exercise of jurisdiction outside the field of criminal law, the only restrictions on cross-examination are those general and well defined exclusionary rules which govern the admissibility of relevant evidence … beyond those restrictions, there is no discretion on the civil side to exclude cross-examination on relevant matters.

16.2.2   The discretion to allow legal representation to prisoners

R v Secretary of State for the Home Department ex p Tarrant and Another; R v Wormwood Scrubs Prison Board of Visitors ex p Anderson and Others (1985): Principles on which discretion to allow representation should be exercised

Facts

The applicants were prisoners who were charged with grave offences against prison discipline. They sought legal representation at inquiries into the charges to be held by Prison Boards of Visitors. In each case, the request was refused, although they would have been entitled to legal representation had their cases been heard in the criminal courts. The applicants sought judicial review of the decisions on the grounds either that they were entitled to legal representation or, alternatively, that the Boards had a discretion to permit legal representation and should have exercised that discretion in the applicants' favour.

Decision

The court held, allowing the application, that the court was bound by the authority of the Court of Appeal in *Fraser v Mudge* (1975) to hold that the applicants had no right to legal representation. However, a Prison Board of Visitors had a discretion to permit legal representation. In deciding how to exercise that discretion, a Board should take into account:

(1)   the seriousness of the charge and of the potential penalty;

(2)   whether any points of law were likely to arise in the proceedings;

(3)   the prisoner's capacity in intellectual and educational terms to present his case;

(4)   the prisoner's difficulty in contacting witnesses;

(5)   the need for reasonable speed in making the adjudication; and

(6)   the need for fairness as between prisoners or as between prisoners and prison officers.

The failure by the Boards to consider the exercise of the discretion to allow legal representation was in all cases a substantial infringement of the applicants' rights, whether or not, if the discretion had been exercised, it would have been exercised in the applicants' favour.

Comment

Although the case specifically concerns prisoners appearing before Prison Boards of Visitors, the factors enumerated by the court may be applied, *mutatis mutandis*, to other matters.

16.2.3   The right to an oral hearing

Overall, case law shows that it is only in rare circumstances that the *audi alteram partem* principle is interpreted to require an oral hearing.

Lloyd v McMahon (1987) QBD: Right of individual to put his case does not necessarily require an oral hearing, even in serious cases

Facts

The appellants were the majority group on Liverpool City Council. They purposely delayed setting a rate for the year 1985–86 in the hope of increasing the city's grant from central government. The district auditor notified the appellants that he proposed to consider whether to certify that the council's loss should fall on them in consequence of their wilful default, making them personally liable for large sums of money. The auditor's notice stated that the appellants could make written representations to him before he reached a decision. The appellants argued before the House of Lords that the auditor's decision to issue a certificate was vitiated by his failure to offer them an oral hearing.

Decision

The court held, dismissing the appeal, that the auditor, like any other decision maker, was under a duty to act fairly. It was not unfair for the auditor to reach a decision on the basis of the written material submitted to him by the appellants.

Per Lord Bridge:

... The so called rules of natural justice are not engraved on tablets of stone. To use the phrase which better expresses the underlying concept, what the requirements of fairness demand when any body, domestic, administrative or judicial, has to make a decision which will affect the rights of individuals depends on the character of the decision making body, the kind of decision it has to make and the statutory or other framework in which it operates. In particular, it is well established that, when a statute has conferred on any body the power to make decisions affecting individuals, the courts will not only require the procedure prescribed by the statute to be followed, but will readily imply so much and no more to be introduced by way of additional procedural safeguards as will ensure the attainment of fairness.

16.2.4   The degree to which the applicant must be told the case against him

R v Gaming Board for Great Britain ex p Benaim and Khaida (1970) CA: Extent of disclosure may be restricted in the public interest

Facts
The applicants, who were the joint managing directors of Crockfords Gaming Club, unsuccessfully applied to the Gaming Board for a licence to carry on their business. Under the Gaming Act 1968, the Board had to be satisfied of the applicants' willingness and ability to run the gaming in accordance with the provisions of the Act, and to do so fairly and properly and without disorder or disturbance. The applicants sought orders of certiorari to quash the decision to refuse the licence, and mandamus requiring the Board to provide them with sufficient information to enable them to answer the case against them.

Decision
The court held, dismissing the application, that the Board had put before the applicants all the information which had led to their suitability being doubted, and had thereby discharged its duty to act fairly. It was not possible to lay down rigid rules as to when the principles of natural justice applied, nor as to their scope or extent. All depended on the subject matter of the decision in question. Here, the Board was not depriving the applicants of an office, or depriving them of their property. In the circumstances, it was enough that the applicants be given notice in broad terms of the Board's opinion of their suitability and the opportunity to argue in their own favour. It was not necessary or desirable for the applicants to be told the sources of the Board's information.

Comment
On this occasion, there were strong public policy reasons for not revealing where the information had come from, not least the need to protect informers from possible underworld reprisals.

16.3   *Nemo judex in causa sua*: the rule against bias

This rule is less concerned with actual bias than with the appearance of potential bias.

16.3.1   The nature of the rule

R v Sussex Justices ex p McCarthy (1924): Not necessary to prove actual bias – appearance of potential bias is sufficient

Facts
A motorist appeared before a bench of magistrates on a charge of dangerous driving. A solicitor, as acting clerk to the justices, accompanied them when they retired to consider their decision. It was proved that the justices did not in fact consult the solicitor during their deliberations and that the solicitor did not proffer any comments prejudicial to the accused. The same solicitor had, however, acted against the accused in an earlier civil case arising from the same motoring incident.

Decision

The court held that the conviction would be quashed, since the circumstances might have created a suspicion that there had been an improper interference with the course of justice.

Per Lord Hewart CJ:

It is not merely of importance, but of fundamental importance that justice should not only be done, but should manifestly and undoubtedly be seen to be done.

16.3.2 Pecuniary interest

Dimes v Grand Junction Canal Proprietors (1852) HL: Any pecuniary interest in the matter at issue disqualifies decision maker

Facts

Dimes, who claimed an interest in land through which the Grand Junction Canal passed, had for many years been involved in litigation with the canal proprietors. The case came before the Lord Chancellor, Lord Cottenham, who affirmed decrees made in favour of the proprietors. Dimes later discovered that the Lord Chancellor held shares in the canal company. He claimed that the Lord Chancellor had been judge in his own cause and that his order was accordingly void.

Decision

The House of Lords held that the Lord Chancellor's order was not void but voidable and would be set aside. No one could suppose that he could have been influenced by his interest in the company, but the rule that no man might be a judge in his own cause was of such importance that it should be seen to be upheld even in these circumstances.

16.3.3 Non-pecuniary interest

Metropolitan Properties v Lannon (1969) CA: Test to be applied in relation to a decision maker with a non-pecuniary interest in the matter

Facts

Mr Lannon, a solicitor, sat as chairman of a rent assessment committee which fixed a 'fair rent' under the Rent Acts for flats in Oakwood Court, West Kensington. The rent fixed was unusually low. Mr Lannon lived with his father who was the tenant of a flat in a similar block. The landlords of the two blocks of flats were companies associated in the same group. Mr Lannon had advised his father about a fair rent for his flat, and had advised other tenants in his father's block in connection with disputes with their landlord. The landlord of Oakwood Court alleged that, since the determination of the rents for Oakwood Court would have an effect on the rents in the second block, Mr Lannon's decision was tainted by an appearance of bias. It was not alleged that he had actually been biased.

Decision

The Court of Appeal held, granting certiorari to set aside the decision of the rent assessment committee, that Mr Lannon had effectively been acting against the landlords. Although, realistically, he could not be said to have a pecuniary interest in the subject matter of the committee's decision, he should not have sat on the committee. *Per* Lord Denning MR: '... there must appear to be a real likelihood of bias. Surmise or conjecture is not enough.'

Edmund-Davies LJ held that a reasonable suspicion of bias was enough to require that the decision be set aside.

R v Gough (1993) HL: Redefinition of test

Facts

The appellant appealed against conviction on the ground that there had been a serious irregularity in his trial. A juror had realised, after conviction and sentence, that she lived next door to the appellant's brother. The appellant argued that the test for bias was whether a reasonable and fair-minded person would reasonably suspect bias. The Crown argued that the test was whether there was a real likelihood of bias.

Decision

The House of Lords held that, on the test applied by the Court of Appeal – namely, whether there had been a real danger of bias – the appeal failed and would be dismissed. The reference to a real danger should be taken to connote a possibility rather than a probability of bias, and if the 'real likelihood' test was to be understood as requiring proof of bias on a balance of probabilities, it was too rigorous. The real danger test should be applicable in all cases of apparent bias, whether concerned with justices or members of other inferior tribunals, or with jurors or with arbitrators. It was not necessary, in formulating the appropriate test, to require that the court should look at the matter through the eyes of a reasonable man, because the court in such cases personified the reasonable man.

R v Inner West London Coroner ex p Dallaglio (1994) CA: Application of test to cases of 'unconscious bias'

Facts

During the adjournment of a coroner's inquests into the deaths of passengers on board the Thames launch *Marchioness*, an application was made to the coroner for an exhumation order in respect of the body of one of the deceased. The application was unsuccessful, but attracted press attention. In the course of an attempt to defuse the situation, the coroner allegedly described the applicant as 'unhinged', and other relatives of the deceased as 'mentally unwell'. Another relative of one of the deceased now applied for judicial review of the coroner's decisions:

(1)   not to remove himself on the grounds of apparent bias; and
(2)   not to resume the inquests.

At first instance, the Divisional Court refused the application.

Decision

The Court of Appeal held, allowing the appeal, that it was impossible to discount the possibility that the coroner had unconsciously allowed himself to be influenced against the applicant and other of the relatives by a feeling of hostility towards them. In the judgment of Sir Thomas Bingham MR, *R v Gough* (above) recognised three classes of case in which bias might arise for consideration:

(1) Cases of actual bias, in which a decision maker is shown to have been influenced in his decision making by prejudice, predilection or personal interest. 'Such cases are very rare ... the law is very clear and very emphatic: where a decision is shown to have been tainted by actual bias, it cannot stand.'

(2) Cases in which the decision maker has a direct pecuniary interest, however small, unless negligible, in the subject matter of the decision. It is irrelevant that the interest has had no effect on the decision in question. 'The nature of the interest is such that public confidence in the administration of justice requires that the decision should not stand ... It is rather as if, in such cases, the law presumes bias.'

(3) Cases in which there is no actual bias and no direct pecuniary interest giving rise to a presumption of bias. 'If, despite the appearance of bias, the court is able to examine all the relevant material and satisfy itself that there was no danger of the alleged bias having in fact caused injustice, the impugned decision will be allowed to stand.'

Sir Thomas Bingham MR added the following comment on the effect of the decision in *R v Gough* on the third class of case:

This decision shows, as it seems to me, that the description 'apparent bias' traditionally given to this head of bias is not entirely apt, for if despite the appearance of bias the court is able to examine all the relevant material and satisfy itself that there was no danger of the alleged bias having in fact caused injustice, the impugned decision will be allowed to stand. The famous aphorism of Lord Hewart CJ in *R v Sussex Justices ex p McCarthy* [see 16.3.1 above] that 'justice ... should manifestly and undoubtedly be seen to be done' is no longer, it seems, good law, save of course in the case where the appearance of bias is such as to show a real danger of bias.

It appears that the *nemo judex* principle will be applied more stringently in relation to judges than other decision makers, such that they may be automatically disqualified from hearing cases in which they have an interest, rather than the test of apparent bias above being applied.

R v Bow Street Magistrate ex p Pinochet Ugarte (No 2) (1999) HL: Example of case in which a judge is automatically disqualified from hearing case

Facts

The present case concerned the conduct of an earlier hearing by the House of Lords of an appeal against the decision of the Divisional Court to quash an international warrant for the arrest and extradition to Spain of Senator Pinochet, a former head of state of Chile. A bare majority of the House (including Lord Hoffmann) had restored the warrant. Leave had been given to the human rights group Amnesty International to intervene in that hearing. Senator Pinochet's solicitors learnt, after the conclusion of the hearing, that Lord Hoffmann was an unpaid director and chairman of the charitable arm of Amnesty International. The present hearing arose from Senator Pinochet's petition to the House to set aside its earlier order on the ground that the decision was marred by the appearance of bias.

Decision

The House of Lords held, setting aside the order and remitting the matter to a differently constituted judicial committee of the House, that, while Lord Hoffmann had had no pecuniary or proprietary interest in the outcome, he was nevertheless to be regarded as having judged in his own cause. Lord Hoffmann had therefore been automatically disqualified from hearing the appeal. It followed in these circumstances that it was not necessary for Senator Pinochet to show a real danger or reasonable suspicion of bias. Lord Browne-Wilkinson noted that the test in *R v Gough* (above) had been criticised as impinging on the traditional requirement that justice should be seen to be done, but added that, in the circumstances of automatic disqualification of a judge, the test was not relevant and therefore did not need to be reviewed.

Locabail (UK) Ltd v Bayfield (and Other Appeals) (1999) CA: Test to be applied to judicial decision makers

The facts are not material.

Decision

In the course of adjudicating upon five appeals concerning the apparent bias of judges, the Court of Appeal (consisting of the Lord Chief Justice, the Master of the Rolls and the Vice Chancellor) observed that the right to a fair hearing before an impartial tribunal was one of the most fundamental principles underlying the administration of justice. After reviewing the principle that an interest in the outcome of a case would automatically disqualify a judge from hearing it (and stating that the rule was not to be extended beyond the bounds set by existing authorities), the court examined the operation of the rule against apparent bias.

Notwithstanding the arguments against attempting to define or list the factors which would give rise to a real danger of bias, the court commented that it could not conceive of circumstances in which an objection could be soundly based on the religion, ethnic or national origin, gender, age, class, means or sexual orientation of a judge. Nor could an objection ordinarily be based on a judge's social, educational, service or employment background, nor that of members of the judge's family; on previous political associations or membership of social, sporting or charitable bodies or Masonic associations; on previous judicial decisions or on extra-judicial pronouncements; on previous receipt of instructions to act for or against any party, solicitor or advocate engaged in the case; nor on membership of the same Inn, circuit, local Law Society or chambers.

A real danger of bias might arise from personal friendship or animosity between a judge and a member of the public engaged in the case; from the judge's close acquaintance with a member of the public, particularly where that person's credibility could be significant; where credibility was an issue to be decided by the judge and he had in previous proceedings rejected that person's evidence in terms which threw doubt on his ability to approach it open-mindedly on any later occasion; from the expression of views by the judge on any question at issue in such extreme terms, particularly in the course of the hearing, as to throw doubt on his ability to try the issue with an open mind; or where, for any other reason, there were real grounds for doubting the judge's objectivity. Adverse comment on a party or on the reliability of a party's evidence in previous proceedings would not of itself provide grounds for objecting to a judge. Where there was real doubt as to the presence of a danger of bias, the doubt should be resolved against the judge continuing to try the matter.

16.3.4 Decision making power co-existing with policy or inalienable interests

The application of the principle may be somewhat modified in relation to local authorities, which may, for example, often be in the position of granting planning applications to themselves.

R v Amber Valley District Council ex p Jackson (1985): Council's duty to act fairly when it is granting right to itself

Facts

The applicant was a member of a local pressure group which opposed a proposed amusement park development. She sought an order of prohibition to prevent the respondent district council from considering an application for planning permission on the ground that its decision was likely to be biased, unfair and contrary to the duty imposed on it by s 29 of the Town and Country Planning Act 1971 to take into account all representations received relating to the application. The same political party had a majority both on the district and the county councils, and its county group had already resolved to support the planning application. The council stated in an affidavit that it would take into account all material considerations.

Decision

The court held, dismissing the application, that the fact that the council had a policy relating to the matter did not disqualify it from adjudicating on the planning application. The council had an obligation to be fair and to consider carefully the evidence; in the light of the council's affidavit, the court was not prepared to doubt that it would discharge that duty.

Per Woolf J:

The rules of fairness or natural justice cannot be regarded as being rigid. They must alter in accordance with the context. Thus, in the case of highways, the department can be both the promoting authority and the determining authority. When this happens, of course any reasonable man would regard the department as being disposed towards the outcome of the inquiry. The department is under an obligation to be fair and to carefully consider the evidence given before the inquiry but the fact that it has a policy in the matter does not entitle the court to intervene. So, in this case, I do not consider that the fact that there is a declaration of policy by the majority group can disqualify a district council from adjudicating on a planning application. It may mean that the outcome of the planning application is likely to be favourable to an applicant and therefore unfavourable to objectors. However, Parliament has seen fit to lay down that it is the local authority which has the power to make the decision ...

R v Sevenoaks District Council ex p Terry (1985): Normal rule against bias is not applicable to cases where the decision maker properly has interest

Facts

The council's planning sub-committee recommended acceptance of a developer's proposal to lease a site from the council. The developer subsequently applied to the council for planning permission and was granted it. The applicant, a local ratepayer, sought certiorari to quash the decision to grant permission, on the grounds that the council had regarded itself as committed to granting the permission, or because it would appear to a reasonable man that the council had regarded itself as being so committed.

Decision

The court held, dismissing the application, that the principle of *Metropolitan Properties v Lannon* (see 16.3.3 above) was not applicable to the case.

Per Glidewell J:

Of course, the Council must act honestly and fairly, but it is not uncommon for a local authority to be obliged to make a decision relating to land or other property in which it has an interest. In such a situation, the application of the rule designed to ensure that a judicial officer does not appear to be biased would, in my view, often produce an administrative impasse.

The question in cases of the present type was whether, before making its decision, the authority had acted in such a way that it was clear that it could not properly exercise its discretion. Here, the Council had not done so, and it was unnecessary for the court to go further to consider what the opinion of a reasonable man would be.

R v Secretary of State for the Environment ex p Kirkstall Valley Campaign (1996): Modified test applicable where the decision maker has an interest in the matter

Facts

In its capacity as local planning authority, an urban development corporation granted outline planning permission to a rugby club for a retail development on part of its land. The chairman of the corporation had an interest in other land which would materially increase in value if the club were able to move premises. This interest had not been declared. Other members of the corporation were members, vice presidents and the professional adviser of the club. The applicant was a community action group concerned with the interests of local residents in the development of the Kirkstall Valley. The respondent minister, in his capacity as successor to the corporation, argued that principles other than those laid down by the House of Lords in *R v Gough* (see 16.3.3 above) applied to non-judicial bodies. The proper test was not whether there was a real danger of bias on the part of any member of the tribunal, but whether the body as a whole could be shown to have gone beyond mere predisposition in favour of a particular course and to have predetermined it.

Decision

The court held, dismissing the application, that, although decisions taken in 1992 and 1993 had been vitiated by apparent bias, the decision challenged was the product of later processes which were so separate as to remain uncontaminated by the earlier flaws. Sedley J held that there was no authority to suggest that the principle in *R v Gough* was limited to judicial or quasi-judicial proceedings. It was appropriate that this should be so, given that, in the modern State, the interests of individuals or of the public might well be more radically affected by administrative than by judicial decisions. An individual with a personal, pecuniary or proprietary interest in the subject matter of a decision was to refrain from playing any part in its making. It was possible that the mere declaration of a disqualifying interest, followed by abstention from discussion or voting, would not always be sufficient.

CHAPTER 17

THE DOCTRINE OF LEGITIMATE EXPECTATION

Introduction

The doctrine of legitimate expectation is closely tied to the principles of natural justice, since a legitimate expectation that a right will be granted (or will continue) may create a requirement that the principles of natural justice be observed. Many decided cases involve legitimate expectation that a particular procedure will be followed – for example, that a particular person or body will be consulted before a decision is made.

17.1 The emergence of the doctrine in English administrative law

Schmidt v Secretary of State for Home Affairs (1969) CA: Individual had legitimate expectation of being heard in response to application, but not that the right applied for would be granted

Facts
The plaintiffs were Scientology students who had applied for an extension to their leave to remain in the UK. Their application was rejected. They sought a declaration that the refusal was *ultra vires* on the grounds that they had not been given an opportunity to be heard.

Decision
The Court of Appeal held, *per* Lord Denning MR, that the question of whether a hearing was required depended on whether the applicants had some right, interest or legitimate expectation of which it would not be fair to deprive them without hearing what they had to say. In respect of their entitlement to remain for the period originally limited, they had; in respect of an extension to that period, they had not.

17.2 Legitimate expectation as a means of establishing *locus standi* to apply for judicial review

O'Reilly v Mackman (1983) HL: Legitimate expectation of being granted a right gave *locus standi* to challenge a contrary decision

Facts
See 9.4 above.

Per Lord Diplock:
… All that each applicant had was a legitimate expectation, based on his knowledge of what is the general practice, that he would be granted the maximum remission … of one-third of his sentence if by that time no disciplinary award of forfeiture of remission had been made against

him ... Such legitimate expectation gave to each appellant a sufficient interest to challenge the legality of the adverse disciplinary award made against him by the board ...

17.3   The recognition of legitimate expectations

Findlay v Secretary of State for the Home Department (1984) HL: Limitations on an individual's legitimate expectation

Facts

In October 1983, the Home Secretary announced his intention to abolish the joint Home Office/Parole Board committee which had recommended when a life sentence prisoner should first be considered by a local review committee for parole, and to determine that date himself in consultation with the judiciary. He further announced that prisoners sentenced for certain classes of offence would in future normally serve at least 20 years of their sentences. The appellants, who were affected by the changes in policy, sought, *inter alia*, an order of prohibition to prevent the Home Secretary from applying the new policy to them, arguing that the policy constituted a fettering of the Home Secretary's discretion and that they had a legitimate expectation of release at the date that would have been set under the previous policy.

Decision

The House of Lords held, dismissing the appeals, that the adoption of the policy did not amount to a fettering of discretion, since it did not preclude the consideration of individual cases and that the expectation contended for by the appellants did not arise.

Per Lord Scarman:

They had good reason under the practice which had prevailed before the adoption of the new policy to expect release much earlier than became likely after its adoption ... But what was their legitimate expectation? Given the substance and purpose of the legislative provisions governing parole, the most that a convicted prisoner can legitimately expect is that his case will be examined individually in the light of whatever policy the Secretary of State sees fit to adopt, provided always that the adopted policy is a lawful exercise of the discretion conferred upon him by the statute.

R v Board of Inland Revenue ex p MFK Underwriting Agencies (1990): Informal and generalised advice does not give rise to legitimate expectation

Facts

With a view to offering an improved investment opportunity to the Lloyds market, certain US banks proposed to issue index-linked US or Canadian dollar securities for the investment of US or Canadian premium income. The banks and their advisers approached the Revenue independently for confirmation that the index-linked element payable on redemption of the securities would be taxed as a capital gain and not as income. The responses of Revenue officials indicated that they considered the index-linked element would be taxable as capital gain rather than income. The applicants purchased index-linked bonds on the basis that they would be so taxed. In fact, the Revenue later decided to tax the index-linked element as income. The applicants sought judicial review of the Revenue's decision, contending that it breached their legitimate expectations and was therefore unfair and amounted to an abuse of power.

Decision

The court held, dismissing the application, that, although the Revenue had informally promulgated guidelines and indicated its likely approach to the taxation question, several factors were required to be proved before its responses could fetter performance of its public duty to collect taxes payable on a proper construction of the relevant law. The taxpayer would have had to have provided full details of the matter on which he sought the Revenue's ruling. He would have had to have made plain that a fully considered ruling was sought and to have specified the use to which he intended to put that ruling. The Revenue would be bound only by a ruling or statement which was clear, unambiguous and devoid of relevant qualification. In the judgment of Bingham LJ, it was one thing to ask an official of the Revenue whether he shared the taxpayer's view of a legislative provision, but quite another to ask whether the Revenue would forgo a claim to tax on any other basis.

R v Inland Revenue Commissioners ex p Unilever plc (1996) CA: Contrast this case with *ex p MFK Underwriting Agencies*

Facts

By s 393 of the Income and Corporation Taxes Act 1988, a taxpayer might make a claim for trading loss relief within two years from the end of the accounting period in which the loss was sustained 'or within such further period as the Board may allow'. For many years, it had been the applicant's practice to offset trading loss against profits when submitting preliminary accounts. However, the offsetting of trading loss was expressly notified only after the finalisation of each year's accounts. As a result of the complexity of the applicant's tax affairs, this notification had fallen outside the statutory time period on 30 occasions. In respect of three recent accounting periods, the Revenue refused to allow the applicant loss relief on the ground that its claim was late.

The applicant argued that:

(1) the preliminary accounts constituted notification of claim within the period; or

(2) in fairness, the Revenue's past acquiescence debarred it from reversing its practice; and

(3) the Revenue should have exercised its statutory discretion in the applicant's favour.

At first instance, the application succeeded on grounds (2) and (3).

Decision

The Court of Appeal held, upholding the decision at first instance, that the claims had not been made within the two year period. However, the Revenue's rejection of the applicant's claims without advance notice was so unfair as to amount to an abuse of power. It was true that the Revenue had made no clear, unambiguous and unqualified representation that it would accept late claims, nor could it be said to have acquiesced in or waived a non-compliance of which it had simply been unaware. However, the facts of the present case were unique. The entitlement to claim trading loss was a fundamental one. There was no useful purpose to be achieved by an insistence on the merely regulatory statutory time limit. The error with regard to the time limit was common to both parties and the Revenue would presumably have alerted the applicant to its prejudicial consequences had it realised it. The tax now claimed was to be regarded as an adventitious windfall accruing to the Revenue through the mistake of an honest and compliant taxpayer. In the circumstances, that claim was so unfair as to amount to an abuse of power. Equally, the Revenue's failure to exercise its statutory discretion to extend the time limit was so unreasonable as to satisfy the public law test of irrationality.

R v Swale Borough Council and Medway Ports Authority ex p The Royal Society for the Protection of Birds (1991): Legitimate expectation of being consulted – test to be applied

Facts

The applicant, a conservation charity with over half a million members, sought to challenge the grant of planning permission by the council to the Authority for the 'land reclamation' of 125 acres of Lappel Bank, a site of recognised environmental importance under domestic and international law. The applicant argued, *inter alia*, that its officer, Dr Clarke, had received an assurance in the course of correspondence that he would be consulted on any application received, and that this legitimate expectation had been breached. The respondents contended that the assurance of consultation had been given only in the context of development proposals already received. It could not reasonably have been taken to extend to any application in the relevant location, and the absence of any immediate protest by the applicants when Dr Clarke was not consulted suggested further that he had, in fact, no legitimate expectation of consultation.

Decision

Simon Brown J noted that Dr Clarke was as convinced that he had been entitled to be consulted as the respondent was that no such entitlement had arisen. The approach to such a misunderstanding being free from authority in public law, Simon Brown J adopted a contractual test; only if the reasonable bystander would regard the promise as being made in the sense contended for by the applicant would his expectation be regarded as not merely reasonable but legitimate also. On the application of this test to the facts, the applicants' contention was to be preferred. However, since they had unduly delayed so that the grant of relief would now be likely to cause substantial prejudice to third parties, their challenge was dismissed.

17.4   Legitimate expectation as a means of securing procedural rights

***Attorney General for Hong Kong v Ng Yuen Shiu* (1983) PC:** Applicant may have legitimate expectation that a particular procedure is followed

Facts
The government of Hong Kong announced that it was terminating its policy of not repatriating illegal immigrants from China who had reached the urban area of Hong Kong. The applicant and others, illegal immigrants of Chinese origin from Macau, sought to clarify their position. They were told by the Secretary for Security that they would be interviewed and that each case would be treated on its own merits. A removal order was made against the applicant.

Decision
The Privy Council held that the removal order would be quashed. Although the applicant, as an illegal immigrant, had no general right to a fair hearing before a removal order was made against him, he had a legitimate expectation of a fair hearing based on what he had been told by the Secretary for Security. When a public authority had promised to follow a certain procedure, it was in the interest of good administration that it should act fairly and should implement its promise, so long as implementation did not interfere with its statutory duty. The quashing of the removal order was, however, entirely without prejudice to the making of a new order once the applicant had been heard.

17.5   Legitimate expectation as a means of securing substantive rights

***R v Secretary of State for the Home Department ex p Khan* (1984) CA:** Applicant may have legitimate expectation that a right will be granted

Facts
The applicant wished to adopt the child of a relative, living with its natural parents in Pakistan. Although the Immigration Rules did not permit a child's entry for these purposes, a Home Office circular stated that, in exceptional circumstances, the Secretary of State would permit entry if specified criteria were met. The criteria appeared to be satisfied in Khan's case, but the Secretary of State applied the additional criterion that the natural parents must be unable to look after the child and refused leave of entry. The applicant sought an order of certiorari.

Decision
The court held, granting the order, that the Home Office circular gave the applicant a legitimate expectation that entry would be granted if the specified criteria were met. The Secretary of State was at liberty to change his policy, but before he did so vis à vis a recipient of the circular, he would be obliged to give full and serious consideration to whether some overriding public interest justified the change.

R v Secretary of State for the Home Department ex p *Ruddock* (1987): Legitimate expectation not limited to right to be heard

Facts

The applicant alleged that the Secretary of State had authorised the interception of her telephone calls in order to gain party political advantage. The criteria governing the issue of interception warrants had been published six times between 1952 and 1982, and adopted by the Secretary of State. The applicant argued that she had a legitimate expectation that the Secretary of State would abide by the criteria when deciding whether to intercept her calls, and that in her case, the criteria were not met. Counsel for the Secretary of State contended that the doctrine of legitimate expectation related only to cases where an applicant's expectation was of being consulted or given the opportunity to make representations before a decision adverse to the applicant was taken. It had no relevance in the present circumstances, where the efficacy of the interception depended on the maintenance of secrecy.

Decision

The court held, dismissing the application, that the applicant's evidence did not establish that the Secretary of State had acted for an improper purpose. However, the applicant did have a legitimate expectation. Although most of the cases on legitimate expectation were concerned with a right to be heard, the doctrine was not so confined. *Per* Taylor J:

> In a case where, *ex hypothesi*, there is no right to be heard, it may be thought the more important to fair dealing that a promise or undertaking given by a Minister as to how he will proceed should be kept.

Here, the expectation arose both from an express promise given on behalf of a public authority, and from the existence of a regular practice which the applicant could reasonably expect to continue. The Secretary of State had adduced evidence that all decisions within his purview had been made in accordance with the criteria, and therefore the applicant's expectation had not been disappointed.

R v Ministry of Agriculture, Fisheries and Food ex p *Hamble (Offshore) Fisheries Ltd* (1995) QBD: Applicant may rely on legitimate expectation that a right will be granted

Facts

See 13.1.1.2 above. Arguing against the substantive legitimate expectation claimed by the applicant (that the beam trawl licence would be transferred to the *Nellie*), counsel for the respondent relied on a passage from the judgment of Laws J in *R v Secretary of State for Transport* ex p *Richmond upon Thames London Borough Council* (1994) to establish that neither precedent nor principle permitted the vindication of substantive legitimate expectations.

Decision

Sedley J noted that *Ruddock* and *Findlay* (*obiter*) had recognised the possibility of substantive legitimate expectations, and continued:

In my respectful view, principle as well as precedent points to these conclusions ... It is difficult to see why it is any less unfair to frustrate a legitimate expectation that something will or will not be done by the decision maker than it is to frustrate a legitimate expectation that the applicant will be listened to before the decision maker decides whether to take a particular step. Such a doctrine does not risk fettering a public body in the discharge of public duties because no individual can legitimately expect the discharge of public duties to stand still or to be distorted because of that individual's peculiar position.

17.6 Considerations overriding legitimate expectations

17.6.1 National security

Council of Civil Service Unions v Minister for the Civil Service (1985) HL: Legitimate expectation that procedure will be followed may be set aside by reason of national security

Facts
See 7.5 above.

Decision
The House of Lords held, proceeding on the basis that the exercise of delegated prerogative powers was justiciable, that, although the staff had no legal right to prior consultation, they had a legitimate expectation to it. Such expectation might arise either from an express promise given by a public authority or, as here, from a regular practice of consultation, which the applicant could reasonably expect to continue. In the absence of evidence that an issue of national security was involved, it would have been proper to grant the declaration sought.

Comment
One of several areas in which the *GCHQ* case broke new ground was that the House of Lords signified that courts would no longer accept submissions that a decision was made on grounds of national security without evidence that national security was actually involved. Previously, assertions of 'national security' had been accepted without inquiry.

17.6.2 The need to preserve freedom of administrative action

R v Secretary of State for Health ex p United States Tobacco (1992): Limitation on circumstances in which legitimate expectation could arise

Facts
The applicant manufactured oral snuff. In 1985, when the government was already aware of a link between oral snuff and cancer, the applicant received a government grant. At the same time, the government obtained the applicant's agreement to place a health warning on its product and not to market it to those aged less than 18 years. In 1988, the Department of Health announced that it intended to ban the manufacture of oral snuff. The applicant sought judicial review on two grounds: first, that the Secretary of State was in breach of a statutory duty to consult it as an affected party and, secondly, that it had a legitimate expectation that it would be permitted to

continue to manufacture snuff as long as it kept to its agreement regarding marketing and the health warning.

Decision
The court held that the applicant would succeed on the first ground and fail on the second. The applicant had no legitimate expectation. *Per* Taylor LJ, the Secretary of State's discretion to change his policy 'could not be fettered by moral obligations to the applicant deriving from the earlier favourable treatment of them'. *Per* Morland J, the applicant 'must have been aware that their expectations could never fetter the Secretary of State's public duty to promote and safeguard the health of the public'.

R v Ministry of Agriculture, Fisheries and Food ex p Hamble (Offshore) Fisheries (1995): Need for balance between public interest and legitimate expectations of individual

Facts
See 13.1.1.2 above.

Decision
The applicant's arguments based on legitimate expectation failed. Legitimacy, in the sense in which it applied to expectations in public law, was not absolute. Its presence was to be gauged by balancing the expectations induced by government and the policy considerations which militated against their fulfilment. Sedley J continued:

> The balance must in the first instance be for the policy maker to strike; but if the outcome is challenged by way of judicial review, I do not consider that the court's criterion is the bare rationality of the policy maker's conclusion. While policy is for the policy maker alone, the fairness of his or her decision not to accommodate reasonable expectations which the policy will thwart remains the court's concern (as of course does the lawfulness of the policy) ... Legitimate expectation is now in effect a term of art, reserved for expectations which are not only reasonable but which will be sustained by the court in the face of changes of policy ... whether this point has been reached is determined by the court, whether on the grounds of rationality, of legality or of fairness, of all of which the court, not the decision maker, is the arbiter.

R v Secretary of State for the Home Department ex p Hargreaves (1996) CA: Test to be applied in deciding cases

Facts
The applicants were three prisoners serving sentences at HMP Risley. Pursuant to rules made by the Secretary of State and in force at the beginning of their sentences, they would have been eligible to apply for periods of home leave after serving one-third of their terms of imprisonment. These rules were communicated to prisoners in the form of a notice and 'compact', setting out responsibilities undertaken by the prison and requiring signed commitments to norms of good behaviour by the prisoners. In response to perceived public concern, the Secretary of State amended the rules by statutory instrument in 1995 with the result that eligibility for home leave accrued only on the completion of half the sentence to be served by a prisoner. The applicants claimed that the change denied them a legitimate expectation on the terms

of the original rules. The Divisional Court dismissed the applications on the grounds that:

(1)   no clear and unambiguous representations had been established; and

(2)   the correct test by which to judge the Secretary of State's change of policy was not the balance of fairness and proportionality, but the public law test of irrationality.

Decision

The Court of Appeal held, upholding the judgment of the Divisional Court, that the principle in *Findlay* (see 17.3 above) disposed of the present case. Although it was to be regretted that the compact and notice had insufficiently stressed the dependence of entitlement to home leave and other privileges upon the regime currently in force, those documents nevertheless suggested that this was the position and certainly contained no contrary indications. Where procedural irregularity was alleged against a minister, it was appropriate to inquire into the fairness of the procedure adopted by him, but where, as in the present case, a substantive defect was alleged, it fell to be judged by the far stricter irrationality test. The contrary suggestion by Sedley J in *Hamble* was inconsistent with authority and heretical.

CHAPTER 18

THE DUTY TO GIVE REASONS

Introduction

The issue of whether and to what extent a decision maker is required to provide persons affected with a statement of reasons for his decision has come to be of increasing importance in recent years. Case law shows that there is no general duty to give reasons, but that a duty based on specific circumstances may arise in individual cases.

18.1   The consequences of failure to give reasons

Padfield v Minister for Agriculture, Fisheries and Food (1968) HL: Failure to give reasons may lead to inference of improper decision

Facts
See 13.4.1 above.

Per Lord Pearce:
If all the *prima facie* reasons seem to point in favour of [the Minister] taking a certain course to carry out the intention of Parliament in respect of a power which it has given to him in that regard, and he gives no reason whatever for taking a contrary course, the court may infer that he has no good reason and that he is not using the power given by Parliament to carry out its intentions.

R v Secretary of State for Trade and Industry ex p Lonrho plc (1989) HL: Restriction of *Padfield* principle

Facts
Lonrho sought judicial review of, *inter alia*, the refusal of the Secretary of State to refer a rival company's acquisition of shares in the House of Fraser group to the Monopolies and Mergers Commission. Lonrho alleged that the refusal to refer was irrational and submitted that the Secretary of State's failure to give reasons for his decision should lead to the conclusion that he had no proper reason for it.

Decision
The House of Lords held, dismissing Lonrho's appeal on these and other grounds, that Lonrho had failed to establish that the Secretary of State had acted irrationally.

Per Lord Keith:
The absence of reasons for a decision where there is no duty to give them cannot of itself provide any support for the suggested irrationality of the decision. The only significance of the absence of reasons is that if all the other known facts and circumstances appear to point overwhelmingly in favour of a different decision, the decision maker who has given no reasons cannot complain if the court draws the inference that he had no rational reason for his decision.

18.2   Circumstances in which the common law imposes a duty to give reasons

***R v Civil Service Appeal Board ex p Cunningham* (1991) CA:** Unusual decision may give rise to duty to give reasons

Facts

The applicant, a prison officer, was dismissed after accusations against him that he had assaulted a prisoner. As a civil servant, he could only seek compensation for unfair dismissal from the Civil Service Appeal Board, rather than from an industrial tribunal. The Board, finding that he had been improperly dismissed, awarded him approximately one-third of the sum he could have expected to receive from an industrial tribunal and gave no reasons for its decision.

Decision

The Court of Appeal held that, in the circumstances, the Board was under a duty to give reasons for its decision. Leggatt LJ considered it obvious that, for reasons of fairness, the applicant should be entitled to know the reasons for the award, so that in the event of error he would be in a position to apply to court for judicial review to challenge it. He had 'a legitimate grievance, because it looks as though his compensation is less than it should be, and yet he has not been told the basis of the assessment'. The absence of reasons did not by itself entitle the court to hold that the award was not supportable, but the unexplained meagreness of the award did compel that inference.

In the view of McCowan LJ, not only had justice not been seen to be done, but also there was no way, in the absence of reasons from the Board, in which it could be judged whether in fact it had been done. McCowan LJ stated that he was influenced by the following factors:

(1)   There was no appeal from the Board's determination of the amount of compensation.

(2)   In making that determination, the Board was carrying out a judicial function.

(3)   The Board was susceptible to judicial review.

(4)   The procedure provided for by the code – the provision of a recommendation without reasons was insufficient to achieve justice.

(5)   There was no statute which required the courts to tolerate that unfairness.

(6)   The giving of short reasons would not frustrate the apparent purpose of the Code for Civil Service Pay and Conditions of Service.

(7)   It was not a case where the giving of reasons would be harmful to the public interest.

Lord Donaldson MR considered that the Board was a judicial body carrying out functions akin to those of an industrial tribunal. Fairness demanded that, just as an industrial tribunal would be under a duty to give reasons by virtue of the Tribunals and Inquiries Act 1958, so the Board should give sufficient reasons for its decision to enable the parties to know the issues to which it addressed its mind and that it acted lawfully.

Doody v Secretary of State for the Home Department (1993) HL: Fairness may give rise to a duty to give reasons

Facts

Mandatory life sentences consisted of two periods of time – a fixed penal period, reflecting the requirements of retribution and deterrence, and the remaining 'risk period', at some time during which the prisoner might be released on licence. There were two inputs into the fixing of the penal period: recommendations made after trial by the trial judge and a decision by the Home Secretary. The applicant argued that he was entitled to be told by the Home Secretary what penal period had been recommended by the judiciary and any departure by the Home Secretary from it. He further claimed that he should be told the reasons both for the judiciary's and the Home Secretary's views. In the Court of Appeal, he succeeded in all but the last of his claims.

Decision

The House of Lords held that he should succeed in the final part of his claim as well. Lord Mustill reiterated that the present law recognises no general duty to give reasons for an administrative decision, but added that in appropriate circumstances a duty might be implied. In the present case, a refusal to give reasons was not fair to the prisoner. It was a matter of unparalleled importance to him. In the case of any other sentence, the prisoner would as a matter of course be told the reasons for it at the time of sentencing:

The prisoner sentenced for murder ... never sees the Home Secretary; he cannot fathom how his mind is working ... I therefore simply ask, is it fair that the mandatory life prisoner should be wholly deprived of the information which all other prisoners receive as a matter of course. I am clearly of opinion that it is not.

Lord Mustill added that he could have arrived at the same conclusion by the route taken in *ex p Cunningham* (above):

I think it important that there should be an effective means of detecting the kind of error which would entitle the court to intervene, and in practice I regard it as necessary for this purpose that the reasoning of the Home Secretary should be disclosed.

R v Mayor, Commonalty and Citizens of London ex p Matson (1996) CA: *Doody* principle applied to non-legal matters

Facts

The applicant sought to be elected an alderman of the Corporation of the City of London (the governing body of the City). The election process consisted of two stages. At the first, the common councilmen of a ward, meeting in a wardmoot, voted whether or not to confirm a candidate as an alderman elect. The applicant received a substantial majority of the votes cast at this stage. At the second stage, the candidate was asked to complete a questionnaire and was then interviewed in private by the court of aldermen. At this stage, his candidacy was rejected by an overwhelming majority. The applicant initially sought either an order of certiorari to quash the decision of the court of aldermen, or an order directing it to reconsider its decision and reach a decision in accordance with the findings of the High Court or the Court of Appeal. On appeal from the rejection of his application by the High Court, the Court of Appeal found that the decision against the applicant could not in itself be impugned on the grounds either of irrationality or procedural unfairness.

Decision

The Court of Appeal held that the applicant's remaining submission that the court of aldermen was under a duty to give reasons for its decision was correct. The decision was not on its face aberrant, but fairness and natural justice required the giving of reasons. This was so because (amongst other considerations) it had been suggested to the applicant in the course of his interview that he had in the past acted in an inappropriate manner and he had been invited to explain himself. In the absence of reasons he had no way of knowing if the refusal of his candidacy arose despite the acceptance of his explanation or because of its rejection. Nor could he know whether to stand for election again and, if so, what further information to supply to the court of aldermen. In the circumstances, his rejection cast a shadow on his reputation. The giving of short reasons would not impede the working of the court of aldermen, but would enable it to ensure that its decisions in every case were sound and manifestly just and in the interests of the City.

R v Secretary of State for the Home Department ex p Al Fayed (1997) CA: Statutory restriction did not oust duty to give reasons

Facts

Section 44(2) of the British Nationality Act 1981 provides:

The Secretary of State ... shall not be required to assign any reason for the grant or referral of any application under this Act the decision on which is at his discretion; and the discretion of the Secretary of State ... on any such application shall not be subject to appeal to, or review in, any court.

The applicants (Mohammed Al Fayed and his brother) sought judicial review of the decision of the Secretary of State to reject their applications for naturalisation. The respondent accepted that s 44(2) did not oust the jurisdiction of the court to review a decision of the Secretary of State under any of the usual heads of judicial review.

Decision

The Court of Appeal held, by a majority, that, in the absence of s 44(2), a duty of fairness was owed to the applicants. The consequences of an adverse decision on naturalisation were of an importance which would give rise to a right to be informed of concerns which might lead to the refusal of the application, and a right to be heard in answer to such concerns. Properly understood, s 44(2) did not negate that duty which, in the instant case, would be met by requiring the Secretary of State to give the applicants sufficient information as to the subject matter of his decision to enable them to make such submissions as they wished. Were it not for s 44(2), the present case was such that reasons for the Secretary of State's refusal should have been given.

18.3 Rationales for the imposition of a duty to give reasons

R v Higher Education Funding Council ex p Institute of Dental Surgery (1994): Circumstances in which duty to give reasons arose

Facts

The Council had power to make grants for research to universities. Grants were awarded according to a rating system administered by the Council. The applicant institute, a university college, had previously been rated three on a scale out of five. In 1992, it was rated two out of five. Its grant was accordingly cut by £270,000. No reasons were given for the downgrading and, in correspondence, the Council refused to give reasons or to permit any appeal. The Institute sought judicial review, contending, *inter alia*, that the Council had acted unfairly in failing to give reasons or, alternatively, that in the absence of reasons, its decision ought to be regarded as irrational.

Decision

The court held, dismissing the application, that no duty would be imposed in the present case. Sedley J reviewed the arguments for and against the requiring of reasons in any given case as follows:

The giving of reasons may among other things concentrate the decision maker's mind on the right questions; demonstrate to the recipient that this is so; show that the issues have been conscientiously addressed and how the result has been reached; or alternatively alert the recipient to a justiciable flaw in the process. On the other side of the argument, it may place an undue burden on decision makers; demand an appearance of unanimity where there is diversity; call for the articulation of sometimes inexpressible value judgments; and offer an invitation to the captious to comb the reasons for previously unsuspected grounds of challenge.

In *Doody*, the nature and impact of the decision itself called for reasons as a routine aspect of procedural fairness. In *Cunningham*, there was a 'trigger factor'; the court could readily evaluate the difference between what the Board had awarded and what an industrial tribunal would have awarded. The court was unable, in the present case, to judge whether the decision of the Council was extraordinary or not; it lacked the necessary academic expertise. In summary, Sedley J said:

(1)   There is no general duty to give reasons for a decision, but there are classes of case where there is such a duty.

(2)   One such class is where the subject matter is an interest so highly regarded by the law – for example, personal liberty – that fairness requires that reasons, at least for particular decisions, should be given as of right.

(3)(a) Another such class is where the decision appears aberrant. Here, fairness may require reasons so that the recipient may know whether the aberration is in the legal sense real (and so challengeable) or apparent.

(3)(b) It follows that this class does not include decisions which are themselves only challengeable by reference to the reasons for them. A pure exercise of academic judgment is such a decision.

CHAPTER 19

PROPORTIONALITY

Introduction

Proportionality is a concept developed in continental jurisdictions rather than by the common law, and involves the premise that a sledgehammer should not be used to crack a nut, so that the measures used to achieve a particular end must be no more than necessary to achieve that end. It did not formally enter English law until the Human Rights Act 1998 came into force, but some movement in this direction can be detected before that date.

19.1 Explicit discussion of disproportionality as a ground of review

19.1.1 The principle as an area for the future development of the common law

Council of Civil Service Unions v Minister for the Civil Service (1985)
HL: Lord Diplock's view

Facts
See 7.5 above.

Per Lord Diplock:
Judicial review has I think developed to a state today when, without reiterating any analysis of the steps by which the development has come about, one can conveniently classify under three heads the grounds on which administrative action is subject to control by judicial review ... That is not to say that further development on a case by case basis may not in the course of time add further grounds. I have in mind particularly the possible adoption in future of the principle of 'proportionality' which is recognised in the administrative law of several of our fellow members of the European Economic Community.

19.1.2 Judicial attitudes to the principle prior to the Human Rights Act

R v Secretary of State for the Home Department ex p Brind (1991)
HL: Proportionality is not part of national law

Facts
See also 3.3.1.

In October 1988, the Secretary of State, acting under the Broadcasting Act 1981, issued directives to the BBC and the IBA prohibiting the broadcasting of 'words spoken' by members or apparent adherents of organisations proscribed under prevention of terrorism legislation. The appellants, who were journalists, alleged, *inter alia*, that the ban infringed their rights to freedom of expression, as guaranteed by the

European Convention on Human Rights, and that it was disproportionate to the ends sought to be achieved.

Decision

The House of Lords held that proportionality was not yet a distinct ground of judicial review. Lord Lowry and Lord Ackner rejected it on the ground that it would inevitably involve consideration of the merits of the decision challenged – a matter entrusted to the decision maker and not to courts of supervisory jurisdiction – though Lord Ackner considered that a decision lacking all proportionality might qualify as *Wednesbury* unreasonable. Lord Lowry added that to accept it would be to encourage a rush of unmeritorious applications for judicial review. Lord Bridge and Lord Roskill accepted that proportionality might in time become an independent ground of review, but denied its application to the present case, Lord Bridge considering that review on the ground of irrationality would achieve a similar end. Lord Templeman, according similar importance to irrationality as a ground of review, noted that proportionality is required by the European Court of Human Rights, and held 'applying these principles' that the Secretary of State's decision was justifiable.

19.2   Implicit use of proportionality in judicial reasoning

R v Secretary of State for Transport ex p Pegasus Holdings (1988): Proportionality may be a factor in deciding whether an executive action is reasonable

Facts

See 16.1.6 above.

Decision

The courts held that, on the facts, there had been no breach of the principles of natural justice or of a duty of fairness. The requirements of fairness had to be considered in all the circumstances of the case.

Per Schiemann J:

One has in the context of fairness to bear in mind, on the one hand, the no doubt substantial economic damage to the applicants and perhaps the irritation and inconvenience that I do not doubt the passengers suffered. On the other hand, one has to bear in mind the magnitude of the risk ...

19.3   Proportionality and the *Wednesbury* test

In *R v Secretary of State for the Home Department ex p Brind* (above), Lord Ackner considered that a decision made with a total lack of proportionality might satisfy the stringent test of *Wednesbury* unreasonableness.

R v Chief Constable of Sussex ex p International Trader's Ferry Ltd (1999) HL: There may be little difference in practical effect between proportionality and *Wednesbury* unreasonableness

Facts

As a result of protests by animal rights groups, the major ferry operators stopped carrying live animals for export during the autumn of 1994. The applicant company began to carry livestock across the Channel from the port of Shoreham on 2 January 1995, and from 4–14 January some 1,125 police officers were deployed in order to allow vehicles to reach the port. The cost of this policing was £1.25 million. The Home Office made it clear that its policy was to refuse to use its powers to award a special grant to Sussex Police in these circumstances. From 14 January, the level of protests was reduced, but policing at the original high level was continued when a shipment took place.

By two 'decision letters' dated 10 and 24 April, the company was informed that this level of policing could not continue, and that the Chief Constable proposed to implement new arrangements which would have the effect of curtailing the company's activities, since police cover would only be provided on two days per week. The decision was based on the impact of this policing on the Chief Constable's resources and on the effective policing of the rest of the force area. The Chief Constable also indicated that, because of the apprehension of a breach of the peace, lorries which attempted to enter the port in the absence of adequate police protection would be turned back. The company could not run economically on this basis and sought judicial review of the Chief Constable's decision.

Decision

The House of Lords held that the Chief Constable was not acting unlawfully. A right to trade lawfully was not an absolute right by which the Chief Constable owed a duty to protect the trader at whatever cost, any more than there was an absolute right to protest lawfully. In a situation where there were conflicting rights and the police had a duty to uphold the law, the police might have to balance a number of factors, not least the likelihood of a serious breach of the peace. In coming to his decisions, the Chief Constable had taken into account the number of men available to him, the rights of others in the area and their protection, and the risk of injury during the demonstration to the drivers, the police and others. He also took account of the right of the company to trade and of the protesters to demonstrate peacefully. It was wrong to overemphasise particular areas where he might have done more or where other chief constables might have reacted in a somewhat different way to particular aspects of the problem.

Per Lord Slynn:

In *Ex p Brind* [above], the House treated *Wednesbury* unreasonableness and proportionality as being different. So in some ways they are, although the distinction between the two tests in practice is in any event much less than is sometimes suggested. The cautious way in which the European Court usually applies this test, recognising the importance of respecting the national authority's margin of appreciation, may mean that whichever test is adopted, and even allowing for a difference in onus, the result is the same.

CHAPTER 20

THE EUROPEAN CONVENTION FOR THE PROTECTION OF HUMAN RIGHTS AND FUNDAMENTAL FREEDOMS

Introduction

This Convention (hereafter 'ECHR' or 'the Convention') was issued in 1951 by the Council of Europe in the political and intellectual milieu of the aftermath of the Second World War and the early years of the Cold War. Recent and current events, the creators of the Convention believed, made it clear that the individual citizen must have positive rights enforceable, if necessary, against the State of which he was a citizen and by a body independent of that State. A European Court of Human Rights ('ECtHR' or 'European Court') was therefore created, with judges representing each of the Member States of the Council of Europe, and a Commission to investigate applications on behalf of the Court.

The UK permitted individuals to make application to the European Court in 1965, but it was only by the Human Rights Act 1998 that the Convention became part of UK domestic law. Cases decided prior to 1 October 2000, when the Human Rights Act took effect, reflect the fact that the UK was bound at the level of international law by the Convention and to give effect to judgments of the European Court (generally by introducing new legislation), but that the Convention was not itself part of national law.

20.1 The Convention and the UK courts before the Human Rights Act

20.1.1 *Statutory discretion need not be exercised in conformity with the Convention*

R v Secretary of State for the Home Department ex p Brind (1991) HL: No scope for interpreting legislation in accordance with Convention principles when there is no ambiguity in that legislation

Facts
In addition to their claim that the consequences of the Secretary of State's decision were disproportionate to the end which he sought to achieve (see 19.1.2 above), the applicants argued that Art 10 of the ECHR was a relevant consideration to which the Secretary of State was bound to have proper regard. Section 29(3) of the Broadcasting Act 1981 conferred on the Secretary of State a discretion to prohibit broadcasting which was otherwise unfettered.

Decision

The House of Lords held that the acceptance of the applicants' submission would result in the effective incorporation of the Convention into English law, and that, since Parliament had refused many opportunities to incorporate it by legislation, Parliament's intention must be deemed to be that the Convention should retain its current status. Lord Ackner acknowledged that reference could be made to the Convention in order to resolve ambiguities in UK legislation, but denied that there was any ambiguity in s 29(3).

R v Morrisey, R v Staines (1997) CA: House of Lords confirms that the Convention is not part of English law

Facts

The appellants, who had been convicted of participation in a financial offence, appealed on the ground that answers given by them in the course of an investigation into the offences had rendered the proceedings unfair and should have been excluded. The answers had been given to an inspector appointed under the Financial Services Act 1986, which provided (by s 177) that such answers should be admissible in evidence. The appellants' argument for exclusion rested on the discretion to exclude contained in s 78 of the Police and Criminal Evidence Act 1984 and on remarks made in *R v Saunders* (1996). In that case, the Court of Appeal had remarked that, if the appellant were to appeal successfully to the ECtHR (which he later did), consideration would have to be given to implementing the effect of that decision in domestic law.

Decision

The Court of Appeal held, dismissing the appeal, that s 177 raised a statutory presumption that the evidence in question was admissible. To exclude the evidence in deference to the decision in the ECtHR would amount to a purported judicial repeal of the domestic law. The ECHR, as interpreted by the ECtHR, remained unenforceable in the English courts. Their Lordships were in express agreement with the appellants' submission that the resulting position was very unsatisfactory, but had no choice but to dismiss the appeal.

R v Director of Public Prosecutions ex p Kebilene and Others (1999): After the Human Rights Act was passed, but before its implementation, courts should have regard to its future effect

Facts

The applicants sought judicial review of the decision of the Director of Public Prosecutions (DPP) to consent to their prosecution for alleged offences under ss 16A and 16B of the Prevention of Terrorism (Temporary Provisions) Act 1989. They argued, *inter alia*, that, pending commencement of the provisions of the Human Rights Act 1998, they had a legitimate expectation that the DPP would exercise his prosecutorial discretion to refuse consent to any prosecution which might be held unsafe after the Convention's incorporation.

Decision

The court held that the claimed expectation did not arise, since the express provisions of the 1998 Act postponing incorporation of the central provisions of the Convention were repugnant to it. However, the compatibility of the Convention with the offences charged was (in the judgment of Lord Bingham of Cornhill CJ) a matter which a conscientious and rational DPP would wish to take into account when exercising his prosecutorial discretion, since an appeal against conviction might well be heard after incorporation of the Convention. On the hypothesis of inconsistency between the offences charged and the Convention, such appeals would be likely to be successful. The DPP had in fact received legal advice on the question of compatibility between the offences and the Convention. It was proper for the court to review the soundness of that advice. In the judgment of Laws LJ, the DPP was obliged to take the compatibility question into account and, since this was a question of law, it was the duty of a court of review to address and decide that issue.

Both judges concluded that the offences were likely to contravene the Convention. The parties were invited to make submissions as to appropriate relief and leave to appeal to the House of Lords was granted in respect of all the questions raised.

20.1.2 *Circumstances justifying reference to the Convention as persuasive authority*

Derbyshire County Council v Times Newspapers Ltd (1992–93) CA and HL: Court of Appeal gives guidance

Facts

The county council brought a libel action against the publishers, editor and two journalists of *The Sunday Times*. The newspapers had printed allegedly defamatory articles concerning the council's management of its superannuation fund. The defendants applied to strike out the statement of claim as disclosing no reasonable cause of action. For the claim to succeed, it was necessary for the plaintiffs to establish that a body corporate should be able to sue for libel. The defendants argued that it should not have that right, since it would be enabled thereby to suppress legitimate criticism of its activities. The defendants submitted that this would be contrary to Art 10 of the European Convention and did not come within the derogation to Art 10. It was unnecessary in a democratic society for a body corporate to have the right to sue for libel, since it could protect its reputation by suing for malicious falsehood or by bringing a prosecution for criminal libel. At first instance, the defendants' submissions were rejected. They appealed to the Court of Appeal.

Decision (1)

The Court of Appeal held, allowing the appeal, that a corporate public authority had no right in common law to sue for libel. In so holding, the court considered Art 10 of the Convention. On the admissibility of the Convention in English courts, Balcombe LJ remarked that, although it had not been incorporated into domestic law, the authorities recognised its relevance in three situations:

(1) Article 10 may be used for the purpose of the resolution of an ambiguity in English primary or subordinate legislation (see *Brind* above).

(2) Article 10 may be used when considering the principles upon which the court should act in exercising a discretion, for example, whether or not to grant an interlocutory injunction (see *AG v Guardian Newspapers Ltd (No 1)* (see 26.1 below).

(3) Article 10 may be used when the common law is uncertain. In *AG v Guardian Newspapers Ltd (No 2)* (see 26.2 below), the courts at all levels had regard to the provisions of Art 10 in considering the extent of the duty of confidence. They did not limit the application of Art 10 to the discretion of the court to grant or withhold an injunction to restrain a breach of confidence.

Even if the common law is certain, the courts will still, when appropriate, consider whether the UK is in breach of Art 10. (As authority for this proposition, Balcombe LJ cited *ex p Choudhury*. See 27.3.2 below.)

The plaintiffs appealed to the House of Lords.

Decision (2)

The House of Lords held, dismissing the appeal, that the judgment of the Court of Appeal would be upheld, but without reliance on the Convention. In the field of freedom of speech, there was no difference in principle between English law and Art 10 of the Convention. Lord Keith added that he found it satisfactory to be able to conclude that the common law of England was consistent with the obligations assumed by the Crown under the Convention in this field.

20.2   Common law procedures for the vindication of fundamental rights

20.2.1   The intensity of judicial review of a decision may be increased proportionately to the importance of the rights which it determines

R v Secretary of State for the Home Department ex p Bugdaycay (1987) HL: Judicial review is more rigorous where rights such as right to life are involved

Facts

The appellants obtained leave to enter the UK by false statements as to their purposes and as to the time for which they intended to stay. In fact, they intended to seek asylum in the UK and, upon being granted entry, each unsuccessfully did so. Orders for their removal were made by the Secretary of State, on the ground that the appellants were illegal entrants. The appellants denied that the facts concealed by them were 'material', in that they were not facts which would have caused the immigration officer to refuse leave to enter. They further claimed that the court had jurisdiction to make a finding on their entitlement to asylum.

Decision

The House of Lords held that the appeals would be dismissed on both grounds. *Per* Lord Bridge:

[The courts are entitled, within limits] to subject an administrative decision to the more rigorous examination, to ensure that it is in no way flawed, according to the gravity of the issue which the decision determines. The most fundamental of all human rights is the individual's right to life and when an administrative decision under challenge is said to be one which may put the applicant's life at risk, the basis of the decision must surely call for the most anxious scrutiny.

20.2.2 The decision maker's failure to maintain a reasonable balance between human rights and competing interests may be subject to review on Wednesbury principles

R v Secretary of State for the Home Department ex p Brind (1991) HL: Failure to uphold Convention rights may be susceptible to judicial review

Facts
See 19.1.2 above.

Decision
With reference to his conclusion that, in the absence of legislation incorporating the Convention into English law, the Secretary of State's decision could not be impugned on the grounds that it did not properly take Art 10 into consideration, Lord Bridge added:

But I do not accept that this conclusion means that the courts are powerless to prevent the exercise by the executive of administrative discretions, even when conferred, as in the instant case, in terms which are on their face unlimited, in a way which infringes fundamental human rights. Thus, Art 10(2) of the Convention spells out and categorises the competing public interests by reference to which the right to freedom of expression may have to be curtailed. In exercising the power of judicial review, we have neither the advantages or the disadvantages of any comparable code to which we may refer or by which we are bound. But, again, this surely does not mean that in deciding whether the Secretary of State, in the exercise of his discretion, could reasonably impose the restriction he has imposed on the broadcasting organisations, we are not perfectly entitled to start from the premise that any restriction of the right to freedom of expression requires to be justified and that nothing less than an important competing public interest will be sufficient to justify it.

20.2.3 The common law requires a substantial public interest justification for the infringement of fundamental rights

R v Cambridge Area Health Authority ex p B (1995) Divisional Court and CA: Decision held unlawful on the basis that applicant's right to life was a relevant factor which had not been taken into consideration

Facts
The applicant, a girl aged 10 years, applied through her father as next friend for certiorari to quash the Authority's decision to refuse her further medical treatment (principally a second bone marrow transplant after the failure of the first). She suffered from leukaemia, and was virtually certain to die in the very near future if the treatment were withheld. Her chances of recovery with the treatment were put at 10–20% at best.

Decision

The court held, *per* Laws J, granting the order and remitting the matter to the Authority, that it had not taken into consideration the wishes of the applicant's father and, further, that it had taken a decision which interfered with the applicant's right to life. Respect for that and other fundamental human rights was not merely a matter of international obligation under the European Convention. It was of the same substance as the English common law. Decisions assaulting such rights could only be justified on substantial public interest grounds. The Authority had not sufficiently explained the priorities which had led it to deprive the applicant of her chance of life. On this (and other) grounds, an order of certiorari would be granted.

Decision on appeal

The Court of Appeal held, on appeal, that the order would be discharged, since the legality of the Authority's decision could not be faulted. The court did not refer to the reasoning of Laws J summarised above.

Comment

The treatment was subsequently funded by an anonymous donor, but the applicant died.

R v Ministry of Defence ex p Smith and Others (1996) CA: Approach of courts when human rights are in issue

Facts

See 14.3 above.

Decision

The test for irrationality proposed by counsel for three of the appellants (and approved by the Court of Appeal) included a direction to take account of human rights issues:

The court may not interfere with the exercise of an administrative discretion on substantive grounds save where the court is satisfied that the decision is unreasonable in the sense that it is beyond the range of responses open to a reasonable decision maker. But in judging whether the decision maker has exceeded this margin of appreciation, the human rights context is important. The more substantial the interference with human rights, the more the court will require by way of justification before it is satisfied that the decision is reasonable in the sense outlined above.

The Court of Appeal did not comment at length on the differential intensity of review made explicit by this approach. In the Divisional Court, however, Simon Brown LJ cited the authorities on judicial review in the human rights context, and stated that:

... They emphasise that, within the limited scope of review open to it, the court must be scrupulous to ensure that no recognised ground of challenge is in truth available to the applicant before rejecting his application ... [However] even where fundamental human rights are being restricted, 'the threshold of unreasonableness' is not lowered. On the other hand, the Minister on judicial review will need to show that there is an important competing public interest which he could reasonably judge sufficient to justify the restriction and he must expect his reasons to be closely scrutinised. Even that approach, therefore, involves a more intensive review process and a greater readiness to intervene than would ordinarily characterise a judicial review challenge.

R v Secretary of State for Home Department ex p McQuillan (1995): Despite the general statements above, a court determining a specific case was bound by precedents relating to the matter at issue

Facts

The applicant, a former member of the Irish Republican Socialist Party, a proscribed organisation, sought review of the decision of the Secretary of State to refuse to revoke successive exclusion orders made against him under the Prevention of Terrorism (Temporary Provisions) Act 1989. He argued that the effect of the order, barring him from entering Great Britain, was to confine him to the one part of the UK where his life and his family's safety were most at risk.

Decision

The court held that, if it were possessed of the information held by the Secretary of State, its task would be to determine whether the Secretary of State's decision lay within the band of rational decisions available in a case which potentially called in question the right to life. Sedley J stated that rationality would be measured in this context by (among other things) asking whether, in the light of its impact, the exclusion order could reasonably be considered an expedient response by a Home Secretary who has given proper weight to the fundamental right thereby put at risk. However, this approach was not available in the present case, where the Crown's evidence had to be regarded in the light of authority as sufficient to invoke national security interests precluding further review.

The applicant had claimed rights under European law. Questions affecting the extent of those rights had already been referred to the European Court of Justice, and the present application would be stayed (without stay of the exclusion order) pending the outcome of those references.

R v Lord Saville of Newdigate and Others ex p A and Others (1999)

See 14.4 above.

20.2.4 *General statutory words are deemed insufficient to permit the infringement of fundamental rights*

Pierson v Secretary of State for the Home Department (1997) HL: If Parliament wishes to oust the protection given to fundamental rights, it must do so in express words

Facts

The appellant was serving two mandatory life sentences for the murder of his parents. The Home Secretary's predecessor increased the tariff period of the sentence to 20 years, beyond that recommended by the judiciary, on the mistaken view that the murders had been characterised by certain aggravating features. His successor, although aware of the error, left the tariff period unaltered. The appellant sought judicial review of the latter decision. The Court of Appeal overturned a first instance decision in the appellant's favour.

Decision

The House of Lords held, by a majority, that the appeal would be allowed. While s 35(2) of the Criminal Justice Act 1991 entrusted the power to take decisions relating to the release of life prisoners to the Home Secretary and was wide enough to authorise the fixing of a tariff, it did not follow that it was wide enough to permit a retrospective increase in the level of punishment once the tariff had been fixed and communicated to the prisoner. The Home Secretary's power was to be subject to the interpretive principle of legality, which was explained by Lord Browne-Wilkinson (dissenting) in the following words:

A power conferred by Parliament in general terms is not to be taken to authorise the doing of acts by the donee of the power which adversely affects the legal rights of the citizen or the basic principles on which the law of the United Kingdom is based unless the statute conferring the power makes it clear that such was the intention of Parliament.

20.3   The attitude of the European Court of Justice

***Nold v Commission of the European Communities* Case 4/73 (1974) ECJ:** International agreements (such as the Convention) have some bearing on EU law

Facts

In 1969, the Commission authorised the merger of the mining companies of the Ruhr into a single company, Ruhrkohle. At a later date, the Commission promulgated new trading rules fixing the conditions required to be met for acquisition of the status of direct wholesaler of coal. Among the conditions was the requirement to buy at least 6,000 tonnes of coal from Ruhrkohle. Nold, a coal wholesaler and building merchant, complained that it could not attain this minimum quota. It claimed that it was the victim of discrimination, since, unlike its competitors, it would now have to deal to its disadvantage through an intermediary. It further argued that its fundamental rights had been violated, namely the right to free development of the personality and the right to freedom of economic action. In the result, its very existence was endangered.

Decision

The Court held that Nold had been treated no differently from any other undertakings, and that it had therefore not been the victim of discrimination. With regard to the matter of fundamental rights, Nold had no more than a commercial interest, the uncertainties of which were part of the very essence of economic activity. It was for Nold to acknowledge the changes which had taken place and to carry out the necessary adaptations. The action would be dismissed. The Court included the following observations in its judgment:

As the Court had already stated, fundamental rights form an integral part of the general principles of law, the observance of which it ensures.

In safeguarding these rights, the Court is bound to draw inspiration from constitutional traditions common to the Member States, and it cannot therefore uphold measures which are incompatible with fundamental rights recognised and protected by the constitutions of those States.

Similarly, international treaties for the protection of human rights on which the Member States have collaborated or to which they are signatories, can supply guidelines which should be followed within the framework of Community law.

CHAPTER 21

THE HUMAN RIGHTS ACT 1998

21.1 Rationale for passing the Act

White Paper: *Rights Brought Home: The Human Rights Bill*, October 1997 (Cm 3782), paras 1.11–1.17:

(a) When the UK ratified the European Convention for the Protection of Human Rights (ECHR) in 1951, the view was taken that the rights and freedoms which the Convention guarantees were already fully protected in UK law.

(b) The European Court of Human Rights (ECtHR) explicitly confirmed that it was not necessary for a Member State to incorporate the Convention into domestic law in order to fulfil the obligations arising under the Convention.

(c) However, since 1951 all the States other than the UK which are parties to the Convention have incorporated or are in the process of incorporating the Convention into domestic law or have domestic legislation guaranteeing similar rights.

(d) As a result of non-incorporation, the Convention rights, originally drafted with major input from British lawyers, are no longer seen as British rights. And enforcing them takes too long and costs too much ... Bringing these rights home will mean that the British people will be able to argue for their rights in the British courts – without this inordinate delay and cost. It will also mean that the rights will be brought much more fully into the jurisprudence of the UK and their interpretation will thus be far more subtly and powerfully woven into our law. And there will be another distinct benefit. British judges will be able to make a distinctively British contribution to the development of the jurisprudence of human rights in Europe.

(e) In the government's view, the approach which the UK has previously adopted towards the Convention does not sufficiently reflect its importance and has not stood the test of time.

(f) This is demonstrated by the number of occasions on which the Commission and ECtHR have found violations of the Convention against the UK, frequently because there has been no domestic framework by which an executive action or decision can be tested against the requirements of the Convention, but only against the requirements of domestic law.

Comment

Note that the White Paper does not allege any large-scale problem of absence of human rights in the UK. Their arguments are more subtle and seem to be concerned with form rather more than substance.

21.2 Summary of the Act's provisions

(1) In all cases where Convention rights are in question, the Act extends and gives 'further effect' to the Convention by:

    (a) obliging UK courts to decide all cases before them (whether under statute or common law) in compatibility with Convention rights unless prevented from doing so by primary legislation which cannot be read compatibly with the Convention, or by delegated legislation made under such primary legislation;

(b) introducing a new obligation on courts to interpret existing and future legislation in compatibility with the Convention where possible;

(c) requiring courts to take ECtHR case law into account in all cases, in so far as they consider it relevant to proceedings before them.

(2) The Act does not make Convention rights directly enforceable in proceedings brought against a private litigant, nor against a quasi-public body acting in its private capacity. However, the Convention has an indirect effect in such cases, through the courts' obligation to construe the law, where possible, in compliance with the Convention.

(3) Section 7 creates directly enforceable rights against public bodies and against quasi-public bodies when exercising their public functions, by:

(a) creating a new ground for judicial review;

(b) creating a new course of action against public bodies which fail to act in compliance with the Convention;

(c) making Convention rights available as a defence in cases brought by public bodies against private bodies.

(4) The Act will not permit the Convention to be used so as to override primary legislation. If a statute that is clear in its terms is incompatible with the Convention, the courts must give it effect. This is also true of delegated legislation made under incompatible primary legislation. This preserves the concept of Parliamentary supremacy. However, in such circumstances the higher courts have power to issue a 'declaration of incompatibility' and the government may make use of a special fast-track procedure under s 10 to amend the legislation so as to remove the incompatibility.

21.3   The Act in detail

Section 1:

(1) 'Convention rights' are those set out in —

(a) Arts 2–12 and 14 of the Convention;

(b) Arts 1–3 of Protocol 1;

(c) Arts 1–2 of Protocol 6

as read with Arts 16–18.

Section 2:

(1) A court or tribunal determining any question which has risen in connection with a Convention right must take into account any —

(a) Judgment, decision, declaration or advisory opinion of the ECtHR;

(b) Opinion of the Commission;

(c) Decision of the Commission;

(d) Decision of the Committee of Ministers of the Council of Europe

whenever made or given, in so far as it is, in the opinion of the court or tribunal, relevant to the proceedings.

Section 3:

(1) *So far as it is possible to do so,* primary legislation and subordinate legislation must be read and given effect in a way which is compatible with the Convention rights.

(2) This section —

(a) Applies to primary and subordinate legislation whenever enacted;

(b) Does not affect the validity, continuing operation or enforcement of any incompatible primary legislation; and

(c) Does not affect the validity, continuing operation or enforcement of any incompatible subordinate legislation if (disregarding any possibility of revocation) primary legislation prevents removal of the incompatibility.

Comment

Note that courts are only required to interpret UK legislation into conformity with the Convention 'so far as is possible'. Further, the courts have no power to set aside UK legislation on the grounds of incompatibility with the Convention. This preserves parliamentary supremacy and would seem to be the true reason for the Act's failure to incorporate Art 13 (requirement to provide effective remedies for breach of Convention rights), although the Act's sponsors have claimed repeatedly that this is not the case. As under the Act a court cannot set aside UK legislation, and a declaration of incompatibility under s 4 does not affect the parties to the case in respect of which it is made, the Act does not go far enough to satisfy Art 13.

Section 4:

(2) If a court is satisfied that a provision of primary legislation is incompatible with a Convention right, it may make a declaration of that incompatibility.

(4) If a court is satisfied that a provision of subordinate legislation, made in accordance with a power conferred by primary legislation, is incompatible with the Convention, it may make a declaration of incompatibility.

(5) 'Court' in this section is limited to —

(a) House of Lords;

(b) Judicial Committee of the Privy Council;

(c) Courts-Martial Appeal Court;

(d) The High Court;

(e) The Court of Appeal.

(6) A declaration of incompatibility —

(a) Does not affect the validity, continuing operation or enforcement of the provision in question; and

(b) Is not binding on the parties to the proceedings in which it is made.

Section 6:

(1) It is unlawful for a *public authority* to act in a way which is incompatible with a Convention right;

(2) Unless as the result of one or more provisions of primary legislation, the authority could not have acted differently.

(3) 'Public authority' *includes* —

(a) A court or tribunal;

(b) Any person *certain* of whose functions are of a *public nature*, but not in relation to acts which are of a *private nature* (s 6(5)), but does not include either House of Parliament or a person exercising functions in connection with proceedings in Parliament, nor the House of Lords in its legislative capacity (s 6(4)).

Section 7:

(1)   A person who claims that a public authority has acted (or proposes to act) in a way contrary to s 6(1) may —
      (a) Bring proceedings against the authority under this Act in the appropriate court or tribunal; or
      (b) Rely on the Convention right or rights concerned in any legal proceedings but only if he is or would be a victim of that unlawful act.

(4)   Proceedings must be brought within one year of the act complained of, unless the court or tribunal sees fit to extend this limit.

Section 8:

(1)   In relation to any act (or proposed act) of a public authority which the court finds is (or would be) unlawful, it may grant such relief or remedy, or make such order, within its powers, as it considers just and appropriate.

(2)   Damages may be awarded only by a court which has power to award damages in civil proceedings.

(3)   No award of damages is to be made unless the court is satisfied that the award is necessary to afford just satisfaction to the person in whose favour it is made, having regard to all the circumstances of the case, including —
      (a) Any other relief or remedy granted;
      (b) The consequences of any decision in relation to the act in question.

(4)   In determining —
      (a) Whether to award damages;
      (b) The amount of any award
      the court must take into account the principles applied by the ECtHR in relation to the award of compensation under Art 41.

Comment

'Public authority' is not defined. See 21.6 below.

Section 10:

(1)   The power in s 10(2) applies if —
      (a) A declaration of incompatibility has been made under s 4 and all rights of appeal have come to an end; or
      (b) If it appears to a Minister of the Crown or Her Majesty in Council that having regard to a finding of the ECtHR made in proceedings against the UK after this section came into force, a legislative provision is incompatible with a UK obligation arising from the Convention.

(2)   If a Minister of the Crown considers that there are *compelling reasons* for proceeding under this section, he may by order and following the procedure set out in sch 2, make such amendments to the legislation *as he considers necessary to remove the incompatibility.*

Comment

'Compelling reason' is not defined, and the remarks of the responsible Ministers during the Committee Stage of the Bill in the Commons suggest that this phrase was introduced in order to assuage the fears of the House that these powers would be used routinely to amend primary legislation. However, the then Home Secretary's words suggest that 'compelling' is less stringent than 'exceptional' and the words of the

Parliamentary Under-Secretary for the Home Department suggest that the phrase 'compelling reason' is intended to be applied in a broad and flexible manner (see *Hansard* HC, 24 June 1998, col 1140 and 21 October 1998 cols 1300–58).

At the date of writing, the powers available under s 10 have yet to be used.

Section 12:

(1)   This section applies if a court is considering whether to grant any relief which, if granted, might affect the exercise of the Convention right to freedom of expression.

(2)   If the person against whom the application for relief is made ('the respondent') is neither present nor represented, no such relief is to be granted unless the court is satisfied —
    (a) That the applicant has taken all practical steps to notify the respondent; and
    (b) That there are compelling reasons why the respondent should not be notified.

(3)   No such relief is to be granted so as to restrain publication before trial unless the court is satisfied that the applicant is likely to establish that publication should not be allowed.

(4)   The court must have particular regard to the importance of the Convention right to freedom of expression, and, where the proceedings relate to material which the respondent claims, or which appears to the court, to be journalistic, literary or artistic material, to —
    (a) The extent to which —
        (i)   The material has, or is about to become, available to the public; or
        (ii) If it is, or would be, in the public interest for the material to be published;
    (b) Any relevant privacy code.

Comment

This section was inserted as an amendment during the passage of the Human Rights Bill through Parliament to placate the newspaper lobby, who were concerned that the incorporation of Art 8 into UK law would unduly restrict their activities. It has been criticised for duplication. It provides that, generally speaking, no injunction to forbid publication will be granted *ex parte*, rather than being granted routinely so as to preserve the status quo between the parties prior to a full trial of the issues. In relation to s 12(4), 'journalistic, literary or artistic material' and 'public interest' are not defined.

Section 19:

(1)   A Minister of the Crown in charge of a Bill before either House of Parliament must, before the Second Reading of the Bill —
    (a) Make a statement [in writing] that in his view the provisions of the Bill are compatible with Convention rights ('a statement of compatibility'); or
    (b) Make a statement to the effect that although he is unable to make a statement of compatibility, the Government nevertheless wishes the House to proceed with the Bill.

21.4   Applying the Act

The Act came into force on 2 October 2000. Case law from before that date is predicated on the fact that the Convention was not part of English law, although it might be used as a tool in the interpretation of law (see Chapter 20 above). Case law since that date shows that where a breach of Convention rights is alleged, the courts will first endeavour to interpret the English law at issue, whether statute or common law, in a manner compatible with the relevant Convention right, and only where this is impossible will they issue a declaration of incompatibility.

The leading cases in this area have dealt with the application of Arts 8 and 10 to the issue of injunctions to prohibit publication by the press of specific material concerning individuals.

Douglas v Hello! Ltd (2001) CA: Approach to interpretation of national law when Arts 8 and 10 are involved

Facts

The claimants, both well known film and television stars, married in New York in November 2000. They gave the third claimants, publishers of *OK!* Magazine, exclusive rights to publish photographs of the wedding and took steps to ensure that no photographs would be taken other than by *OK!*'s photographers. *Hello!* obtained unauthorised photographs and the claimants sought an injunction to prevent publication. An interim injunction was obtained until trial or further order and *Hello!* appealed. Following the coming into force of the Human Rights Act, the Court of Appeal considered the inter-relationship between the right to respect for private life contained in Art 8, the right to freedom of expression in Art 10, and the provisions of s 12 of the Human Rights Act. In particular, under s 12(3), no relief was to be granted so as to restrain publication before trial unless the court was satisfied that the applicant was likely to establish that publication should not be allowed.

Decision

(1)   The Court of Appeal held that, on its true construction, s 12(3) did not seek to give priority to one Convention right over another. It simply dealt with the interlocutory stage of proceedings and the approach the court should take in advance of any ultimate balance which might be struck between rights which were in potential conflict. The court had to consider the merits of the case, including the application of the exceptions in Art 10(2), rather than merely considering, as under the common law, whether there was a serious issue to be tried.

(2)   Here, the first two claimants were likely to establish that publication should not be permitted on confidentiality grounds, or were likely at trial to establish an actionable breach of their privacy. However, the dominant feature of the case was that the greater part of their privacy had been traded as a commodity in the hands of the publishers of *OK!* That could be dealt with by an award of damages, so that the injunction would be discharged.

Venables and Thompson v News Group Newspapers Ltd (2001) Family Division: Approach where Convention rights conflict, and right to life is involved

Facts

In November 1993, the appellants, both then aged 11, were convicted of the murder of two year old James Bulger. The facts and circumstances of the murder were unusually shocking and not only received wide media publicity, but aroused intense public feeling. The appellants were sentenced under s 53(1) of the Children and Young

Persons Act 1933 to be detained at Her Majesty's pleasure. They were placed in separate local authority secure units and injunctions were imposed to prevent publicity about them or their whereabouts, to last until they reached the age of 18. Both reached the age of 18 in August 2000. In July 2000, they made application for injunctions in the same terms to continue indefinitely. There was evidence that the appellants would be at risk of death or serious injury from vengeful members of the public following their release if their identities and whereabouts became known.

Decision

The court held:

(1)   In private law actions such as this, the Convention did not give rise to freestanding causes of action based on Convention rights, but the court, as a public authority, was required to act in a manner compatible with Convention rights when adjudicating on common law causes of action. By virtue of s 12(4) of the Human Rights Act, the court was required to give direct effect to the right of freedom of expression under Art 10.

(2)   By virtue of Art 10(1), the freedom of the media to publish could not be restricted unless the grounds for restriction fell within the exceptions in Art 10(2), which were to be construed narrowly. The onus lay on those seeking the restrictions to show that they were in accordance with the law, necessary in a democratic society to achieve one of the pressing social needs contained in Art 10(2) and proportionate to the aim pursued.

(3)   Taking into account the Convention rights secured by Arts 2 and 3 (right to life and prohibition of torture and inhuman or degrading treatment), together with the right to respect for a person's private life, home and correspondence in Art 8, the law of confidence could, exceptionally, cover information as to the identity or whereabouts of individuals where disclosure would put them at risk of death or serious injury. In such circumstances, the need for restrictions on freedom of expression would fall within the exceptions contained in Art 10(2).

(4)   On the evidence, the disclosure of the new identities to be granted to the claimants on release would have disastrous consequences for them, and in order to afford them the protection to which they were entitled, the court would grant permanent injunctions against the world protecting information as to their identities, whereabouts and appearance.

Per Dame Elizabeth Butler-Sloss P:

… The starting point is … the well recognised position of the press, and their right and duty to be free to publish … I am being asked to extend the domestic law of confidence to grant injunctions in this case. I am satisfied that I can only restrict the freedom of the media to publish if the need for those restrictions can be shown to fall within the exceptions set out in Article 10(2). In considering the limits to the law of confidence, and whether a remedy is available to the claimants within those limits, I must interpret narrowly those exceptions. In doing so and having regard to Articles 2, 3 and 8 it is important to have regard to the fact that the rights under Articles 2 and 3 are not capable of derogation, and the consequences to the claimants if those rights were to be breached. It is clear that, on the basis that there is a real possibility that they may be the objects of revenge attacks, the potential breaches of Articles 2, 3 and 8 have to be evaluated with great care.

Dame Elizabeth Butler-Sloss P went on to say that protection of the claimants' future identities was critical as that was the key to protecting them from revenge attacks, and that the risk of such attacks displaced the right of the media to publish information about the claimants without any restriction imposed by the court. Further, the grant of the proposed injunction answered the 'pressing social need' of protecting the claimants, and its terms as drafted were proportionate to the aim. The injunction therefore fell within the exceptions to the Art 10 principle of freedom of expression contained in Art 10(2).

21.5   Declaration of incompatibility

***R (on the Application of Alconbury Developments Ltd) v Secretary of State for the Environment, Transport and the Regions* (2001) HL:** Availability of judicial review of administrative decisions might satisfy requirements of Art 6

Facts
It was argued, in a number of conjoined applications, that various of the Secretary of State's powers under the Town and Country Planning Acts were incompatible with Art 6(1), as the Secretary of State's role in the making of policy meant that he had such an interest in individual decisions that he could not be regarded as an independent and impartial tribunal, and there was no appeal from his decisions on issues of fact or merit. The Queen's Bench Divisional Court ruled that the availability of judicial review did not render the provisions compatible with Art 6(1) and so granted declarations of incompatibility. The Secretary of State appealed to the House of Lords.

Decision
The House of Lords held that the powers at issue were not incompatible with Art 6(1). The jurisprudence of the ECtHR did not require judicial control of administrative decisions made by ministers answerable to Parliament to constitute an appeal on the merits. Judicial review of such decisions was sufficient to satisfy the requirements of Art 6(1).

***Wilson v First County Trust Ltd* (2001) CA:** First occasion on which a declaration of incompatibility is granted – guidance as to circumstances in which a declaration should be made

Facts
In January 1999, the claimant signed a loan agreement with the defendant pawnbroker, using her car as security. This constituted a regulated agreement under the Consumer Credit Act 1974, which provided that a regulated agreement which had not been executed in accordance with the terms of s 61(1) was only enforceable by the creditor if a court made an order under s 65(1). Under s 127(3), such an order could only be made if the debtor had signed a document containing all the 'prescribed terms' of the agreement, including the 'amount of the credit' (the sum actually borrowed). The issue between the parties was whether the amount of the credit stated should or should not have included a 'document fee' of £250. The Court of Appeal, on

appeal by the claimant from the making of a s 65(1) order, held that the amount of the credit had not been correctly stated, that the agreement fell within s 127(3) and was therefore unenforceable. The Court of Appeal also indicated that it was considering whether to make a declaration under s 4 of the Human Rights Act that s 127(3) was incompatible with the right to a fair hearing under Art 6(1) and the prohibition against depriving a person of his possessions under Art 1 of the First Protocol of the Convention. On its adjourned hearing on the issue of compatibility, the Court of Appeal was required to determine whether:

(1)   the relevant provisions of the HRA had any application, given that the loan agreement pre-dated the implementation of the Act;

(2)   if so, the provisions of s 127(3) were incompatible with a Convention right granted to the pawnbroker;

(3)   if so, it was possible to give effect to s 127(3) in a way which was compatible with that Convention right.

If that were not possible, a declaration of incompatibility should be granted.

Decision

The Court of Appeal held:

(1)   Section 127(3) was incompatible with the pawnbroker's Convention rights, which were engaged by the restriction on the enforcement of the creditor's contractual rights.

(2)   The critical question was whether the exclusion of any judicial remedy in a case such as this was legitimate. The policy aim of s 127(3) was a legitimate one, but it did not automatically follow that the means of achieving it were also legitimate. The means would not be legitimate if Convention rights were infringed to an extent which was disproportionate to the policy aim. This was the effect of the prohibition imposed by s 127(3) against the making of an enforcement order in cases where the document signed by the debtor did not include the prescribed terms. There was no reason why the legitimate policy aim should not be achieved by giving the court power to do what was just in each individual case.

(3)   It was not possible to interpret s 127(3) in a way compatible with the pawnbroker's Convention rights. The court should exercise its discretion to make a declaration of incompatibility for three reasons:

   (a)   the point had been fully identified and argued at a special hearing for that purpose alone;

   (b)   since the court had held that the order which it would have been required to make by a non-Convention interpretation of s 127(3) was incompatible with Convention rights, it could not lawfully make that order unless satisfied that s 127(3) could not be interpreted in a way compatible with Convention rights, thereby giving jurisdiction to make a declaration of incompatibility;

   (c)   a declaration provided a basis for a Minister of the Crown to consider whether there were compelling reasons for making amendments to the legislation by means of a remedial order under s 10 of and Sched 2 to the Human Rights Act.

R v Shayler (2002) HL: Example of case in which declaration was not granted

Facts
The defendant, a former member of the Security Service, was charged with unlawful disclosure of secret information to the press contrary to ss 1 and 4 of the Official Secrets Act 1989. He claimed that these disclosures had been made in the public and national interest. The judge held a preparatory hearing under the Criminal Procedure and Investigations Act 1996, at which he ruled, *inter alia*, that no public interest defence was available to the defendant, and that ss 1 and 4 were compatible with the right to freedom of expression under Art 10. The defendant appealed to the Court of Appeal and thence to the House of Lords.

Decision
(1) Sections 1 and 4 were compatible with Art 10. Although there could be no doubt that they restricted the defendant's *prima facie* right to freedom of expression, the need to preserve the secrecy of information relating to intelligence and military operations in order to counter terrorism and other hostile activities had been recognised by both the European Court and the European Commission. The acid test was whether, in all the circumstances, the interference with the individual's right of free expression was greater than required to meet the State's legitimate object (a proportionality argument).

(2) The 1989 Act had to be taken in context. The prohibition on disclosure imposed by the Act on a former member of the Security Service was not absolute, but rather a ban on disclosure without lawful authority. Under s 7(3), there were two circumstances in which disclosure might be made lawfully:

    (a) if he had concerns about, *inter alia*, the lawfulness of what the Service was doing, he might make disclosure as appropriate to a staff counsellor, the Attorney General, the Director of Public Prosecutions, the Commissioner of the Metropolitan Police, or the Prime Minister or other ministers (s 7(3)(a));

    (b) if, following such disclosure, effective action was not taken or there remained facts which should, in the public interest, be revealed to a wider audience, the former member might seek official authorisation to make disclosure to such an audience (s 7(3)(b)). Judicial review was available in respect of a decision to refuse such authorisation.

Further, by s 9(1), the consent of the Attorney General was required for prosecution under the Act.

These procedures, properly applied, provided sufficient safeguards to ensure that unlawful acts could be reported to those with power to take effective action, that the power to withhold authorisation to publish was not abused and that proper disclosures were not stifled. It was necessary that a former member of the Security Service should avail himself of the procedures available under the Act. Such a person, prosecuted for making an unauthorised disclosure, could not defend himself by claiming that disclosure under s 7(3)(a) or seeking authorisation under s 7(3)(a) would have brought no result.

21.6   Public authority

Under s 6, a 'public authority' will act unlawfully if it acts in a way which contravenes a Convention right, unless UK legislation makes it impossible to act in accordance with the Convention. Effectively, therefore, s 6 creates an additional ground for judicial review, with the extra element over normal judicial review that the courts are permitted to apply the doctrine of proportionality, and so consider issues of merit as well as legality.

'Public authority' is not defined in the Act and is capable of being construed to include any body which has some functions which are public in nature, when exercising one of those functions, although the two Houses of Parliament are specifically excluded from being 'public authorities' for the purpose of the Act. As yet, the issue of what is a public authority has not been specifically addressed by the courts.

Lord Irvine of Lairg, House of Lords, Second Reading (*Hansard* HL, 16 November 1997, col 1231):

We decided ... that a provision of this kind should apply only to public authorities, however defined, and not to private individuals ... We also decided that we should apply the Bill to a wide rather than a narrow range of public authorities, so as to provide as much protection as possible to those who claim that their rights have been infringed.

[Section 6] is designed to apply not only to obvious public authorities such as government departments and the police, but also to bodies which are public in some respects but not in others. Organisations of this kind will be liable ... for any of their acts, unless the act is of a private nature. Finally, [s 6] does not impose a liability on organisations which have no public functions at all.

Lord Irvine of Lairg, House of Lords, Committee Stage (*Hansard* HL, 24 November 1998, col 784):

... I tend to believe that the important function of the Press Complaints Commission to adjudicate on complaints from the public about the press may well be held to be a function of a public nature, so that ... the PCC might well be held to be a public authority under the Human Rights Bill ... There are some bodies which are obviously public authorities, such as the police, the courts, government departments and prisons. They are obviously public authorities ... However, under s 6(3)(c) the term 'public authority' includes, 'any person certain of whose functions are functions of a public nature' ... [One should] abstain from asking the question: is this a public authority just looking at the body in the round? That is what [s 6(1)] invites us to do. However, [s 6(3)(c)] asks whether the body in question has certain functions – not all – which are functions of a public nature. If it has any functions of a public nature, it qualifies as a public authority. However, it is certain acts by public authorities which this Act makes unlawful ... Railtrack, as a public utility, obviously qualifies as a public authority because some of its functions, for example its functions in relation to safety on the railway, qualify it as a public authority. However, acts carried out in its capacity as a private property developer would no doubt be held by the courts to be of a private nature and therefore not caught by the [Act].

Jack Straw, House of Commons, Second Reading (*Hansard* HC, 16 February 1998, col 775):

Under the Convention, the government are answerable in Strasbourg for any acts or omissions of the State about which an individual has a complaint under the Convention. The government have a direct responsibility for core bodies, such as central government and the police, but they also have a responsibility for other public authorities, in so far as the actions of such authorities impinge on private individuals.

The Bill had to have a definition of a public authority that went at least as wide and took account of the fact that, over the past 20 years, an increasingly large number of private bodies, such as companies or charities, have come to exercise public functions that were previously exercised by public authorities. Under UK domestic law, such bodies have increasingly been held to account under the processes of judicial review ... It was not practicable to list all the bodies to which the Bill's provisions should apply. Nor would it have been wise to do so. What was needed instead was a statement of principle to which the courts could give effect. [s 6] therefore adopts a non-exhaustive definition of a public authority. Obvious public authorities, such as central government and the police, are caught in respect of everything they do. Public – but not private – acts of bodies that have a mix of public and private functions are also covered.

Comment

Do these statements clarify matters at all? One might argue that even bodies which Mr Straw categorises as entirely public authorities still have some functions which are essentially private in nature. The Ministry of Defence is a very considerable landowner, for example, and some of that land is let to tenant farmers. Would its actions in respect of its tenant farmers be caught by s 8?

CHAPTER 22

THE POLICE

Introduction

Traditionally, police officers have a unique status, as 'public officers' responsible to the law. Control over policing is not vested in any one body, but instead 'control functions' are split between the Chief Constable, a police authority partly composed of independent members, and the Home Secretary, along with councillors and magistrates.

22.1 Legal status of police officers

Fisher v Oldham Corp (1930): Police are servants of the Crown, not of local government

Facts

A warrant for the arrest of Russell, who was suspected of obtaining money on false pretences, was issued by a magistrate in Oldham. Russell could not be found in Oldham. A London police officer arrested the plaintiff, who was mistakenly thought to be Russell. The plaintiff was detained overnight at a London police station, handed over to the Oldham police, and detained for several more hours before the mistake was discovered. The plaintiff brought an action against Oldham Corporation for wrongful arrest and detention. His statement of claim alleged that the defendant Corporation 'acting through their watch committee, are the police authority for the county borough of Oldham and are the employers of the police for the said county borough'. The question for the court was whether the relationship between the Corporation and the police was such as to make the Corporation liable in law to the plaintiff.

Decision

The court held that it was not, and that the action therefore failed. The police had not acted as the servants or agents of the Corporation, but had been fulfilling their duties as public servants holding office under the Crown. This appeared from a review of the relevant common law authorities and of statute. However, were it otherwise and local authorities were to be liable in such a case, it would entitle them equally to demand a full measure of control over the arrest and prosecution of all offenders.

22.2   The courts and the duty of the police to enforce the law

R v Metropolitan Police Commissioner ex p Blackburn **(1968) CA:**
Court will not interfere in matters of operational discretion

Facts

The Betting, Gaming and Lotteries Act 1963 made certain forms of gaming unlawful. Some gaming clubs in London attempted to avoid compliance with the provisions of the Act. When enforcement of its terms became increasingly difficult, the Metropolitan Police Commissioner issued a secret circular to senior officers, stating that, in future, no actions would be taken against gaming clubs for breaches of part of s 32 of the 1963 Act, unless there were complaints of cheating or clubs had become the haunt of criminals. Blackburn sought an order of mandamus to compel the Commissioner to carry out his public duty.

Decision

The Court of Appeal held that the Commissioner owed a duty to the public to enforce the law. If circumstances made it necessary, his performance of that duty would be enforced by the court. Chief officers had a wide discretion as to the means by which they carried out that duty, and provided their actions were directed towards discharging it, the courts would not interfere. Judicial review would lie in an extreme case against a policy decision which amounted to an abandonment of that duty. However, since the circular had been withdrawn before the conclusion of the proceedings, no relief was required.

Comment

Case law since then has shown this principle to be well established. Courts will not interfere in matters considered to be within the operational discretion of chief constables, such as the relative priority to be given to dealing with different types of crime.

R v Chief Constable of Sussex ex p International Trader's Ferry Ltd **(1999) HL:** Allocation of resources is a matter within chief constables' operational discretion

Facts

As a result of protests by animal rights groups, the major ferry operators stopped carrying live animals for export during the autumn of 1994. The applicant company began to carry livestock across the Channel from the port of Shoreham on 2 January 1995, and from 4–14 January some 1,125 police officers were deployed in order to allow vehicles to reach the port. The cost of this policing was £1.25 million. The Home Office made it clear that its policy was to refuse to use its powers to award a special grant to Sussex Police in these circumstances. From 14 January, the level of protests was reduced, but policing at the original high level was continued when a shipment took place.

By two 'decision letters' dated 10 and 24 April, the company was informed that this level of policing could not continue, and that the Chief Constable proposed to implement new arrangements which would have the effect of curtailing the company's activities. The decision was based on the impact of this policing on the Chief Constable's resources and on the effective policing of the rest of the force area. The Chief Constable also indicated that, because of the apprehension of a breach of the peace, lorries which attempted to enter the port in the absence of adequate police protection would be turned back. The company could not run economically on this basis and sought judicial review of the Chief Constable's decision.

Decision

The House of Lords held that the Chief Constable had not abdicated his responsibility to enforce the law, and that he was entitled to have regard to the finite nature of his resources and to competing priorities in deciding how those resources were to be allocated.

R v Chief Constable of Sussex ex p International Trader's Ferry Ltd (1998) HL: Chief Constable entitled to have regard to finite resources and need to balance conflicting demands when exercising discretion in operational matters

Facts

After several months of providing police cover for daily sailings, the Chief Constable decided that the cost in both financial resources and manpower was interfering with the efficient policing of the county. He accordingly reduced the level of cover to two consecutive days per week, or four consecutive days per fortnight, and on days when no cover was provided, his officers turned back livestock lorries if it was believed that a breach of the peace might otherwise occur.

Decision

The House of Lords held that the Chief Constable was not acting unlawfully.

Per Lord Slynn:

A right to trade lawfully was not an absolute right by which the Chief Constable owed a duty to protect the trader at whatever cost, any more than there was an absolute right to protest lawfully. In a situation where there were conflicting rights and the police had a duty to uphold the law, the police might, in deciding what to do, have to balance a number of factors, not the least of which was the likelihood of a serious breach of the peace. That involved balancing judgment and discretion.

In coming to his decisions, the Chief Constable had taken into account the number of men available to him, his financial resources, the rights of others in the area and their protection, and the risk of injury during the demonstration to the drivers, the police and others. He also took account of the right of the company to trade and of the protesters to demonstrate peacefully. It was wrong to overemphasise particular areas where he might have done more or where other chief constables might have reacted in a somewhat different way to particular aspects of the problem. The whole picture had to be considered.

Per Lord Hoffmann:

The fact that a Chief Constable considered that certain resources were needed to prevent some kind of criminal behaviour did not mean that he was obliged to provide them. He might, for example, decide that the only way to prevent muggings on the streets of Brighton would be to have many more constables on patrol and spend large sums on vehicles and communications equipment. That could not create a duty to find the resources at the expense of other policing activities. There was no distinction between the interests of Trader's Ferry in obtaining protection from demonstrators and those of the people of Brighton in obtaining protection from muggers.

Comment
On this basis:
(1) the police may restrain lawful activity in order to prevent a breach of the peace which might be provoked by that lawful activity;
(2) the police have no general enforceable duty to protect or assist particular members of the public.

22.3 The police have no general duty to individual members of the public

Hill v Chief Constable of West Yorkshire (1989) HL: Police have no duty to protect individual members of the public from crime

Facts
A 20 year old student was among the murder victims of Peter Sutcliffe, the so-called Yorkshire Ripper. Sutcliffe had committed a number of similar offences in the area over a period of years. The estate of the deceased brought an action against the police authority, alleging that it had been negligent in investigating the previous offences, and had thereby failed to catch Sutcliffe and so to prevent the murder of the deceased.

Decision
The House of Lords held that no duty of care would be recognised. The deceased had been merely a member of the public at large and any risk the alleged negligence presented to her was no different from the risk to thousands of other young women, any one of whom might equally have been Sutcliffe's victim. Although the imposition of a duty of care might in many cases be for the public benefit in increasing safety, to impose a duty in this area could lead to the police carrying on their investigations in a detrimentally defensive manner. Challenges in the courts would involve adjudication on matters of police policy and discretion, which the courts were ill suited to consider, and would divert police resources to the defending of such action. In reality, the plaintiff estate was seeking to mount an investigation into the efficiency of a police force. That task could be undertaken only by the national or local authorities which were responsible to the public for police efficiency.

However, a duty of care towards individuals may arise in special circumstances.

Rigby v Chief Constable of Northamptonshire (1985) QBD: Duty of care arose where police had themselves created risk of foreseeable harm

Facts
The plaintiff's premises were destroyed by fire when police threw CS gas canisters into them in an attempt to flush out a criminal who had taken refuge in there. The plaintiff argued that it was negligent on the part of the Chief Constable to purchase CS gas canisters, knowing them to be inflammable.

Decision

Taylor J rejected that part of the claim on the basis that the Chief Constable had not acted improperly in the exercise of his statutory discretion, but held that the use of the cylinders in the absence of fire fighting equipment was negligent and, under the normal principles of vicarious liability, the Chief Constable was liable.

CHAPTER 23

THE COURTS AND POLICE POWERS

23.1 Police duties and the nature of the citizen's duty to assist the police

Rice v Connolly (1966): No general duty to assist the police with their inquiries

Facts

In the early hours of the morning, police constables were patrolling an area of Grimsby in which a number of burglaries had taken place earlier that night. The officers saw the appellant behaving suspiciously and asked him where he was going, where he was coming from, and his name and address. The appellant gave only partial (although accurate) details and refused to provide more information. When he refused to accompany the constables to a police box to confirm his identity, he was then arrested on the grounds that he had wilfully obstructed a police constable in the exercise of his duty. The appellant was convicted and appealed to the Divisional Court.

Decision

The court held that the appeal would be allowed. It was clear that the appellant had obstructed the police and that the police had been acting throughout in accordance with their duty. It was part of the obligations and duties of a police constable (*per* Lord Parker CJ):

... to take all steps which appear to him necessary for keeping the peace, for preventing crime or for protecting property from criminal injury. There is no exhaustive definition of the powers and obligations of the police, but they are at least those, and they would further include the duty to detect crime and to bring an offender to justice.

However, it was necessary for the prosecution to prove that the obstruction was 'wilful', which in the context meant not merely 'intentional', but connoted something which was done without lawful excuse. Here, the question was whether the appellant had a lawful excuse for failing to answer the questions which had been put to him. In the judgment of Lord Parker CJ, he had; while every citizen had a moral or social duty to assist the police, there was no legal duty to that effect, and the appellant was therefore within his rights to refuse to answer the questions put to him.

23.2   The requirement of legal justification for police action

R v Waterfield and Lynn (1964): The police, as an executive body, cannot act without legal justification

The facts are not material.

Per Ashworth J:

In the judgment of this court, it would be difficult, and in the present case it is unnecessary, to reduce within specific limits the general terms in which the duties of police constables have been expressed. In most cases, it is probably more convenient to consider what the police constable was actually doing and in particular whether such conduct was *prima facie* an unlawful interference with a person's liberty or property. If so, it is then relevant to consider whether

(a)   such conduct falls within the general scope of any duty imposed by statute or recognised at common law; and

(b)   whether such conduct, albeit within the general scope of such a duty, involved an unjustifiable use of powers associated with the duty.

23.3   The exercise of specific powers

23.3.1   *Arrest*

23.3.1.1   The meaning of 'reasonable suspicion' giving rise to power of arrest

Castorina v Chief Constable of Surrey (1988) CA: Test of reasonable suspicion

Facts

Section 2(4) of the Criminal Law Act 1967 provided as follows: 'Where a constable, with reasonable cause, suspects that an arrestable offence has been committed, he may arrest without warrant anyone whom he, with reasonable cause, suspects to be guilty of the offence.' Detectives, who reasonably suspected that the burglary of a company's premises was an 'inside job', interviewed the respondent and arrested her. They had been informed that the documents taken by the burglar would have been useful to a person who had a grudge against the company. The respondent was detained at the police station for three and a quarter hours, interrogated, and released without charge. She claimed damages for wrongful arrest and detention.

The court at first instance upheld her claim, holding that 'reasonable cause' required an 'honest belief founded on reasonable suspicion leading an ordinary cautious man to the conclusion that the person arrested was guilty of the offence'. It was further stated that an ordinary man would have sought more information from the suspect before arresting her, including an examination of whether she held any grudge against the company. The respondent was awarded £4,500. The Chief Constable appealed to the Court of Appeal.

Decision

The Court of Appeal held, allowing the appeal, that in objective terms there was sufficient information available to the arresting officers to give them reasonable cause to suspect that the respondent was guilty of the burglary. The remaining question, therefore, was whether, before arresting her, the officers should have sought further information and explanation from her. Purchas LJ reviewed the authorities and concluded that they imposed no such requirement. Although the failure to follow an obvious course of questioning might, in exceptional circumstances, render the decision to arrest subject to challenge under the *Wednesbury* principle (*Associated Provincial Picture Houses Ltd v Wednesbury Corp* (see 14.1 above)), the court should have been concerned in the present action only to establish whether the arresting officers had reasonable cause for suspicion, and not with any further inquiries which the officers might have carried out. The judge at first instance had not so confined himself, and had therefore directed himself wrongly in law in applying the provisions of the Criminal Law Act 1967.

23.3.1.2   *The requirement to inform the suspect of the grounds for his arrest*

Christie v Leachinsky (1947) HL: Suspect must be informed of grounds at time of arrest

Facts
The appellant was a rag merchant. He was arrested by two police officers of the Liverpool police force and charged under the Liverpool Corporation Act 1921 with the unlawful possession of a bale of cloth he had earlier acquired in Leicester. He was detained in custody for a day, brought before a magistrate and twice remanded for periods of a week. At the hearing, he was discharged, but was re-arrested later the same day. The Leicester police then charged him with larceny and took him to Leicester in order to commit him for trial. The Leicester magistrates dismissed the charge. The appellant brought an action against the Liverpool police officers for false imprisonment and for trespass to the person.

Decision
The court held that, under the Liverpool Corporation Act 1921, the police could arrest without a warrant in these circumstances only if the name and address of the suspect were unknown and could not be ascertained. That was not the case here and the arrest was therefore unlawful. Further, the common law power of arrest was limited to arrest on a specific charge. Viscount Simon considered that the authorities established the following propositions:

(1)   If a policeman arrests without warrant on a reasonable suspicion of felony, or of other crime of a sort which does not require a warrant, he must in ordinary circumstances inform the person arrested of the true ground of arrest. He is not entitled to keep the reason to himself or to give a reason which is not the true reason. In other words, a citizen is entitled to know on what charge or on suspicion of what charge he is seized.

(2)   If the citizen is not so informed, but is nevertheless seized, the policeman, apart from certain exceptions, is liable for false imprisonment.

(3)   The requirement that the person arrested should be informed of the reason why he is seized naturally does not exist if the circumstances are such that he must know the general nature of the alleged offence for which he is detained.

(4)   The requirement that he should be so informed does not mean that technical or precise language need be used. The matter is a matter of substance, and turns on the elementary proposition that in this country a person is, *prima facie*, entitled to his freedom and is only required to submit to restraint on his freedom if he knows in substance the reason why it is claimed that this restraint should be imposed.

(5)   The person arrested cannot complain that he has not been supplied with the above information as and when he should be, if he himself produces the situation which makes it practically impossible to inform him, for example, by immediate counter-attack or by running away.

Comment

Prior to the Police and Criminal Evidence Act 1984, powers of arrest were scattered through a wide range of statutes, as well as the common law, but there was no over-arching legislation in this area.

Lewis and Another v Chief Constable of the South Wales Constabulary (1991) CA: An originally unlawful arrest may become lawful when suspect is informed of grounds

Facts

The appellants were arrested for burglary. They were not informed of the reason for the arrest until their arrival at the police station. This took place 10 minutes after arrest in the case of the first appellant and some 23 minutes after arrest in the case of the second appellant. Section 28(3) of the Police and Criminal Evidence Act 1984 provided that 'no arrest is lawful unless the person arrested is informed of the ground for the arrest at the time of, or as soon as practicable after, the arrest'. The appellants brought an action against the Chief Constable for wrongful arrest and false imprisonment.

The trial judge held that the arrest, although originally unlawful, was a continuing action and became lawful once the appellants were told the reasons for it. The jury awarded each appellant £200 in damages. The appellants argued on appeal that the arrest was a nullity, that an originally unlawful arrest could not later become lawful, and that they were accordingly entitled to damages in respect of the entire period of detention (some five hours).

Decision

The court held, dismissing the appeal, that the authorities showed that arrest was to be regarded as an ordinary English word and not a legal concept. Therefore, the question whether a person had been arrested depended on the fact of deprivation of liberty and not on the legitimacy of the arrest. The case of *Holgate-Mohammed v Duke* (see 23.3.1.4) showed that arrest was a continuing act and remained good law in the light of the Police and Criminal Evidence Act 1984. There was nothing inconsistent with s 28(3) in holding that, from the time the appellants had been informed of the reason for their arrest, the arrest became lawful.

23.3.1.3 Limits on restraint of suspects outside arrest

Kenlin v Gardiner (1967): Police officer cannot detain suspect without arrest

Facts
Two plainclothes police officers became suspicious of the behaviour of two boys who were visiting the homes of members of their school rugby team in order to remind them about a forthcoming match. One of the officers approached the boys, asked them what they were doing, and showed his warrant card. The boys failed to realise that the men were police officers and one of them attempted to run away. The officer took hold of the boy by the arm in order to prevent his escape. A struggle then took place, one of the officers was struck, and the boys ran away. They were charged under s 51(1) of the Police Act 1964 and appealed against conviction.

Decision
The Court of Appeal held that the appeal would be allowed. Winn LJ considered whether the officer had been entitled in law to take hold of the boy by the arm, and continued:

I feel myself compelled to say that the answer to that question must be in the negative. This officer might or might not in the particular circumstances have possessed a power to arrest these boys. I leave that question open, saying no more than that I feel some doubt whether he would have had a power of arrest; but on the assumption that he had a power of arrest, it is to my mind perfectly plain that neither of these officers purported to arrest either of these boys. What was done was not done as an integral step in the process of arresting, but was done in order to secure an opportunity, by detaining the boys from escape, to put to them or to either of them the question which was regarded as the test question to satisfy the officers whether or not it would be right in the circumstances, and having regard to the answer obtained from that question, if any, to arrest them.

I regret to say that I think there was a technical assault by the police officer ...

Comment
Only where the 'stop and search' provisions of s 1 of the Police and Criminal Evidence Act 1984 apply may the police detain without arrest.

R v Inwood (1973) CA: Fact of arrest must be communicated to suspect

Facts
The appellant was charged with assaulting a police constable in the exercise of his duty. He had attended voluntarily at a police station for questioning in connection with alleged thefts. During this procedure, a detective constable had told the appellant that he proposed to charge him with theft and handling stolen goods, and had cautioned him. The police then carried out the formalities associated with arrest, including fingerprinting the appellant. The appellant later attempted to leave the police station. The police sought to prevent his departure, and in the ensuing struggle, two officers were injured. At trial, the judge directed the jury that the appellant had been legally arrested. The appellant was convicted.

Decision

The court held, allowing the appeal, that the question whether it had been made clear to the appellant that he was under arrest was one of fact and should have been left to the jury. It would depend on the circumstances of individual cases whether enough had been done to demonstrate that a man had been arrested, and no particular formula would suit every case. Different procedures might have to be followed with different persons depending on their age, ethnic origin, knowledge of English, intellectual qualities or mental disabilities. In every case, there would be an obligation to make it plain to the suspect by what was said and done that he was no longer a free man. Here, without the judge's direction, the jury might or might not have found sufficient to have been done. The conviction would therefore be quashed.

23.3.1.4   Challenge to the exercise of statutory powers of arrest

Holgate-Mohammed v Duke (1984) HL: Exercise of police discretion to arrest is subject to scrutiny by court

Facts

A police officer suspected the appellant of the theft of jewellery, but considered that he needed further evidence in order to secure the appellant's conviction. Rather than interviewing the appellant under caution, the officer decided to arrest her and take her to a police station for questioning. The county court judge found the officer's intention was to subject the appellant 'to the greater stress and pressure involved in arrest and deprivation of liberty in the belief that if she was going to confess she would be more likely to do so in a state of arrest' (though it was not suggested that any impropriety took place). The judge awarded the appellant £1,000 damages for false imprisonment. The Court of Appeal allowed an appeal by the Chief Constable. The appellant appealed to the House of Lords.

Decision

The House of Lords held, dismissing the appeal, that the powers under which the arrest had been made were not common law powers, but derived from s 2(4) of the Criminal Law Act 1967. Accordingly, the court was concerned with the exercise of a discretion conferred by statute. It could be challenged only by reference to the *Wednesbury* principles. Applying those principles, Lord Diplock noted that it had been found as fact by the county court judge that the officer had acted in good faith. The court therefore had only to determine whether the officer's exercise of his discretion had been reasonable. This depended on whether the officer's motivation constituted an irrelevant consideration. Lord Diplock was of the opinion that it did not. Accordingly, the arrest was lawful.

23.3.2   Other powers

23.3.2.1   *A suspect's rights may not be infringed unless that necessity appears on the facts of the individual case*

Lindley v Rutter (1981): Police cannot adopt blanket policies, but must apply discretion to each individual case

Facts
The appellant was arrested for disorderly behaviour while drunk. She was taken to a police station where she refused to be searched. Two women police officers then forcibly searched her and removed her brassiere. In the course of the search, the appellant assaulted one of the officers. The officers believed that they were acting in accordance with standing orders of the Chief Constable, which they understood to require them to search every female prisoner and remove her brassiere for her own protection. The appellant argued that the woman police officer had not been acting in the course of her duty when the appellant assaulted her.

Decision
The Court of Appeal held, allowing the appeal, that the appellant's argument was correct, since the officer had exceeded her duty at the time of the assault.

Per Donaldson LJ:
It is the duty of the courts to be ever zealous to protect the personal freedom, privacy and dignity of all who live in these islands. Any claim to be entitled to take action which infringes these rights is to be examined with very great care. But such rights are not absolute. They have to be weighed against the rights and duties of police officers, acting on behalf of society as a whole. It is the duty of any constable who lawfully has a prisoner in his charge to take all reasonable measures to ensure that the prisoner does not escape or assist others to do so, does not injure himself or others, does not destroy or dispose of evidence and does not commit further crime such as, for example, malicious damage to property ...

What can never be justified is the adoption of any particular measures without regard to all the circumstances of the particular case. This is not to say that there can be no standing instructions ... But the officer having custody of the prisoner must always consider, and be allowed and encouraged to consider, whether the special circumstances of the particular case justify or demand a departure from the standard procedure either by omitting what would otherwise be done or by taking additional measures. So far as searches are concerned, he should appreciate that they involve an affront to the dignity and privacy of the individual. Furthermore, there are degrees of affront involved in such a search. Clearly, going through someone's pockets or handbag is less of an affront than a body search. In every case, a police officer ordering a search or depriving a prisoner of property should have a very good reason for doing so.

23.3.2.2   A suspect must be informed of the reason for an infringement of his rights

Brazil v Chief Constable of Surrey (1983): Suspect must be informed of reason for search

Facts

The appellant was asked, but refused to leave a public house, and was arrested by police officers for conducting herself in a way likely to cause a breach of the peace. Upon being taken to the police station, she was informed by a woman police officer that everyone brought into the police station had to be searched for their own safety. The appellant then assaulted the officer. At this stage, the police did not suspect the appellant of being in possession of controlled drugs. The officer in charge of the police station, Inspector Martin, subsequently ordered the appellant to be searched by force. The appellant then assaulted the woman police officer who was carrying out the search. Martin did now suspect the appellant of being in possession of controlled drugs, but he did not inform her that this was the reason for the search. The appellant contended that the first assault could not be an assault on a police officer in the execution of her duty, because the justification given for the search was not a proper justification. With regard to the second search, the appellant argued, *inter alia*, that it was unlawful because she had not been informed of the reason for it.

Decision

The court held, allowing the appeal and quashing the appellant's convictions, that both submissions were correct. In so holding, the court applied the reasoning of Donaldson LJ in *Lindley v Rutter* (above) in respect of the first search, and obtained guidance from *Christie v Leachinsky* (above) in respect of the second.

23.3.3   Protection of the subject through the exclusion of evidence

23.3.3.1   The considerations governing exercise of the common law discretion to exclude evidence

Jeffrey v Black (1978): Exclusion should only take place in exceptional circumstances

Facts

The respondent was arrested by members of the police drug squad for the theft of a sandwich from a public house. He was taken to a police station. Before he was charged, he was asked to give his consent to his flat being searched. The respondent accompanied the police to his flat and unlocked the door. In the course of the search, the police found cannabis and cannabis resin. The magistrates found as fact that the respondent had not given his consent to the search of his flat. They therefore exercised their common law discretion to exclude evidence found as a result of the search and dismissed the charges. The prosecution appealed by way of case stated to the Divisional Court, asking, *inter alia*: '... Were the justices right in ruling that the evidence of the finding of the articles was inadmissible if they found that the respondent had not given his consent to the search?'

Decision

The court held that there was no discretion to exclude relevant evidence solely on the ground stated, and the case would be sent back to be re-heard before a different bench. The test for the admissibility of evidence was whether the evidence was relevant to the matters in issue. The magistrates, in common with any other English court, had a general discretion to decline to allow any evidence to be called by the prosecution if they thought that it would be unfair or oppressive to allow that to be done. However, it would be appropriate to exercise the discretion only in exceptional circumstances.

Per Lord Widgery CJ:

... if the case is exceptional, if the case is such that not only have the police officers entered without authority, but they have been guilty of trickery or they have misled someone, or they have been oppressive or they have been unfair, or in other respects they have behaved in a manner which is morally reprehensible, then it is open to the justices to apply their discretion and decline to allow the particular evidence to be let in as part of the trial.

23.3.3.2 *There is no discretion at common law to exclude evidence on the ground that it was obtained by entrapment*

R v Sang (1980) HL

Facts

In the course of the appellant's trial on charges of conspiracy in connection with counterfeit bank notes, his counsel sought to persuade the judge to rule against the admissibility of the prosecution's evidence, on the ground that it related to offences which the appellant would not have committed unless he had been induced to do so by police officers acting as *agents provocateurs*. The judge ruled that he had no discretion to exclude evidence on this ground, and therefore refused to hear the evidence by which the entrapment was intended to be established. The appellant then changed his plea to one of guilty. His appeal against the judge's ruling was dismissed by the Court of Appeal. He renewed it before the House of Lords.

Decision

The House of Lords held, dismissing the appeal, that the judge's ruling had been correct. The court was concerned not with how evidence was gathered, but rather with the use made of it at the trial. To allow the exclusion of evidence on the basis for which the appellant contended would effectively be to introduce into English law a defence of entrapment. No such defence existed.

Per Lord Diplock:

... the function of a judge at a criminal trial as respects the admission of evidence is to ensure that the accused has a fair trial according to the law. It is no part of a judge's function to exercise disciplinary powers over the police or prosecution as respects the way in which evidence to be used at the trial is obtained by them. If it was obtained illegally there will be a remedy in civil law; if it was obtained legally but in breach of the rules of conduct for the police, this is a matter for the appropriate disciplinary authority to deal with ...

23.3.3.3 Statutory exclusion of evidence

The Police and Criminal Evidence Act 1984 gives the courts a much wider discretion to exclude evidence obtained improperly.

R v Keenan (1989) CA: Approach to be taken by courts when statutory power of exclusion arises

Facts

Police officers stopped the appellant's car, arrested the appellant for taking and driving the car away without authority, and searched the car in the appellant's absence. They found a home made spear in it. The appellant was charged with driving offences and with possession of an offensive weapon. After his committal, at which the only evidence relating to the spear was provided by the officers who had found it, further evidence was served in which two other officers alleged that the appellant had been asked about the spear. They stated that he had admitted that he knew it was in the car, but denied it was his. In breach of provisions of the Code of Practice for the Detention, Treatment and Questioning of Persons by Police Officers issued under s 66 of the Police and Criminal Evidence Act 1984, the alleged interview had not been properly recorded or documented by the police. The appellant maintained that it had never taken place. He was convicted and appealed on the ground that evidence of the alleged interview should not have been admitted.

Decision

The court held, allowing the appeal and quashing the conviction, that the breaches of the code had been serious and substantial. To admit the evidence was to penalise the appellant if he intended to exercise his right to remain silent at the trial, or to force him to challenge it and thereby open his past record to cross-examination or to put him at a disadvantage since there was no contemporaneous record of the interview. The evidence should therefore have been excluded under s 78 of the 1984 Act.

Per Hodgson J:

The provisions [of the 1984 Act and the Codes of Practice issued under it] will only be workable if and when compliance with them becomes the habitual practice of the police ... It is to be hoped that in future no police officer will display the ignorance of even the important provisions in issue in this case as these officers did ... We think that, in cases where there have been 'significant and substantial' breaches of the 'verballing' provisions of the Code, the evidence so obtained will frequently be excluded. We do not think that any injustice will be caused by this. It is clear that not every breach or combination of breaches of the code will justify the exclusion of interview evidence under s 76 or s 78: see *R v Hallett* (1989). They must be significant and substantial. If this were not the case, the courts would be undertaking a task which is no part of their duty; as Lord Lane CJ said in *R v Delaney* ((1989) at p 341): 'It is no part of the duty of the court to rule a statement inadmissible simply in order to punish the police for failure to observe the Codes of Practice.'

23.4   Article 5 of the European Convention on Human Rights

(1)   Everyone has the right to liberty and security of person. No one shall be deprived of his liberty save in the following cases and in accordance with a procedure prescribed by law:
    (a)   the lawful detention of a person after conviction by a competent court;
    (b)   the lawful arrest or detention of a person for non-compliance with the lawful order of a court or in order to secure the fulfilment of any obligation prescribed by law;
    (c)   the lawful arrest or detention of a person effected for the purpose of bringing him before the competent legal authority on reasonable suspicion of having committed an offence or when it is reasonably considered necessary to prevent his committing an offence or fleeing after having done so;
    (d)   the detention of a minor by lawful order for the purpose of educational supervision or his lawful detention for the purpose of bringing him before the competent legal authority;
    (e)   the lawful detention of persons for the purpose of the prevention of the spreading of infectious diseases, of persons of unsound mind, alcoholics or drug addicts, or vagrants;
    (f)   the lawful arrest or detention of a person to prevent his effecting an unauthorised entry into the country or of a person against whom action is being taken with a view to deportation or extradition.

(2)   Everyone who is arrested shall be informed promptly, in a language which he understands, of the reasons for his arrest and of any charge against him.

(3)   Everyone arrested or detained in accordance with the provisions of para 1(c) of this Article shall be brought promptly before a judge or other officer authorised by law to exercise judicial power and shall be entitled to trial within a reasonable time or to release pending trial. Release may be conditioned by guarantees to appear for trial.

(4)   Everyone who is deprived of his liberty by arrest or detention shall be entitled to take proceedings by which the lawfulness of his detention shall be decided speedily by a court and his release ordered if the detention is not lawful.

(5)   Everyone who has been the victim of arrest or detention in contravention of the provisions of the Article shall have an enforceable right to compensation.

CHAPTER 24

PROTECTION OF PRIVACY

Introduction

This is an area of law which is becoming highly controversial, not least as 'celebrities' seek to invoke some form of law of privacy so as to control their exposure in the media and maintain a favourable impression of themselves in the minds of the public. UK case law maintains that there is no right of privacy as such in domestic law, even after the Human Rights Act. Article 8 of the European Convention on Human Rights creates a right to respect for an individual's private life, home and correspondence, which may be limited or even abrogated altogether on the grounds stated in Art 8(2), but that is not of itself a right of privacy. Application of Art 8 also requires a balancing act with the right to freedom of expression guaranteed by Art 10, which is particularly significant where the press is alleged to have breached an individual's 'right to privacy'.

However, the equitable doctrine of breach of confidence has developed in a way which provides a limited right to privacy, the more so since the Human Rights Act 1998 came into force.

24.1   The absence of a general right to privacy at common law

***Kaye v Robertson* (1991) CA:** There is no general right to privacy at common law

Facts

The plaintiff, a well known television actor (star of the comedy series *Allo, Allo*), was seriously injured when debris fell on his car during a gale. As he was recovering in hospital after brain surgery, a journalist and photographer from the *Sunday Sport* entered his room, interviewed him and took photographs of his injuries. Medical evidence indicated that at that time he was in no condition to appreciate what was happening. The plaintiff obtained an injunction against publication of the interview or the photographs, basing his application upon claims for libel, malicious falsehood, trespass to the person and the tort of passing off, since the law recognised no general right to privacy. The defendants applied to the Court of Appeal for the discharge of the injunction.

Decision

The court held, allowing the appeal in part, that the injunction had wrongly been granted on the basis of the claim of libel, though it would be upheld in modified form on the basis of the malicious falsehood claim.

Per Leggatt LJ:
We do not need a First Amendment to preserve the freedom of the press, but the abuse of that freedom can be prevented only by the enforcement of a right to privacy. This right has so long been disregarded here that it can be recognised now only by the legislature. Especially since there is available in the US a wealth of experience of the enforcement of this right both at common law and also under statute, it is to be hoped that the making good of this signal shortcoming in our law will not be long delayed.

Malone v Metropolitan Police Commissioner (No 2) (1979): Undesirability of wide and indefinite right to privacy

Facts
See 2.1.2 above.

Decision
Sir Robert Megarry VC addressed, *inter alia*, the contention that the tapping of the plaintiff's telephone had contravened his right of privacy. He observed that there was no general right of privacy recognised by English law, but added that, if the existing rules, in combination with the requirements of justice and common sense, pointed to the existence of such a right, a court would not be deterred from acknowledging it. The creation of a wholly new right was a different matter, however, and a court would have to bear in mind that its function was judicial, not legislative. Further, the right claimed was broad in its scope:

> The wider and more indefinite the right claimed, the greater the undesirability of holding that such a right exists. Wide and indefinite rights, while conferring an advantage on those who have them, may well gravely impair the position of those who are subject to the rights. To create a right for one person, you have to impose a corresponding duty on another. In the present case, the alleged right to hold a telephone conversation in the privacy of one's own home without molestation is wide and indefinite in its scope … In any case, why is the telephone to be subject to this special right of privacy when there is no general right?

24.2   Breach of confidence

24.2.1   *The development of the equitable doctrine of breach of confidence*

Albert v Strange (1849): The principle emerges

Facts
Queen Victoria and Prince Albert made etchings of their children. The Royal Family kept them privately, although a few copies were given to friends. The plates of the etchings were entrusted to a printer for further copies to be made. Without the printer's knowledge, one of his employees made further copies. The defendant purchased them, intending to exhibit them, and prepared a catalogue listing and describing them. The plaintiff obtained an injunction to prevent both the exhibition and the publication of the catalogue. In further proceedings, the defendant applied for the variation of the injunction to permit him to publish the catalogue, although he accepted that the exhibition should not be held. On appeal, counsel for the defendant

contended that the injunction could be based only on breach of trust or on the property rights of the plaintiff.

Decision
The court held that a breach of trust, the protection of property rights, contract or a breach of confidence would justify the continuance of the injunction as originally made. The plaintiff undoubtedly had property rights in his own work. On the evidence adduced by the plaintiff and the absence of any explanation from the defendant, the court was bound to assume that the possession of the etchings by the defendant had been obtained in breach of trust, breach of an implied contract, or in breach of confidence.

24.2.2 The doctrine is independent of other legal rights

Duchess of Argyll v Duke of Argyll (1967): Individual need not have contract or property right for obligation of confidence to arise

Facts
Following the failure of his marriage to the plaintiff, the Duke of Argyll intended to publish a series of articles in *The People* relating to their married life. The first two instalments were published and the plaintiff sought injunctions against the Duke and against the editor and publisher of *The People* to restrain further publication of 'secrets … relating to her private life, personal affairs or private conduct, communicated to the first defendant in confidence during the subsistence of his marriage to the plaintiff and not hitherto made public property'.

Decision
The court held, following a review of the authorities, that an obligation of confidence could arise from property rights or from contract, but that these were not the only grounds on which a court could intervene.

Per Ungoed-Thomas J:
These cases, in my view, indicate:
(1)   that a contract or obligation of confidence need not be express but can be implied;
(2)   that a breach of confidence or trust or faith can arise independently of any right of property or contract;
(3)   that the court in the exercise of its equitable jurisdiction will restrain a breach of confidence independently of any right at law.
The confidential nature of a marital relationship was of its essence, and so obviously implicit in it that it did not need to be expressed. In the protection of that confidence:
    … The court is not to be deterred merely because it is not already provided with fully developed principles, guides, tests, definitions and the full armament for judicial decision. It is sufficient that the court recognises that the communications are confidential, and their publication within the mischief which the law as its policy seeks to avoid, without further defining the scope and limits of the jurisdiction; and I have no hesitation in this case in concluding that publication of some of the passages complained of is in breach of marital confidence …

A v B (A Company) **(2002) CA:** Development of law of confidence in context of sexual relationships, as affected by the Human Rights Act 1998

Facts

The claimant, a professional footballer who was married with children, had brief adulterous affairs with two women, C and D, who both sold their stories to a national newspaper. In order to prevent his wife from learning of the adultery, the claimant obtained an interim injunction to prevent publication. The newspaper subsequently applied for the injunction to be discharged. Re-imposing the injunction, the judge held, *inter alia*, that:

(1)   the protection of confidentiality which applied to sexual relations within marriage should also be applied to sexual relations outside marriage;

(2)   there was a substantial distinction between communication of confidential matters to family and friends and to the press;

(3)   the claimant had a right to respect for his private life under Art 8 of the European Convention on Human Rights and there was no countervailing public interest in the publication of the articles.

The newspaper appealed.

Decision

The Court of Appeal, allowing the appeal, stated that, even after the implementation of the Human Rights Act 1998, there was no free-standing tort relating to privacy in English law. In the great majority of cases, where the protection of privacy was justified, that protection could be achieved through an action for breach of confidence. A duty of confidence would arise whenever the party subject to the duty either knew or ought to have known that the other person could reasonably expect his privacy to be protected. If there was an intrusion into privacy in such circumstances, that intrusion would be capable of giving rise to liability for breach of contract unless that intrusion could be justified. If one party wished to exercise his right to freedom of expression under Art 10, that impacted on the other's right to maintain confidentiality. In the case of a sexual relationship outside marriage, the fact that the confidence was a shared confidence, which only one of the parties wished to preserve, did not extinguish that party's right to have the confidence preserved, but it did undermine that right. While recognising the special status of marriage, the courts had to recognise and give appropriate weight to the extensive range of relationships that now existed.

Here, the trial judge had made no allowance for the very different nature between the relationships which the claimant had had with C and D and lawful marriage, and the difference in the confidentiality which applied to them. Further, the fact that C and D had chosen to disclose their relationships with the applicant affected his right to preservation of confidentiality. Any other conclusion would fail to acknowledge their right to freedom of expression.

A public figure was entitled to have his privacy respected in appropriate circumstances, but should recognise that because of his public position he must accept that his actions would be more closely scrutinised by the media. Conduct which would not be the appropriate subject of comment in the case of a private individual might be so in that of a public figure. Such a person might be a legitimate subject of public attention whether or not he had courted publicity. In balancing the interests of the parties, the courts should not act as censors or arbiters of taste.

Campbell v Mirror Group Newspapers Ltd (2002) CA: Principles relating to disclosure of confidential information in the public interest

Facts

In the course of media interviews, Naomi Campbell, a well known model, falsely stated that she did not take drugs. A newspaper published by the defendants revealed that she had become addicted to drugs and was receiving treatment through Narcotics Anonymous. The claimant accepted that in view of her previous dishonesty, the newspaper was entitled in the public interest to reveal that she was a drug addict and was receiving treatment. However, she sought damages for breach of confidence in respect of the publication of specific details of her treatment, and for breach of the provisions of the Data Protection Act 1998. The judge at first instance found in her favour under both heads of claim. The newspaper appealed.

Decision

On the issue of whether the newspaper's entitlement to disclose that Miss Campbell was a drug addict and was being treated for drug addiction carried an entitlement to publish details of the treatment, the Court of Appeal held that in a case where publication of particular confidential information was justified in the public interest, a journalist had to be given reasonable latitude as to the way in which the information was conveyed to the public. Any other conclusion would inhibit his right to freedom of expression under Art 10. Here, publication of the details of the claimant's treatment had been justified in order to give credibility to the newspaper's accounts of her drug addiction. In any event, publication of those details had not been sufficiently significant to amount to a breach of confidence.

Per curiam:
(1) The fact that an individual has achieved public prominence does not mean that his private life may be laid bare by the media. It is not necessarily in the public interest to reveal that a person who has been adopted as a role model, without seeking that distinction, has feet of clay.
(2) The unjustifiable publication of information about a person's private life is more properly described as breach of privacy rather than breach of confidence.

24.2.3 Factors affecting the availability of the protection

24.2.3.1 Rights to confidentiality are incompatible with interests in publicity

Woodward v Hutchins (1977) CA: Litigant cannot rely on right of confidentiality when he is actively seeking publicity

Facts

The plaintiffs were well known pop singers (they included Tom Jones). The defendant, their press relations agent, contracted with a national newspaper to write a series of articles about the plaintiffs, giving details of their personal lives. The plaintiffs sued for libel, breach of contract and breach of confidence. At first instance, an injunction was granted to prevent breach of confidence, but not on the other two grounds. The defendants appealed.

Decision

The Court of Appeal held that the injunction would be discharged.

Per Lord Denning MR:

There is no doubt whatever that this pop group sought publicity. They wanted to have themselves presented to the public in a favourable light so that audiences would come to hear them and support them ... If a group of this kind seek publicity which is to their advantage, it seems to me that they cannot complain if a servant or employee of theirs afterwards discloses the truth about them. If the image which they fostered was not a true image, it is in the public interest that it should be corrected. In these cases of confidential information, it is a question of balancing the public interest in maintaining the confidence against the public interest in knowing the truth ...

Comment

This deals neatly with the classic problem concerning 'celebrities', since many actively court publicity for themselves and their activities, but only on their own terms. How far should the law go in enabling them to do this? This was considered afresh in a more recent case.

Douglas and Zeta Jones v Hello! Ltd (2003) Ch D: Position since the Human Rights Act

Facts

See 21.4 above. After the injunction was discharged by the Court of Appeal on the basis that damages would be a sufficient remedy, the photographs were published in *Hello!* and elsewhere. The claimants then sought damages under heads of claim which included:

(1) breach of a duty of confidence, since the wedding was a private occasion or, alternatively, that the wedding was an occasion exploited for gain and thus a commercial or trade secret;

(2) breaches of the Data Production Act 1998;

(3) breach of privacy.

Decision

(1) The claimants had a valuable trade asset, whose value depended in part on its content first being kept secret and then being made public in ways controlled by them. Photographic representation of the wedding thus had the quality of confidence.

(2) The photographer knew, or ought to have known, that the claimants reasonably expected the private character of the event and its photographic representation to be protected. The consciences of the defendants were therefore affected; they were not acting in good faith, nor by way of fair dealing.

(3) The claimants suffered detriment by the publication of the unauthorised photographs.

(4) Striking a balance as required by s 12 of the Human Rights Act between freedom of expression and confidentiality, there was no public interest claimed for the

unauthorised pictures, which also represented a breach of the Press Complaints Commission Code.

(5)   Regarding the claimants' case as one either of commercial confidence or a hybrid kind in which, by reason of the event having become a commodity, elements which would otherwise have been merely private became commercial, the defendants had acted unconscionably and, by reason of breach of confidence, they were liable to the claimants to the extent of the detriment that was caused to each of them.

Per curiam (Lindsay J):

(1)   The modern law relating to personal confidence contained in cases such as *Campbell v MGN* represented a fusion between the common law of confidence and the rights and duties arising under the Human Rights Act 1998 and European Convention on Human Rights. There was no presumption of priority to freedom of expression when it was in conflict with other rights under the Convention or with the law of confidence. It would be pointless of Art 10(2) to make freedom of expression subject to these rights if it invariably overrode them.

(2)   The law of confidence could encompass photographs of an event such as a wedding.

(3)   The starting point was whether the information was already public knowledge. It was not a question of whether the information was 'private' in the sense that its disclosure would be significantly harmful. At the relief stage equity should balance confidentiality and freedom of expression, and in doing so could take account of the degree of offensiveness of the activity complained of and its propensity to injure.

(4)   There were conflicting views in the authorities as to whether there was an existing law of privacy under which the claimants were entitled to relief. They were on these facts protected by the law of confidence, and the issue of privacy was better left to Parliament.

24.2.3.2   Other considerations

Stephens v Avery (1988): Basis of confidentiality of information relating to sexual misconduct

Facts

A man was convicted of the manslaughter of his wife, whom he had found in a compromising position with another woman. The plaintiff told the defendant, expressly in confidence, that she had had a lesbian relationship with the wife. The defendant allegedly informed *The Mail on Sunday,* which then stated in print that the plaintiff was the woman who had been found with the wife. The plaintiff brought proceedings for breach of confidence, and the defendant applied for the claim to be struck out as disclosing no reasonable cause of action. The defendant argued that:

(1)   the law did not protect information which related to grossly immoral behaviour;

(2)   the law did not protect mere tittle-tattle or trivial gossip;

(3)   information relating to sexual contact was inevitably known to both parties to it, and therefore not confidential; and

(4)   in the absence of a legally enforceable contract or a pre-existing relationship such as that of employer and employee, doctor and patient or priest and penitent, no legal duty of confidence arose.

The master refused to strike out the claim and the defendant appealed.

Decision

The court held that the appeal would be dismissed. It was correct to say that the law afforded no protection to information about grossly immoral conduct, but there was no longer any generally recognised code of sexual morality to which a judge would be justified in making reference. The triviality of the information sought to be protected went to the exercise of the court's discretion to afford an equitable remedy, and not to the nature of the plaintiff's right. Furthermore, the information in the present case either was not trivial or could not be judged to be so until trial. The mere fact that two people knew a secret did not deprive it of its quality of secrecy. *Attorney General v Guardian Newspapers (No 2)* (see 26.1 below) was authority for the proposition that information only ceased to be capable of protection as confidential when it was in fact known to a substantial number of people. No legally enforceable contract or pre-existing relationship was required by law.

Per Sir Nicholas Browne-Wilkinson VC:

The basis of equitable intervention to protect confidentiality is that it is unconscionable for a person who has received information on the basis that it is confidential subsequently to reveal that information. Although the relationship between the parties is often important in cases where it is said that there is an implied as opposed to express obligation of confidence, the relationship between the parties is not the determining factor. It is the acceptance of the information on the basis that it will be kept secret that affects the conscience of the recipient.

24.2.4   The defence of public interest compelling disclosure

It is frequently argued in individual cases that although an individual has received information in circumstances which give rise to a duty of confidence, there exists a public interest in disclosure which provides a complete defence to an action for breach of that duty of confidence.

Francome v Mirror Group Newspapers (1984) CA: Public interest in disclosure may arise in rare circumstances

Facts

The first plaintiff was a well known steeplechase jockey. He was approached by journalists who wished to confirm the authenticity of tapes of his telephone conversations. The tapes, which had been made by other unidentified persons in tapping his telephone without his knowledge (itself a criminal act under the Wireless Telegraphy Act 1949), were said to reveal that he had breached the rules of racing in relation to betting on horses. The plaintiff brought proceedings against the journalists and the newspaper for which they wrote, claiming, *inter alia*, damages for breach of confidence. He obtained an interlocutory injunction to restrain publication based on the tapes until trial. On appeal, the defendants sought the discharge of the injunction. They argued in defence to breach of confidence that they had acted in the public interest in revealing the plaintiff's suspected wrongdoing.

Decision

The court held that an injunction had been properly granted, but would be upheld in amended terms. It was indeed in the public interest that the allegations against the plaintiff should be investigated by the proper authorities, and the injunction would be varied to permit the disclosure of the tapes to such authorities with the permission of the appropriate Minister of the Crown. The editor of the *Daily Mirror* had asserted a right in the public interest to publish a story based on the tapes, although he admitted that publication would probably be an offence under s 5(b) of the Wireless and Telegraphy Act 1949.

Sir John Donaldson MR regarded this as a claim to be bound by the law only in so far as it remained expedient in the public interest (as conceived by the editor) to be so bound, and rejected it on the basis that while it was in the public interest for the material to be disclosed to the Jockey Club and the police, publication in the *Daily Mirror* was solely in the interests of the *Daily Mirror*. Reviewing the circumstances in which a subject might feel obliged to break the law, he added:

... I nevertheless recognise that, in very rare circumstances, a situation can arise in which a citizen is faced with a conflict between what is, [*sic*] in effect, two inconsistent laws. The first law is the law of the land. The second is a moral imperative, usually, but not always, religious in origin ... However, I cannot overemphasise the rarity of the moral imperative. Furthermore, it is almost unheard of for compliance with the moral imperative to be in the financial or other best interests of the persons concerned ...

24.2.5 Revelation of wrongdoing is not the only acceptable rationale for disclosure

Lion Laboratories Ltd v Evans (1985) CA: Public interest in disclosure not confined to cases of crime or other actionable wrongdoing

Facts

The plaintiffs were the manufacturers of the Lion Intoximeter 3000, used by the police for measuring the blood alcohol levels of motorists suspected of drink driving offences. Two former employees of the plaintiff passed company documents detailing the plaintiff's and the Home Office's doubts about the reliability and accuracy of the Intoximeter to the *Daily Express*. The plaintiff applied for and received an *ex parte* injunction to prevent publication of the documents, claiming breach of copyright or breach of confidence. The *Daily Express* subsequently published an article based on the documents. The defendants appealed against the injunction.

Decision

The court held, allowing the appeal and discharging the injunction, that the issue raised by the defendants was a serious question concerning the life and liberty of an unascertainable number of Her Majesty's subjects. Although the information regarding the working of the Intoximeter was confidential and had been unlawfully taken in breach of confidence, the defendants would not be restrained from putting that information before the public. In the evidence before the court, no misconduct was alleged against the plaintiffs. However, it was incorrect to assert that the publication of confidential information would be in the public interest only if it revealed wrongdoing on the part of the person to whom it was confidential. The revelation of wrongdoing was merely one instance of an occasion on which there might be just cause for breaching confidence.

24.3   Article 8 of the European Convention on Human Rights

(1)   Everyone has the right to respect for his private and family life, his home and his correspondence.

(2)   There shall be no interference by a public authority with the exercise of this right except such as is in accordance with the law and is necessary in a democratic society in the interests of national security, public safety or the economic well being of the country, for the prevention of disorder or crime, for the protection of health or morals, or for the protection of the rights and freedoms of others.

24.3.1   Effect of Art 8 on the law of confidence

Douglas v Hello! Ltd (2001) CA: Application of Art 8 to existing common law of confidence

Facts
See 21.4 above.

Decision
Sedley LJ stated that the law of confidence had developed very largely in response to individual cases, rather than larger-scale public policy. However, law and equity had reached a point of providing protection for personal privacy to a degree appropriate to the circumstances of each individual case. Equity and common law now recognised that everyone was entitled to some private space in the face of increasing risk of invasion, and the Human Rights Act meant that English courts were now required to give appropriate effect to the right to respect for private life, home and correspondence contained in Art 8 of the European Convention on Human Rights. Sedley LJ considered that ss 2 and 6 of the Human Rights Act, requiring the UK courts to act compatibly with the Convention, acted as the final impetus to the recognition of a free-standing right of privacy in English law.

Such a right was important in this case because the unauthorised photographs may have been taken by a person who was an intruder at the wedding reception and so, arguably, not covered by the duty of confidence which applied to the invited guests and those persons in a contractual relationship with the claimants.

Comment
When the action for damages arising from this matter was heard, it was reiterated that in the majority of cases the law of confidence is able to provide appropriate protection, and did so on this occasion, presumably on the basis that the photographer was indeed a guest at the wedding or an employee of the hotel. See 24.2.3.1 above.

Campbell v Mirror Group Newspapers Ltd (2002) CA: The Master of the Rolls proposes a change in terminology

Facts
See 24.2.2 above.

Per Lord Phillips of Worth Matravers MR:

The development of the law of confidentiality since the Human Rights Act 1998 came into force has seen information described as 'confidential' not where it has been confided by one person to another, but where it relates to an aspect of an individual's private life which he does not choose to make public. We consider that the unjustifiable publication of such information would better be described as breach of privacy rather than breach of confidence.

A v B (A Company) (2002) CA: Interplay between Art 8 and Art 10

Facts

See 24.2.2 above.

Per Lord Woolf CJ:

The manner in which the two articles operate is entirely different. Article 8 operates so as to extend the areas in which an action for breach of confidence can provide protection for privacy. It requires a generous approach to the situations in which privacy is to be protected. Article 10 operates in the opposite direction. This is because it protects freedom of expression and to achieve this it is necessary to restrict the area in which remedies are available for breaches of confidence. There is a tension between the two Articles which requires the court to hold the balance between the conflicting interests they are designed to protect. This is not an easy task but it can be achieved by the courts if, when holding the balance, they attach proper weight to the important rights both Articles are designed to protect. Each Article is qualified expressly in a way which allows the interests under the other Article to be taken into account.

CHAPTER 25

PUBLIC ASSEMBLY AND PUBLIC ORDER

Introduction

This is an area in which the law has to reconcile a number of competing demands: the protection of freedom of peaceful assembly, protection of the interests of non-protestors, and prevention of public disorder in what may be highly volatile situations. Common law in this sphere rests on the ancient concept of the Queen's peace and the duty of the police to act pre-emptively in order to prevent breaches of the peace. Statutory intervention included the Riot Act 1715, which gave lords-lieutenant of counties power to use militia against rioters who failed to obey an order to disperse. The statutory framework in this sphere is now based on the Public Order Act 1986, which gives the police powers to intervene to prevent disorder additional to those available under the common law.

25.1   What is a breach of the peace?

R v Howell (1982) CA: Current definition

Facts
In the course of attempting to disperse a group of people who had congregated on the street and were behaving in a disorderly manner, police arrested the appellant. During his arrest, the appellant struck a police officer in the face. He was convicted of an assault occasioning actual bodily harm. On appeal, he argued that there had been no breach of the peace before the arrest, that the arrest was consequently unlawful, and that he had used reasonable force to prevent it.

Decision
The court held that the appeal would be dismissed. In so holding, Watkins LJ considered the definition of 'breach of the peace':

A comprehensive definition of the term 'breach of the peace' has very rarely been formulated ... Nevertheless, even in these days when affrays, riotous behaviour and other disturbances happen all too frequently, we cannot accept that there can be a breach of the peace unless there has been an act done or threatened to be done which actually harms a person, or in his presence his property, or is likely to cause such harm, or which puts someone in fear of such harm being done. There is nothing more likely to arouse resentment and anger in him, and a desire to take instant revenge, than attacks or threatened attacks upon a person's body or property ...

R v Chief Constable of Devon and Cornwall ex p CEGB (1982) CA: A broader definition?

Facts
The Central Electricity Generating Board (CEGB) was obstructed by demonstrators in its attempts to exercise its statutory powers to survey land for suitability as a site for

a nuclear power station. The police attended at the site, but refused to intervene, on the grounds that there was no actual or threatened breach of the peace. The CEGB sought an order of mandamus to compel the police to remove or to assist in the removal of the demonstrators.

Decision

The Court of Appeal held that it would not be appropriate to order mandamus. Lord Denning MR, however, considered that there had been or was likely to be a breach of the peace. It might be constituted either by the physical steps taken by CEGB employees to prevent the obstruction, whether or not such reaction might be justified as a matter of self-help, or by the conduct of the demonstrators themselves. Lord Denning MR continued:

> ... The lifting up of a recumbent obstructor would be a battery unless justified as being done in the exercise of self-help. But in deciding whether there is a breach of the peace or the apprehension of it, the law does not go into the rights and wrongs of the matter – or whether it is justified by self-help or not. Suffice it that the peace is broken or is likely to be broken by one or another of those present ...
>
> If I were wrong on this point, if there were here no breach of the peace nor apprehension of it, I would give a licence to every obstructor and every passive resister in the land. He would be able to cock a snook at the law as these groups have done. Public works of the greatest importance could be held up indefinitely. This cannot be. The rule of law must prevail.

Comment

Case law is uncertain on this point, as Lord Denning's views have not been overruled, but Watkins LJ's narrower definition has been followed in cases since. Note that both postulate 'conduct likely to lead to a breach of the peace' as conduct which may provoke a breach of the peace by some other person.

25.2 Restriction of freedom of assembly for the avoidance of public disorder

***Beatty v Gillbanks* (1882):** Police cannot take action on the basis that actions of peaceful protesters may provoke violent reaction from others

Facts

The Salvation Army organised processions in the streets of Weston-Super-Mare. The processions were accompanied by another organised body called the Skeleton Army, which opposed itself to the Salvation Army. Factions supporting each of the two groups developed and violent disorder broke out. After a major disturbance, a justices' notice requiring the cessation of assemblies to the disturbance of the public peace was posted in the town and served on the appellant organisers of the Salvation Army. The Salvation Army continued to march. They were met and stopped by the police, who told the appellants that they must obey the notice. The appellants refused, were arrested, and as a result of being charged with 'unlawfully and tumultuously assembling with others to the disturbance of the public peace, and against the peace of the Queen', were bound over to find sureties to keep the peace. They appealed to the Queen's Bench Divisional Court.

Decision

The court held, allowing the appeal, that, as regarded the appellants themselves, there was no disturbance of the peace. The appellants' aims were wholly lawful, if not indeed laudable. The disturbance which had taken place had been caused entirely by the unlawful and unjustifiable interference of the Skeleton Army.

Per Field J:

I entirely concede that everyone must be taken to intend the natural consequences of his own acts, and it is clear to me that, if this disturbance of the peace was the natural consequence of the acts of the appellants, they would be liable, and the justices would have been right in binding them over. But the evidence set forth in the case does not support this contention ... The law relating to unlawful assemblies, as laid down in the books and the cases, affords no support to the view of the matter for which the learned counsel for the respondent was obliged to contend, viz, that persons acting lawfully are to be held responsible and punished merely because other persons are thereby induced to act unlawfully and create a disturbance.

Duncan v Jones (1936): Distinction for this purpose between moving an assembly and prohibiting it altogether

Facts

A meeting was to be held outside an unemployed training centre in Deptford to protest against the Incitement to Disaffection Bill (which, as it passed into law in 1934, made it an offence to seek to seduce a member of the Armed Forces from his duty or his allegiance to the Crown and gave the authorities extensive powers to act to prevent or detect the offence).

The appellant had addressed a meeting at the same location more than a year previously, and on that occasion there had been disturbances at the centre. The appellant was told by a police inspector that the meeting could not be held at the intended venue, but could take place some 175 yards away in a different street. The appellant told the inspector that she was going to hold the meeting in any event, stepped onto a platform, and began to address the audience. The inspector then arrested her, to which she submitted without resistance. She was charged with obstructing the inspector in the execution of his duty contrary to s 12 of the Prevention of Crimes Act 1871. Upon conviction, she appealed to the London Quarter Sessions. The Deputy Chairman of Quarter Sessions held, dismissing the appeal, that:

(1)   the appellant must have known of the probable consequence of her holding the meeting – namely, a disturbance and possibly a breach of the peace – and was not unwilling that such consequences should ensue;

(2)   the respondent reasonably apprehended a breach of the peace;

(3)   it therefore became the respondent's duty to prevent the holding of the meeting; and

(4)   by attempting to hold the meeting, the appellant obstructed the respondent when in the execution of his duty.

The appellant appealed by way of case stated to the King's Bench Divisional Court.

Decision

The court held that the deputy chairman had been entitled to come to the conclusion to which he came on the facts which he had found. The case was a plain one. The *ratio* of *Beatty v Gillbanks* (above) was not in point, and the judgments in that case did not carry the matter any further. There was in any event no positive right of assembly in English law, merely a freedom to assemble to the extent to which it was not unlawful.

Thomas v Sawkins (1935): Police might attend public meeting on private premises in order to prevent a breach of the peace

Facts
A public meeting to protest against the Incitement to Disaffection Bill was held on private premises. The organisers of the meeting had previously made it clear to the police that they were not welcome. Police officers nevertheless attended, and the appellant took hold of one of them in order to eject him. The officer resisted and the appellant brought a private prosecution for assault. At first instance, the case was dismissed and the appellant appealed to the Divisional Court.

The question arose whether the police officers had been lawfully on the premises.

Decision
The court held that the decision to dismiss the case would be upheld. The police had been lawfully on the premises in the exercise of a power to enter and remain in order to deal with a breach of the peace or to prevent an anticipated breach of the peace. The court rejected the appellant's argument that no such power existed where a breach was merely expected by the police.

Per Avory J:
I think it is very material in this particular case to observe that the meeting was described as a public meeting ... and that the public was invited to attend. There can be no doubt that the police officers who attended the meeting were members of the public and were included in that sense in the invitation to attend. It is true that those who had hired the hall for the meeting might withdraw their invitation from any particular individual who was likely to commit a breach of the peace or some other offence, but it is quite a different proposition to say that they might withdraw the invitation from police officers who might be there for the express purpose of preventing a breach of the peace or the commission of an offence ...

Avory J was satisfied that the police had reasonable grounds for believing that a breach of the peace would occur if they did not remain on the premises for the duration of the meeting, and in order to prevent such a breach they were entitled to enter and remain on the premises.

25.3   Restriction of freedom of assembly in the interest of private rights

Hubbard v Pitt (1975) CA: Freedom of assembly may be limited in interests of property owners

Facts
The defendants, who were opposed to property redevelopment in Islington, organised a campaign against the plaintiffs, a firm of local estate agents. They assembled outside the plaintiffs' offices with placards and leaflets, stating that they would continue this picketing until the plaintiffs complied with their demands. The pickets were orderly and peaceful, co-operated with the police, and left sufficient room for pedestrians to

pass along the pavement. The plaintiffs obtained an injunction to prevent the defendants from 'besetting' their offices, claiming that it was substantially interfering with their business. The defendants appealed.

Decision

The Court of Appeal held, by a majority, that the appeal would be dismissed. The balance of convenience was in favour of maintaining the injunction until full trial. However, Lord Denning dissented on the basis that peaceful and orderly protest should not be restricted.

Per Lord Denning MR (dissenting):

Finally, the real grievance of the plaintiffs is about the placards and leaflets. To restrain these by an interlocutory injunction would be contrary to the principle laid down by the court 85 years ago in *Bonnard v Perryman* and repeatedly applied ever since. That case spoke of the right of free speech. Here we have to consider the right to demonstrate and the right to protest on matters of public concern. These are rights which it is in the public interest that individuals should possess; and, indeed, that they should exercise without impediment as long as no wrongful act is done ... As long as all is done peaceably and in good order without threats or incitement to violence or obstruction to traffic, it is not prohibited: see *Beatty v Gillbanks* [above]. I stress the need for peace and good order. Only too often violence may break out, and then it should be firmly handled and severely punished. But, so long as good order is maintained, the right to demonstrate must be preserved.

25.4   Restriction in the interest of public rights

Hirst and Agu v Chief Constable of West Yorkshire (1986): Test to be applied by the courts

Facts

The appellants, who were animal rights activists, carried on a protest outside a shop selling animal furs. They stood in various parts of the street outside the shop, holding a banner and handing out leaflets. The street was a spacious but busy pedestrian precinct. They were convicted of obstructing the highway contrary to s 137 of the Highways Act 1980 and appealed to the Divisional Court by way of case stated.

Decision

The court held, allowing the appeal, that the Crown Court had been wrong to regard the appellants' activities as unlawful merely because they were not incidental to the lawful use of the highway to pass and re-pass. Where the activity on which the charge was based was not of itself contrary to law, a court should consider whether:

(1)   a more than negligible obstruction had been caused;

(2)   the obstruction was deliberate; and

(3)   it was caused without lawful authority or excuse.

In answering the third question, the court was to consider, as a question of fact, whether the activity was reasonable.

***Director of Public Prosecutions v Jones* (1999) HL:** Peaceful and non-obstructive demonstration constitutes lawful use of the highway

Facts
The appellants, who had held what was agreed to have been a peaceful and non-obstructive demonstration on the verge of the A344 adjacent to the perimeter fence of Stonehenge, were convicted of taking part in a 'trespassory assembly' on a highway in respect of which an order prohibiting such assemblies had been made, contrary to s 14B(2) of the Public Order Act 1986 (as inserted by s 70 of the Criminal Justice and Public Order Act 1994). They appealed successfully to the Crown Court, but their convictions were reinstated following an appeal by the Director of Public Prosecutions to the Divisional Court. The appellants appealed to the House of Lords.

Decision
The court held, allowing the appeal, that the case raised a point of fundamental constitutional importance, namely, the limits of the public's rights of access to the public highway. The common law contained observations to the effect both that the right of the public upon a highway was limited to passing and re-passing over it, and that there may be reasonable or usual (and therefore non-trespassory) uses of the highway which are not limited or ancillary to mere passage. The latter were to be preferred.

Per Lord Irvine of Lairg LC:
In truth very little activity could accurately be described as 'ancillary' to passing along the highway; perhaps stopping to tie one's shoe lace, consulting a street map, or pausing to catch one's breath. But I do not think that such ordinary and usual activities as making a sketch, taking a photograph, handing out leaflets, collecting money for charity, singing carols, playing in a Salvation Army band, children playing a game on the pavement, having a picnic, or reading a book, would qualify. These examples illustrate that to limit lawful use of the highway to that which is literally 'incidental or ancillary' to the right of passage would be to place an unrealistic and unwarranted restriction on commonplace day-to-day activities. The law should not make unlawful what is commonplace and well accepted.

25.5   Insulting words and behaviour

***Jordan v Burgoyne* (1963):** Insulting words likely to cause a breach of the peace – test of whether breach of peace is likely to be caused is a subjective one

Facts
The respondent was a leader of the extreme right wing National Socialist movement. He addressed a rally in Trafalgar Square. A group of communists, Campaign for Nuclear Disarmament (CND) supporters and Jewish activists attended the rally, intending to prevent it taking place. Jordan used the following words:

… More and more people every day are opening their eyes and coming to say with us 'Hitler was right'. They are coming to say that our real enemies … were not Hitler and the National Socialists of Germany, but world Jewry and its associates in this country.

At this point, there was turmoil, and the police stopped the rally. Jordan was convicted of using insulting words whereby a breach of the peace was likely to be occasioned, contrary to s 5 of the Public Order Act 1936. His appeal to quarter sessions was allowed on the ground that, although his words had been insulting, they would not have been likely to lead ordinary, reasonable people to commit a breach of the peace. The prosecutor appealed to the Divisional Court.

Decision
The court held, allowing the appeal, that it was difficult to imagine any reasonable person not being provoked beyond endurance by the respondent's words, but that there was no room for any test as to whether any member of the audience was a reasonable man or an ordinary citizen.

Per Lord Parker CJ:
This is … a Public Order Act, and if in fact it is apparent that a body of persons are present – and let me assume in the defendant's favour that they are a body of hooligans – yet if words are used which threaten, abuse or insult them – all very strong words – then that person must take his audience as he finds them, and if those words to that audience are likely to provoke a breach of the peace, then the speaker is guilty of an offence.

Brutus v Cozens (1973) HL: Meaning of 'insulting'

Facts
During a tennis match at Wimbledon which involved a South African player, the appellant stepped onto the court blowing a whistle, threw leaflets around, attempted to give one to a player and sat down on the court. Other protesters then made their way onto the court. Play was stopped. The appellant was charged with using insulting behaviour whereby a breach of the peace was likely to be caused, contrary to s 5 of the Public Order Act 1936. The magistrates held that the appellant's behaviour could not be described as 'insulting'. The prosecutor appealed to the Divisional Court, which defined the word 'insulting' and held that the evidence established that the appellant had used insulting behaviour. The appellant appealed to the House of Lords.

Decision
The House of Lords held, allowing the appeal, that the meaning of the word 'insulting' was a matter of fact, not law, and that the question for the Divisional Court had therefore been whether the magistrates had acted unreasonably in holding that the appellant's behaviour was not insulting. They had not so acted. The Divisional Court had defined 'insulting' behaviour as that which affronted others and tended to evidence a disrespect or contempt for their rights.

Per Lord Reid:
I cannot agree with that. Parliament had to solve the difficult question of how far freedom of speech or behaviour must be limited in the general public interest. It would have been going much too far to prohibit all speech or conduct likely to occasion a breach of the peace because determined opponents may not shrink from organising or at least threatening a breach of the peace in order to silence a speaker whose views they detest.

25.6   Article 11 of the European Convention on Human Rights

(1)   Everyone has the right to freedom of peaceful assembly and to freedom of association with others, including the right to form and to join trade unions for the protection of his interests.

(2)   No restrictions shall be placed on the exercise of these rights other than such as are prescribed by law and are necessary in a democratic society in the interests of national security or public safety, for the prevention of disorder or crime, for the protection of health or morals or for the protection of the rights and freedoms of others. This Article shall not prevent the imposition of lawful restrictions on the exercise of these rights by members of the armed forces, of the police or of the administration of the State.

CHAPTER 26

FREEDOM OF EXPRESSION

Introduction

The law relating to freedom of expression is essentially the other side of the same coin as that of privacy and confidentiality. A major difficulty concerns the proper balance to be struck between freedom of expression on the one hand and confidentiality on the other, along with the weight to be given to such public interests as the protection and detection of crime and the proper administration of justice. Much case law concerns the freedom of the press to publish confidential information and information which may have been acquired by unlawful means.

26.1   Common law

Schering Chemicals v Falkman Ltd **(1982) CA:** Importance of press freedom – though press may be liable in damages where publication is improper in some way

Facts

The plaintiff, the manufacturer of a pregnancy testing drug, sought an injunction to prevent the broadcasting of a television documentary which concerned allegations that the drug had caused abnormalities in children born to women who had used it. The plaintiff claimed that the producer of the documentary, who was formerly its employee, had used material confidential to the plaintiff.

Decision

The Court of Appeal held, by a majority, that the injunction granted to the plaintiff would be upheld. Although the material in question was said already to be in the public domain, its re-publication would cause further damage to the plaintiff.

Per Lord Denning MR (dissenting):

The freedom of the press is extolled as one of the great bulwarks of liberty. It is entrenched in the constitutions of the world. But it is often misunderstood. I will first say what it does not mean. It does not mean that the press is free to ruin a reputation or to break a confidence, or to pollute the course of justice or to do anything that is unlawful. I will next say what it does mean. It means that there is to be no censorship. No restraint should be placed on the press as to what they should publish … The press is not to be restrained in advance from publishing whatever it thinks right to publish. It can publish whatever it chooses to publish. But it does so at its own risk. It can 'publish and be damned'. Afterwards – after the publication – if the press has done anything unlawful – it can be dealt with by the courts. If it should offend – by interfering with the course of justice – it can be punished in proceedings for contempt of court. If it should damage the reputation of innocent people, by telling untruths or making unfair comment, it may be made liable in damages. But always afterwards. Never beforehand. Never by previous restraint.

Attorney General v Guardian Newspapers (No 1) (1987) HL: Fundamental importance of freedom of expression

Facts

Peter Wright, a former member of the British security service MI5, sought to publish a book in Australia giving an account of his experiences in the service. The Crown obtained an interim injunction in New South Wales against publication in Australia and injunctions to prevent the publication of extracts from the book in British newspapers. Contempt of court proceedings were also prosecuted against newspapers which had published in disregard of the injunctions. Certain of the newspapers applied for the discharge of the injunctions, arguing that the contents of the book were now in the public domain. By the time the appeals reached the House of Lords, the book had been published in its entirety in several countries and no attempt was made to prevent individuals from freely importing copies into the UK.

Decision

The House of Lords held, by a majority, that the injunctions would be upheld and broadened.

Per Lord Bridge (dissenting):

… Having no written constitution, we have no equivalent in our law to the First Amendment to the Constitution of the United States of America. Some think that puts freedom of speech on too lofty a pedestal. Perhaps they are right … [In the past] I have had confidence in the capacity of the common law to safeguard the fundamental freedoms essential to a free society including the right to freedom of speech which is specifically safeguarded by Art 10 of the Convention. My confidence is seriously undermined by your Lordships' decision …

   Freedom of speech is always the first casualty under a totalitarian regime. Such a regime cannot afford to allow the free circulation of information and ideas among its citizens. Censorship is the indispensable tool to regulate what the public may and what they may not know. The present attempt to insulate the public in this country from information which is freely available elsewhere is a significant step down that very dangerous road.

26.2   Compatibility of English law and the Convention

Attorney General v Guardian Newspapers (No 2) (1990) HL: Common law on freedom of expression and restrictions thereon had developed in a matter compatible with Art 10

Facts

The Attorney General sought permanent injunctions to prevent the publication of material obtained directly or indirectly from Mr Wright, a general injunction against the future publication by certain newspapers of material derived from Mr Wright or other members of the security service, and an account of profits made by another newspaper which had begun to serialise the book.

Decision

The House of Lords held, on the first issue by a majority only, that the permanent injunctions would not be granted because publication would not be contrary to the public interest. This was because the information in question was already in the public domain. The Crown was entitled to an account of the profits from that part of the serialisation which had already been published, but not with regard to future serialisation. The claim for general injunctions would be refused. In the course of his speech, Lord Goff considered the compatibility of the English law on confidentiality with Art 10 of the European Convention on Human Rights:

Finally, I wish to observe that I can see no inconsistency between English law on this subject and Art 10 of the European Convention on Human Rights ... The only difference is that, whereas Art 10 of the Convention, in accordance with its avowed purpose, proceeds to state a fundamental right and then to qualify it, we in this country (where everybody is free to do anything, subject only to the provisions of the law) proceed rather upon an assumption of freedom of speech, and turn to our law to discover the established exceptions to it ...

The exercise of the right to freedom of expression under Art 10 may be subject to restrictions (as are prescribed by law and are necessary in a democratic society) in relation to certain prescribed matters, which include 'the interests of national security' and 'preventing the disclosure of information received in confidence'. It is established in the jurisprudence of the European Court of Human Rights that the word 'necessary' in this context implies the existence of a pressing social need, and that interference with freedom of expression should be no more than is proportionate to the legitimate aim pursued. I have no reason to believe that English law, as applied in the courts, leads to any different conclusion.

26.3 Article 10 of the European Convention on Human Rights

(1)   Everyone has the right to freedom of expression. This right shall include freedom to hold opinions and to receive and impart information and ideas without interference by public authority and regardless of frontiers. This Article shall not prevent States from requiring the licensing of broadcasting, television or cinema enterprises.

(2)   The exercise of these freedoms, since it carries with it duties and responsibilities, may be subject to such formalities, conditions, restrictions or penalties as are prescribed by law and are necessary in a democratic society in the interests of national security, territorial integrity or public safety, for the prevention of disorder or crime, for the protection of health or morals, for the protection of the reputation or rights of others, for preventing the disclosure of information received in confidence, or for maintaining the authority and impartiality of the judiciary.

CHAPTER 27

FREEDOM OF RELIGION

27.1 The definition of 'religion'

***Barralet v Attorney General* (1980):** Religion defined in broad terms

Facts

The South Place Ethical Society had as its objects:
(1) 'the study and dissemination of ethical principles'; and
(2) 'the cultivation of a rational religious sentiment'.
In pursuit of both these objects, the Society had as its aim to rely on the methods of reason, rather than on instruction by supernatural revelation and, in the second of its objects, the word 'religious' was used in a sense devoid of supernatural content. By an originating summons, the Society asked the court to declare whether or not its objects were charitable. The court considered whether the objects fell under the charitable heads of the advancement of religion, the advancement of education, or whether they were for purposes beneficial to the community.

Decision

The court held that the Society's objects came under the latter two heads, but could not be brought under the first head. The Society had contended that a sincere belief in ethical qualities was religious, because such qualities as truth, love and beauty were sacred, and the advancement of any such belief was the advancement of religion. Although it was true that such beliefs might occupy a place in the minds of their possessors parallel to that of religious beliefs, the two could not be equated.

***Per* Dillon J:**

In a free country ... it is natural that the court should not desire to discriminate between beliefs deeply and sincerely held, whether they are beliefs in a god or in the excellence of man or in Platonism or some other scheme of philosophy. But I do not see that that warrants extending the meaning of the word 'religion' so as to embrace all other beliefs and philosophies. The two are not the same, and are not made the same by sincere inquiry into the question, what is God ... There is a further point. It seems to me that two of the essential attributes of religion are faith and worship.

27.2 The extent of the association between Christianity and the law

***Bowman v Secular Society* (1917) HL:** Christianity not of itself part of English law

Facts

The Society's objects included the following: '... to promote ... the principle that human conduct should be based upon natural knowledge, and not upon supernatural belief, and that human welfare in this world is the proper end of all thought and action.' The appellants challenged the validity of a testamentary gift to the Society on the grounds that acts done in pursuance of its objects were illegal.

Decision

The House of Lords held, by a majority, dismissing the appeal, that such acts would not now be regarded as contrary to the law. Lord Sumner stated that the case gave rise to the question whether Christianity was part of the law of England and, if so, in what sense it was. While it was true that England was a Christian State, that the national religion was Christianity and that the English family was built on Christian ideals, the maxim that 'Christianity was part of the law of England' was rhetoric and not law. Lord Sumner continued:

English law may well be called a Christian law, but we apply many of its rules and most of its principles, with equal justice and equally good government, in heathen communities, and its sanctions, even in courts of conscience, are material and not spiritual ... In the present day, reasonable men do not apprehend the dissolution or downfall of society because religion is publicly assailed by methods not scandalous. Whether it is possible that in the future irreligious attacks, designed to undermine fundamental institutions of our society, may come to be criminal in themselves, as constituting a public danger, is a matter that does not arise. The fact that opinion grounded on experience has moved one way does not in law preclude the possibility of its moving on fresh experience in the other; nor does it bind succeeding generations, when conditions have again changed.

27.3   The law of blasphemy

27.3.1   The protection of Christianity

Whitehouse v Lemon (1979) HL: Common law of blasphemy protects Christianity only

Facts

The magazine *Gay News* published a poem entitled 'The Love that Dares to Speak its Name'. This, in the words of Lord Diplock, purported 'to describe in explicit detail acts of sodomy and fellatio with the body of Christ immediately after His death and to ascribe to Him during his lifetime promiscuous homosexual practices with the Apostles and with other men'. A private prosecution was brought against the magazine and its editor by Mary Whitehouse. Although the common law offence of blasphemous libel had been thought to have become a 'dead letter' (described thus by Lord Denning in *Freedom Under the Law* (1949)), the defendants were convicted. They appealed to the House of Lords on the grounds that to sustain a conviction, it was necessary to prove the accused's specific intent to shock believing Christians.

Decision

The House of Lords held, by a majority, that the appeal would be dismissed. The Court of Appeal had correctly concluded that blasphemous libel was a crime of strict liability. It was sufficient to show an intent to publish the material in question; the motive for publication was irrelevant. Although the judge at first instance had stated that he would have been prepared if necessary to extend the protection of the law against blasphemous libel to other religions, the House made it clear that, at present, it applied exclusively to Christianity. It was not for the judiciary to broaden it.

Per Lord Scarman:

My Lords, I do not subscribe to the view that the common law offence of blasphemous libel serves no purpose in the modern law. On the contrary, I think that there is a case for legislation extending it to protect the religious beliefs and feelings of non-Christians. The offence belongs to a group of criminal offences designed to safeguard the internal tranquillity of the kingdom. In an increasingly plural society, it is necessary not only to protect the differing religious beliefs, feelings and practices of all but also to protect them from scurrility, vilification, ridicule and contempt.

27.3.2 The position of other religions

R v Chief Metropolitan Stipendiary Magistrate ex p Choudhury (1991): Law of blasphemy does not apply to non-Christian beliefs

Facts

The applicant sought judicial review of the Chief Magistrate's refusal to issue a summons alleging blasphemous libel and seditious libel against the publisher of Salman Rushdie's novel *The Satanic Verses*.

Decision

The court held, refusing the application, that, on the present state of the law, the offence of blasphemous libel did not extend to protect any religion other than Christianity. If the law were to be changed in this respect, it was for Parliament and not the courts to change it. Were it open to the present court to change it, it would not in any event do so, since the extension of the protection would give rise to difficult questions of definition, and put the issue of the libel itself beyond the common understanding of a jury. Furthermore, in so far as the protection afforded by the common law of blasphemous libel was discriminatory, Watkins LJ considered that state of affairs objectively justified:

The offence of blasphemous libel is an offence of strict liability ... If the offence is extended to cover attacks upon religious doctrines, tenets, commandments, or practices of religions other than Christianity, the existence of such an extended law of blasphemy would encourage intolerance, divisiveness and unreasonable interference and interferences with freedom of expression ... An extended law of blasphemy which applied to all religions could be used as a weapon between Protestants and Roman Catholics in Northern Ireland, or by fringe religions, such as the Church of Scientology. The fact that the offence was committed only in cases of scurrilous attacks would mitigate, but would not eliminate, the resulting intolerance, divisiveness, and unreasonable interference with freedom of expression ...

Comment

Nevertheless, there has in recent years been much discussion and controversy over, on the one hand, abolishing the law of blasphemy altogether and, on the other, extending it to cover at least the major world religions besides Christianity.

27.4   Religious discrimination and testamentary freedom

Blaythwayt v Baron Cawley (1976) HL: Clause in will restricting religious freedom of beneficiary not void on grounds of public policy

Facts
A testator, who died in 1936, had settled property upon certain persons, subject to a forfeiture clause providing that, if any person who became entitled as tenant for life or tenant in tail male to possession of the estate should 'be or become a Roman Catholic … the estate hereby limited to him shall cease and determine and be utterly void and my principal estate shall thereupon go to the person next entitled …'. The question arose whether this clause was void for reasons of public policy.

Decision
The House of Lords held that it was not. Lord Wilberforce noted that the European Convention referred to freedom of religion and to enjoyment of that and other freedoms without discrimination on the ground of religion. He acknowledged that conceptions of public policy should move with the times, but was of the opinion that to introduce a rule of law avoiding the clause would be to uphold one freedom only at the cost of a substantial reduction in another – the freedom of testamentary disposition. The provision in question was a matter of choice, not of discrimination, and private choice was not a matter of public policy.

Per Lord Cross of Chelsea:
Turning to the question of public policy, it is true that it is widely thought nowadays that it is wrong for government to treat some of its citizens less favourably than others because of differences in their religious beliefs; but it does not follow from that that it is against public policy for an adherent of one religion to distinguish in disposing of his property between adherents of his faith and those of another. So to hold would amount to saying that, though it is in order for a man to have a mild preference for one religion as opposed to another, it is disreputable for him to be convinced of the importance of holding true religious beliefs and the fact that his religious beliefs are the true ones.

Comment
Here the court had essentially to determine the proper balance between two conflicting public interests, of religious freedom and testamentary freedom respectively.

27.5   Freedom of worship under the common law

Ahmad v ILEA (1978) CA: Matters relating to freedom of religious worship given a narrow interpretation

Facts
The applicant, a Muslim, was employed as a full-time teacher and formed a habit of attending Friday prayers at his local mosque which caused him to be late for his afternoon classes. On being told that if he continued to be late for his afternoon classes he must move to a part-time post, he resigned and claimed that he had been

constructively and unfairly dismissed, relying on s 30 of the Education Act 1944, which provides that:

... No person shall be disqualified by reason of his religious opinions, or of his attending or omitting to attend religious worship, from being a teacher ... and no teacher ... shall ... receive any less emolument or be deprived of, or disqualified for, any promotion or other advantage ... by reason of his religious opinions or of his attending or omitting to attend religious worship.

Decision
The Court of Appeal held (Lord Scarman dissenting) that s 30 should not be construed to permit Mr Ahmad to take time off work.

Per Lord Denning MR:
[After referring to Art 9 of the European Convention, he continued:] The Convention is not part of our English law, but, as I have often said, we will always have regard to it. We will do our best to see that our decisions are in conformity with it. But it is drawn in such vague terms that it can be used for all sorts of unreasonable claims and provoke all sorts of litigation. As so often happens with high-sounding principles, they have to be brought down to earth ... If it should happen that, in the name of religious freedom, [Muslims] were given special privileges or advantages, it would provoke discontent, and even resentment among those with whom they work. As, indeed, it has done in this very case. And so the cause of racial integration would suffer. So, while upholding religious freedom to the full, I would suggest that it should be applied with caution, especially having regard to the setting in which it is sought.

Lord Denning went on to say, in robust fashion, that Mr Ahmad's right to 'manifest his religion in practice and observance' must be subject to the rights of the education authorities under the contract and to the interests of his pupils, ending: 'I see nothing in the European Convention to give Mr Ahmad any right to manifest his religion on Friday afternoons in derogation of his contract of employment: and certainly not on full pay.'

Comment
Twenty-five years later, Lord Denning's views seem mainly of historical interest, although the decision in *Ahmad* remains good law.

27.6 Article 9 of the European Convention on Human Rights

(1) Everyone has the right to freedom of thought, conscience and religion; this right includes freedom to change his religion or belief, and freedom, either alone or in community with others and in public or private, to manifest his religion or belief, in worship, teaching, practice and observance.

(2) Freedom to manifest one's religion or beliefs shall be subject only to such limitations as are prescribed by law and are necessary in a democratic society in the interests of public safety, for the protection of public order, health or morals, or for the protection of the rights and freedoms of others.

CHAPTER 28

FREEDOM OF MOVEMENT

Introduction

EC law provides for freedom of movement for citizens of Member States within the EC, but rights of entry and residence for non-EC citizens are much more restricted.

28.1 Freedom to travel abroad

The Immigration Act 1971 states as follows:

1(1) All those who are in this Act expressed to have the right of abode in the UK shall be free to live in, and to come and go into and from, the UK without let or hindrance except such as may be required under and in accordance with this Act to enable their right to be established or as may be otherwise lawfully imposed on any person.

2(1) A person is under this Act to have the right of abode in the UK if:

(a) he is a British citizen ...

28.2 Exclusion orders: legal challenge

R v Secretary of State for the Home Department ex p Stitt (1987): Orders under anti-terrorist legislation excluding individuals from the British mainland were susceptible to judicial review, but not when made on grounds of national security

Facts

The applicant sought judicial review of the Secretary of State's refusal to revoke an exclusion order made under the Prevention of Terrorism (Temporary Provisions) Acts 1976 and 1984. Additionally, he applied to order the Secretary of State to give reasons for the making of the exclusion order.

Decision

The court held, refusing the application, that the 1976 Act was comprehensive in its provision of rights to those against whom the legislation operated, and no such rights of the applicant had been breached. Further, the Secretary of State's refusal to give reasons was based on considerations of national security. Once there was *bona fide* evidence that security was involved, the court would not examine the strength of justification for the Secretary of State's actions.

28.3   Deportation

28.3.1   *Considerations governing the discretion to make a deportation order after conviction*

The Home Secretary has power to deport aliens convicted of criminal offences in the UK, which is normally exercised in the case of persons convicted of serious offences on completion of their prison sentences.

R v Nazari (1980) CA: Principles on which power of deportation should be exercised

Facts

Following their convictions for various offences, the three defendants, all of whom were immigrants, were recommended to be deported. The Court of Appeal laid down the following principles for general application in cases where there was jurisdiction to make a deportation order:

(1)   The court was to consider whether the offender's continued presence in the UK would be to the country's detriment. The country had no use for criminals of other nationalities. The more serious the crime and the longer the offender's criminal record, the more obvious it was that a deportation order should be made.

(2)   The court would not be concerned with the political systems operating in the country to which the offender would be deported. This was a matter for the Home Secretary to take into account at the end of the offender's sentence of imprisonment in this country.

(3)   The court would consider the effect that an offender's deportation would have on innocent persons not before the court, such as the offender's family.

(4)   Where an offender states his intention to return to his country voluntarily at the end of his sentence, the court would be unwise to allow such a statement much weight.

(5)   Where an offender is found to be an illegal immigrant, a deportation order should normally be made.

28.3.2   *Legal challenge to the decision to deport*

R v Governor of Brixton Prison ex p Soblen (1963) CA: Principles to be applied when granting relief against deportation

Facts

Soblen was convicted of espionage in the US. He then disappeared while on bail pending an appeal and went to Israel, from which his extradition was sought by the Americans. During a flight returning him from Israel to the US, he inflicted wounds upon himself as the plane neared London, in order to force it to land. A deportation order was made against him by the Secretary of State, who let it be known that he intended Soblen to be placed on a flight to the US. Soblen sought a writ of habeas corpus on the grounds, *inter alia*, that the deportation order was calculated to amount to extradition, and that the Secretary of State had accordingly acted for an improper purpose; no power to extradite in fact existed with respect to Soblen's offence. At first instance, Soblen's application was refused.

Decision

The Court of Appeal held, dismissing the appeal, that two principles were to be weighed together. First, the Crown had power to surrender a fugitive offender to another country only in so far as it might do so in accordance with the Extradition Acts. Secondly, the Secretary of State could deport an alien if he considered it to be conducive to the public good. It was necessary to inquire what the Secretary of State's purpose had been in making the order. If the deportation order was a mere sham, designed to achieve an unlawful extradition, then the court could overturn it. Here, however, there was no evidence that the Secretary of State had acted to achieve an improper purpose, and there were grounds on which he could genuinely have come to the conclusion that Soblen's deportation would be to the public good.

R v Secretary of State for the Home Department ex p Hosenball (1977) CA: Position where a person is deported in interests of national security

Facts

The applicant, a US citizen, had been living and working in the UK as an investigative journalist for several years. He was informed by the Secretary of State that he was to be deported on the ground of national security. The applicant sought further information from the Secretary of State, who considered the request but stated that it was to be refused in the interests of national security.

By the terms of the Immigration Rules and of an undertaking given by the Secretary of State to the House of Commons, a person proposed to be deported was to be given a hearing and such particulars of the allegations against him as would not entail disclosure of sources of evidence. The applicant received a hearing, but was given no particulars of the case against him. He sought judicial review of the decision to issue a deportation order against him, on the grounds that the Secretary of State was required, either by the principles of natural justice or by the Rules or undertaking, to distinguish between disclosable and non-disclosable allegations upon which the order was based.

The application was dismissed at first instance, and the applicant appealed to the Court of Appeal.

Decision

The Court of Appeal held, dismissing the appeal, that the demands of national security could prevail over the requirements of natural justice. The balance between the demands of national security and natural justice was a matter for the Secretary of State. He had considered the applicant's request for further information and he was entitled to refuse it. He would be answerable to Parliament, and not to the courts, for his judgment.

Per Lord Denning MR:

There is a conflict here between the interests of national security on the one hand and the freedom of the individual on the other. The balance between these two is not for a court of law.

It is for the Home Secretary. He is the person entrusted by Parliament with the task. In some parts of the world national security has on occasions been used as an excuse for all kinds of infringements of individual liberty. But not in England.

R v Secretary of State for the Home Department ex p Cheblak (1991) CA: Limited role of courts when a decision to deport is made on grounds of national security

Facts
Shortly after the outbreak of hostilities in the Gulf in 1991, the applicant, a Lebanese citizen and a known pacifist, was arrested and served with a notice of the Home Secretary's intention to make a deportation order against him on the grounds of national security. The risk was later stated by the Home Department to arise from the applicant's association with an organisation which, it was believed, might indulge in terrorist activity in the UK. The Secretary of State subsequently stated in an affidavit that national security prevented the disclosure of further details of the case in favour of deportation. The applicant, arguing that the Secretary of State's decision was contrary to natural justice, irrational, and made in disregard of relevant considerations, sought judicial review and a writ of habeas corpus. Both applications were refused at first instance and the applicant appealed to the Court of Appeal.

Decision
The Court of Appeal held, dismissing the appeal, that the challenge failed on all three grounds. Concluding his judgment, Lord Donaldson MR noted that responsibility for decisions made on grounds of national security rested not with the courts, but with government. The courts would intervene if the Secretary of State were to be shown to have acted in bad faith or to have exceeded his statutory powers. Otherwise, the court would accept that the Secretary of State had good grounds for his decision without requiring him to adduce evidence to that effect. Although it was true that tensions might arise between considerations of individual liberty and the requirements of national security, and that there would be cases where the latter would prevail over the former, it was relevant to remember that national security was in fact the foundation of all civil liberties.

28.3.3   Deportation and the rights of third parties

Singh v Immigration Appeals Tribunal (1986) HL: Effect on third parties is a relevant factor in making a decision to deport

Facts
The applicant, a Sikh musician, overstayed his leave to remain in the UK by more than three years. He appealed unsuccessfully to an immigration adjudicator and thence to the Immigration Appeals Tribunal against a deportation order made by the Secretary of State. He then sought judicial review of the Tribunal's decision. Before the House of Lords, he contended that the damaging effect of his deportation on the Sikh community was either a compassionate circumstance or part of the relevant circumstances which the immigration authorities were bound, by the 1982

Immigration Rules, to take into account in considering an appeal against a deportation order.

Decision

The House of Lords held, allowing the appeal, that the respondent Tribunal had misdirected itself in law. The prejudice to third parties which would be caused by the applicant's deportation was a relevant factor under the Immigration Rules. Further, under principles of general law, it was a factor which the Secretary of State had been bound to consider by virtue of its bearing on the matter before him. It was therefore a matter which the Tribunal should have directed itself to consider, since it was bound by s 19(1)(a) of the Immigration Act 1971 to decide whether the Secretary of State's decision was 'in accordance with the law'.

28.4 Protocols 4 and 7 of the European Convention on Human Rights

Protocol 4, Art 2:

(1) Everyone lawfully within the territory of a State shall, within that territory, have the right to liberty of movement and freedom to choose his residence.

(2) Everyone shall be free to leave any country, including his own.

(3) No restrictions shall be placed on the exercise of these rights other than such as are in accordance with law and are necessary in a democratic society in the interests of national security or public safety, for the maintenance of 'order public', for the prevention of crime or for the protection of the rights and freedoms of others.

(4) The rights set forth in para 1 may also be subject, in particular areas, to restrictions imposed in accordance with law and justified by the public interest in a democratic society.

Protocol 7, Art 1:

(1) An alien lawfully resident in the territory of a State shall not be expelled therefrom except in pursuance of a decision reached in accordance with law and shall be allowed:

    (a) to submit reasons against his expulsion;

    (b) to have his case reviewed;

    (c) to be represented for these purposes before the competent authority or a person or persons designated by that authority.

(2) An alien may be expelled before the exercise of his rights under para 1(a), (b) and (c) of this Article, when such expulsion is necessary in the interests of public order or is grounded upon reasons of national authority.

CHAPTER 29

PRISONERS' RIGHTS

Introduction

This is another controversial area, as it is often argued that a prisoner should lose nothing by his imprisonment but his physical liberty.

29.1 Judicial review is available to vindicate the residual rights of prisoners

R v Board of Visitors of Hull Prison ex p St Germain (No 1) (1979) CA: Prisoners may argue breach of principles of natural justice in disciplinary proceedings

Facts

As a result of their part in riots at Hull Prison, the applicants were subjected to various disciplinary penalties by the Board of Visitors. They sought orders of certiorari to quash the disciplinary awards, on the grounds that the Board had failed to observe the principles of natural justice. Their applications were refused by the Divisional Court, on the preliminary ground that the determinations of the Board of Visitors in these circumstances could not be subject to judicial review, but concerned merely internal and domestic disciplinary matters. Further, recognition of the right of prisoners to apply for judicial review of decisions relating to prison discipline would render the position of the prison authorities intolerable. The applicants appealed to the Court of Appeal.

Decision

The Court of Appeal held, allowing the appeals and remitting the case to the Divisional Court, that the supervisory jurisdiction of the High Court was, in principle, sufficiently broad for an order of certiorari to issue against the disciplinary award of a Prison Board of Visitors. Shaw LJ cited provisions of the Prison Rules 1964, made under the Prison Act 1952, and concluded that '... despite the deprivation of his general liberty, a prisoner remains invested with residuary rights appertaining to the nature and conduct of his incarceration'. He continued:

Now the rights of a citizen, however circumscribed by a penal sentence or otherwise, must always be the concern of the courts unless their jurisdiction is clearly excluded by some statutory provision. The courts are in general the ultimate custodians of the rights and liberties of the subject whatever his status and however attenuated those rights may be as the result of some punitive or other process ... Once it is acknowledged that such rights exist, the courts have function and jurisdiction. It is irrelevant that the Secretary of State may afford redress where the rules have been infringed or their application has been irregular or unduly harsh. An essential characteristic of the right of a subject is that it carries with it a right of recourse to the courts unless some statute decrees otherwise.

R v Deputy Governor of Parkhurst Prison ex p Hague; Weldon v Home Office (1991) HL: Limited extent of prisoners' rights of legal action

Facts

The applicant in the first case sought judicial review of the prison governor's decision to transfer him between prisons and to segregate him from other prisoners, and included a claim for damages for false imprisonment. The Court of Appeal granted his application in part, but held that a claim for damages by a prisoner for breach of the Prison Rules did not lie, and a claim for false imprisonment would be maintainable only if the prisoner had been deprived of his residual liberty in bad faith, or the conditions of his imprisonment were 'intolerable'. In the second case, a prisoner claimed damages against the Home Office for assault and battery, and for false imprisonment. The Home Office appealed to the House of Lords from the Court of Appeal's refusal to strike out the part of the claim relating to false imprisonment. The House heard the cases as conjoined appeals.

Decision

The House of Lords held, dismissing the prisoner's appeal in the first case and allowing the Home Office's appeal in the second case, that a prisoner had no claim for damages arising from a breach of the Prison Rules, and could not maintain an action for false imprisonment on either of the grounds identified by the Court of Appeal. The second of these claims rested on the proposition that a prisoner had, despite his confinement, a residual liberty amounting to a right which the law would protect. That was incorrect. While it was true that the law would provide a remedy where the prisoner's conditions of detainment were intolerable, the remedy thus granted would be one which would not impugn the legality of the detainment.

Rejecting the concept of residual liberty, Lord Bridge said as follows:

Can the prisoner then complain that his legal rights are infringed by a restraint which confines him at any particular time within a particular part of the prison? It seems to me that the reality of prison life demands a negative answer to this question ... Thus, the concept of the prisoner's 'residual liberty' as a species of freedom of movement within the prison enjoyed as a legal right which the prison authorities cannot lawfully restrain seems to me quite illusory. The prisoner is at all times lawfully restrained within closely defined bounds and if he is kept in a segregated cell, at a time when, if the rules had not been misapplied, he would be in the company of other prisoners at the workshop, at the dinner table or elsewhere, this is not the deprivation of his liberty of movement, which is the essence of the tort of false imprisonment, it is the substitution of one form of restraint for another.

29.2   Prisoners' rights of access to legal advice and to the courts

Raymond v Honey (1983) HL: Principles applicable

Facts

Raymond, a prisoner, applied to commit the prison governor for contempt of court. The governor had intercepted and decided not to forward a letter written by Raymond to his solicitor which related not only to pending legal proceedings, but also contained allegations against an assistant governor. Raymond's application to commit the governor was also intercepted by him. Orders made under s 47 of the Prison Act 1952 permitted correspondence between a prisoner who was party to any legal proceedings and his solicitor, and gave the prison governor power to stop letters containing allegations against prison officers, requiring him to explain the correct complaints procedure to the prisoner. The Divisional Court held that the stopping of the first letter did not constitute contempt of court, but that the stopping of the second letter did. The governor appealed and Raymond cross-appealed.

Decision

The House of Lords held that both the appeal and the cross-appeal would be dismissed. Two principles governed the case. The first was derived from *R v Gray* (1900). Any act calculated to obstruct or interfere with the course of justice, or the lawful process of the courts, was a contempt of court. The second principle, stated in *R v Board of Visitors of Hull Prison ex p St Germain (No 1)* (see 29.1 above), was that a convicted prisoner retained all civil rights which were not expressly or by necessary implication taken from him. The Prison Act 1952 did not confer power to make regulations which would deny or interfere with a prisoner's right to have unimpeded access to a court. The orders made under s 47 of the Prison Act 1952 would be interpreted narrowly in order to avoid ascribing to them that effect (which would have rendered them *ultra vires*). The governor had temporarily denied Raymond's access to the court by stopping the second letter, and had therefore committed a contempt.

R v Secretary of State for the Home Department ex p Leech (No 2) (1993) CA: Prison governors' powers in respect of prisoners' correspondence with their legal advisers to be construed narrowly

Facts

The appellant, a prisoner, sought certiorari to quash the power of a prison governor under the Prison Rules 1964 to censor inmates' correspondence with their solicitors in respect of legal proceedings not yet commenced. At first instance, the court rejected the contention that the relevant part of the Rules (r 33(3)) was *ultra vires* s 47(1) of the Prison Act 1952, which conferred power to 'make rules for the regulation and management of prisons'. The prisoner appealed to the Court of Appeal.

Decision

The Court of Appeal held, allowing the appeal, that it was necessary to consider whether there was an objective need for a rule as wide as r 33(3), which empowered a prison governor to stop any letter or communication on the grounds that its contents were objectionable or that it was of inordinate length. While both a power to examine correspondence between prisoners and their legal advisors to ascertain whether it was *bona fide*, and a power to stop objectionable correspondence could be justified, neither the distinction between proceedings already begun and those contemplated, nor the reference to the length of the correspondence were required. Since r 33(3) was therefore wider than necessary and created a substantial impediment to the exercise of the prisoner's basic rights as expounded in *Raymond v Honey* (above), it was *ultra vires*, so far as it purported to apply to correspondence between prisoners and their legal advisers.

R v Secretary of State for the Home Department ex p Simms (1999) HL: Prisoners' entitlement to access to journalists

Facts

Two prisoners serving life sentences, who claimed that they had been the victims of miscarriages of justice, sought interviews with journalists in order to publicise their grievances. It was the policy of the Home Secretary, relying on paras 37 and 37A of the Prison Service Standing Order 5A (made under s 47(1) of the Prison Act 1952) to allow the interviews only if the journalists signed undertakings not to use any part of the interviews for professional purposes. The justification for the policy was that the interviews would tend to undermine discipline and control within the prison environment. The journalists refused to sign the undertakings, and the prisoners sought judicial review of the policy as a fetter upon their access to justice. They were successful at first instance. The Court of Appeal allowed an appeal by the Home Secretary. The prisoners appealed to the House of Lords.

Decision

The House of Lords held, allowing the appeal, that investigative journalism had been shown on the evidence to play an important role in leading to the detection and remedying of miscarriages of justice. It was hard to conceive of a more pressing justification for the assertion of a right to free speech. The fact that fundamental and basic rights were being invoked mandated the application of the principle of legality to the construction of paras 37 and 37A. So interpreted, the two paras were not *ultra vires* s 47(1) of the Prison Act 1952, but to base upon them an absolute rule against the publication of interviews was unlawful.

INDEX